KV-510-426

Justifying Same-Sex Marriage

A Philosophical Investigation

Louise Richardson-Self

ROWMAN &
LITTLEFIELD
INTERNATIONAL
London • New York

Published by Rowman & Littlefield International, Ltd.
Unit A, Whitacre Mews, 26–34 Stannary Street, London SE11 4AB, United Kingdom
www.rowmaninternational.com

Rowman & Littlefield International, Ltd. is an affiliate of Rowman & Littlefield
4501 Forbes Boulevard, Suite 200, Lanham, Maryland 20706, USA
With additional offices in Boulder, New York, Toronto (Canada), and London (UK)
www.rowman.com
All rights reserved. No part of this book may be reproduced in any form or by any electronic or mechanical means, including information storage and retrieval systems, without written permission from the publisher, except by a reviewer who may quote passages in a review.

British Library Cataloguing in Publication Information Available
A catalogue record for this book is available from the British Library
ISBN: HB 978-1-78348-321-1
ISBN: PB 978-1-78348-322-8
ISBN: EB 978-1-78348-323-5

Library of Congress Cataloging-in-Publication Data
Richardson-Self, Louise.
Justifying same-sex marriage : a philosophical investigation / Louise Richardson-Self.
pages cm
Includes bibliographical references and index.
ISBN 978-1-78348-321-1 (cloth : alk. paper) -- ISBN 978-1-78348-322-8 (pbk. : alk. paper) -- ISBN 978-1-78348-323-5 (electronic)
1. Same-sex marriage. 2. Gay rights. 3. Human rights. I. Title.
HQ1033.R53 2015
306.84'8--dc23
2014050348
∞™ The paper used in this publication meets the minimum requirements of American National Standard for Information Sciences Permanence of Paper for Printed Library Materials, ANSI/NISO Z39.48-1992.
Printed in the United States of America

Justifying Same-Sex Marriage

C016151688

Contents

Acknowledgments ix

Introduction: Same-Sex Marriage and LGBT Nondiscrimination 1

1 Rights, Norms, and Small Change 13

2 Assimilative Justifications of Same-Sex Marriage 35

3 Feminist Criticisms of Human Rights 57

4 Towards a Feminist Human Rights Framework: The Intersubjective Justification Theory 81

5 Advancing the Intersubjective Justification Theory: The Politics of Sexuate Difference 105

6 A Combined Approach: Aiming for LGBT Equal Regard 127

Conclusion: Reflections on Same-Sex Marriage 149

Bibliography 159

Index 165

Acknowledgments

My sincerest gratitude goes to my colleagues at the University of Sydney. Foremost, to Moira Gatens: I have been privileged to work with and have the support of such an inspiring scholar. I must also thank Thomas Besch, Justine McGill, John Grumley, Anik Waldow, Kristie Miller, Caroline West, and Tom Dougherty.

In addition, I would like to thank the staff and graduate students at the Universiteit Utrecht media and cultural studies department. My gratitude goes to Rosemarie Buikema, Gloria Wekker, Berteke Waaldijk, Chiara Bonfiglioli, Rosi Braidotti, Iris van der Tuin, and Domitilla Olivieri. I would also like to thank Kees Waaldijk, Universiteit Leiden.

I am greatly appreciative for feedback on my research from Luce Irigaray, offered at the 2013 Luce Irigaray International Seminar, University of Bristol. I am also grateful to the participants, who each enthusiastically engaged with my work.

I must also thank the people who took time away from their research to read and comment on my research for this book. They are Lucy Cane, Millie Churcher, Tama Coutts, Ben Cross, Kari Greenswag, Shu Yi Huang, Trista Lini, Sarah Drews Lucas, Laura MacDonald, Nick Malpas, Krizia Nardini, Iwo Nord, Inja Stracenski, Jennifer Upchurch, Emma Wood, and Elena Walsh. The support of these generous people was immense. I would like to make a special mention of Freya de Mink. Freya put in a substantial effort when responding to my research. I found her insights and suggestions to be particularly beneficial, and I am indebted to her.

My sincerest gratitude goes to Marguerite La Caze, Rosemarie Buikema, Georgia Warnke, and Jyl Josephson for their detailed and helpful suggestions on the manuscript.

Finally, I would like to thank my friends and family and make a special mention of Libby Cassidy, Ian and Gail Richardson, Ilusha Moroz, and Jenny Self.

Portions of this book have appeared elsewhere in a different form. I would like to thank the publishers for permission to make use of the following materials:

'Questioning the Goal of Same-Sex Marriage', *Australian Feminist Studies* 27, no. 72 (2012): 205–19, available at http://www.tandfonline.com/doi/full/10.1080/08164649.2012.678572, for a portion of chapters 1 and 6.

'Same Sex Marriage: The Road to Social Justice?' *Australian Review of Public Affairs: Digest*, May 2014, available at http://www.australianreview.net/digest/2014/05/richardson-self.html, for a portion of chapters 1 and 6.

'Coming Out and Fitting In: Same-Sex Marriage and the Politics of Difference', *M/C Journal: A Journal of Media and Culture* 15, no. 6 (2012), available at http://journal.media-culture.org.au/index.php/mcjournal/article/viewArticle/572, for a portion of chapter 2.

'Same-Sex Marriage: Zero Tolerance', *Parrhesia: A Journal of Critical Philosophy* 21 (December 2014): 113–24, available at http://www.parrhesiajournal.org/parrhesia21/parrhesia21_richardson-self.pdf, for portions of chapters 4 and 5.

'Irigarayan Insights on the Problem of LGBT Inequality', in *Everyday Feminist Research Praxis: Doing Gender in the Netherlands*, ed. Koen Leurs and Domitilla Olivieri, (Newcastle upon Tyne, UK: Cambridge Scholars Press, 2014), 40–55, for a portion of chapter 5. Published with the permission of Cambridge Scholars Publishing.

Introduction

Same-Sex Marriage and LGBT Nondiscrimination

Since Denmark became the first country to implement a registered partnership scheme for same-sex couples in 1989, and the Netherlands became the first country to legalize same-sex marriage in 2001, legal relationship recognition of same-sex couples has increased rapidly, especially among Western states. Eleven Western European countries have legalized same-sex marriage at the time of this writing: the Netherlands (2001), Belgium (2003), Spain (2005), Sweden (2009), Norway (2009), Iceland (2010), Portugal (2010), Denmark (2012), France (2013), England (2013), Wales (2013), and Luxembourg (2015). Other notable Western European countries, including Germany, Finland, Scotland, Switzerland, and Ireland, have instead implemented alternative formal partnership recognition for same-sex couples. In 2013, the United States' Defense of Marriage Act of 1996 (DOMA), which defined marriage, for federal purposes, as exclusively between one man and one woman, was ruled unconstitutional. At the time of this writing, thirty-two American states recognize same-sex marriage. They are Alaska, Arizona, California, Colorado, Connecticut, Delaware, Hawaii, Idaho, Illinois, Indiana, Iowa, Maine, Maryland, Massachusetts, Minnesota, Nevada, New Hampshire, New Jersey, New Mexico, New York, North Carolina, Oklahoma, Oregon, Pennsylvania, Rhode Island, Utah, Vermont, Virginia, Washington, West Virginia, Wisconsin, and Wyoming. Canada, alternatively, was relatively early in its implementation of same-sex marriage, which took place in 2005. In 2013, New Zealand became the first country in the Asia-Pacific region to legalize same-sex marriage, and in Australia, the question of whether to legalize same-sex marriage has a prominent place in the political spotlight, being briefly legal in the Australian Capital Territory in 2013.

The purpose of this book is to investigate the extent to which legalizing same-sex marriage may contribute to ending the discrimination and social stigma against lesbian, gay, bisexual, and transgender men and women (LGBT). Foremost, it is important to clarify that I am taking 'same-sex marriage' to be a legal union that would be entered into by same-sex attracted couples. While support for same-sex marriage continues to increase, there is much opposition to reform. Importantly, not all opposition is based in conservativism. Many feminists have criticized the institution of marriage as a whole: some argue that marriage is wrong in principle, since it can only be understood in relation to the past it perpetuates, and makes what should be a spontaneous impulse into rights and duties. According to Simone de Beauvoir, for a woman to 'love her husband and to be happy is a duty to herself and society'; however, the practical, social, and moral ties—or normative expectations—demanded within a marriage, such as life-long commitment and fidelity, are inconsistent with the fleeting feelings of sentiment and eroticism (conjugal love) on which the union is supposedly based.[1] The effect of these practical, social, and moral ties is that the couple becomes 'a community whose members have lost their autonomy without escaping their solitude; they are statically assimilated to each other instead of sustaining a dynamic and lively relation together'.[2] In addition, feminists have argued that marriage is an essentially patriarchal institution, that it is an ownership relation, and that it is conducive to violence and mayhem. They claim that it contributes to the systematic oppression of women by shaping their default expectations about how they ought to structure their lives, providing them with a double burden of 'wife work', and teaching them that their highest purpose is to be wives and mothers.[3]

There is also disagreement about the desirability of same-sex marriage in both the academic realm and the queer community. Some believe that same-sex marriage is not desirable because it fails to recognize the different modes that queer intimacies can take. Thus, same-sex marriage would simply redraw the boundaries of legitimacy to include those same-sex couples who assimilate to heteronormative, Eurocentric relationship structures, while continuing to exclude those LGBTs who do not fit the bill.[4] In other words, the argument holds that regarding marriage as an intrinsically valuable institution and providing justifications for same-sex marriage on the basis of LGBT 'sameness' to heteronormative couples is ultimately likely to perpetuate hierarchies of inequality. This is because assimilative arguments implicitly endorse and legitimize already existing unequal social and legal institutions. Assimilative arguments thereby create a further distinction between 'good' LGBT people, who abide by heteronorms, and 'bad' LGBT people, who continue to act deviantly.

As such, my central research question is can same-sex marriage bring about full equality for LGBT people? The answer to this question will, of course, depend on what is meant by 'equality' and what it would mean for LGBT people to be socially included. I postulate a basic claim which holds that what is at stake in the same-sex marriage debate is the *equal regard* of LGBT people. That is to say, *what matters in the same-sex marriage debate is LGBT people coming to be respected as equivalent in dignity, in recognition of (the potential for) difference(s).* If the overarching goal is to achieve nondiscrimination of LGBTs, coming to respect them in recognition of their (potential for) difference(s) is necessary. Thus, equal regard requires that the LGBT rights movement should contribute to the end of stigmatization and the fostering of LGBT identities in this cultivation of difference(s).[5] Therefore, this position maintains that LGBT people need not match heteronormative conceptions of 'appropriate' intimacies and the 'traditional family' in order to be worthy of equal regard. Since assimilative arguments do not cultivate a space in which difference(s) can be fostered, they ought to be avoided.

I have said that LGBT people ought not to be required to match heteronormative standards of acceptability in order to be held in equal regard. It would be wise, then, to define 'heteronormativity' and the 'traditional family'. Heteronormativity involves centralized institutions and localized practices privileging heterosexual relationships as natural and fundamental within society. Heterosexuality is not simply a sexual preference for the other sex; rather, heterosexuality is an assumed way of being oriented in the social world. It is taken for granted in social interactions, advertising, film and television representations, modes of flirting, dating, and so forth. It is ultimately a way of organizing social life. In this way, heterosexuality is institutionalized. Thus, the assumption that underpins institutionalized heterosexuality/heteronormativity is that heterosexuality is the natural, nonpathological orientation.[6]

In 1980 Adrienne Rich famously introduced us to the concept of 'compulsory heterosexuality'.[7] Heterosexuality is 'compulsory' insofar as there is widespread belief that 'male bodies find their natural expression in masculine identities while female bodies find their natural expression in feminine identities. Natural desires, for their part, are all heterosexual'.[8] When this is held to be fundamentally and ahistorically true, heterosexuality cannot be perceived as anything other than normal, proper, and correct. It is presumed that people will be sexually interested in the other sex, and society is structured so as to prepare people for heterosexual encounters and to encourage them to unfold in a certain way.

One may be tempted to object that the increasing visibility of LGBT people nullifies the compulsoriness of heterosexuality. However, this is largely untrue. Leena-Maija Rossi argues that, despite the increase of LGBT visibility in popular media, 'only a certain specific order based on the heterosexual couple and the nuclear family around it continues to be socially, both visually and verbally, privileged and naturalised'.[9] Similarly, Kathy Miriam argues that 'the compulsory dimension of heterosexuality remains mystified/naturalized in the contemporary life-world, and indeed . . . heterosexuality remains compulsory despite the visibility—and to some extent cultural legitimacy—of diverse sexual identities'.[10] Rich herself states (over two decades since the release of *Compulsory Heterosexuality and Lesbian Existence*), 'That new generations of young women have met with that critique [of compulsory heterosexuality] for the first time in my essay only indicates how deeply the presumption still prevails.'[11]

The advent of compulsory heterosexuality is sustained, in part, by the phallocentric logic which designates heterosexuality as normal. Phallocentrism can be defined as 'thinking in terms of an ostensibly disembodied, but implicitly masculine rationalism'.[12] Phallocentrism thus refers to 'the ways in which patriarchal systems of representation always submit women to models and images defined by men'.[13] Phallocentric logic assumes heterosexuality and dictates that a particular kind of subject is 'normal' and the marker for humanity. This subject is an individual; he is male, heterosexual, adult, white, able-bodied, rational, and competent.

Importantly, even what it is to be a citizen has been imagined through the lens of compulsory heterosexuality and the figure of the phallocentric subject. But it is not simply any version of heterosexual interaction that counts in this context. Rather, 'it is heterosexuality *as marriage and the traditional, middle-class nuclear family* which is commonly held up as a model of good citizenship, necessary for ensuring national security and a stable social order'.[14] What defines traditional marriage and the nuclear family? Marriage is thought to encompass the emotional and spiritual unity of two persons, and this unity requires certain features, such as monogamy, long-term commitment, sexual fidelity, companionship, and economic support. This basic unit also ensures the correct environment for childrearing.[15] Thus, the nuclear family is that unit formed of children raised by parents who are engaged in a marital union. Importantly, this union has been imagined, until recently, to be exclusively heterosexual.

Now, in this research, the concepts of traditional marriage and the nuclear family are considered with reference to their figuration in a *dominant shared Western social imaginary*. This point is important, since such normative figurations have real influences on the intimate and familial choices people make. 'Imaginaries' are made up of 'images, symbols, metaphors and narratives that help structure forms of embodied identity and belonging'.[16] Imaginaries are plural and can be social, political, legal, philosophical, and so on. Social imaginaries, in particular, make sense of social bodies (that is, of actual people), and contribute to the determination of their value, status, and appropriate treatment.[17] These imaginaries create a set of *social norms* which then receive dominant uptake. A social norm can be defined as 'a collective expectation about what is to count as appropriate behaviour for a particular identity in a particular context'.[18] Georgia Warnke notes that norms are double-edged swords. They bind individuals together and form the basis of ethical and political claims. But norms are also coercive. Norms dictate what counts as evaluatively normal and what actions or behaviours are deauthorized.[19] Together, the norms within imaginaries create *meaning-generating narratives*. Meaning-generating narratives are the stories we are invested in. They are those stories which give us reasons to act in one particular way rather than another or to believe in or value one thing rather than another. The dominant shared Western social imaginary is constituted of multiple imaginaries working together to create common perspectives, providing people with meaningful reasons for action. These narratives effectively 'legitimize' certain normative behaviours and institutions.

Thus, in this introduction I have not defined what marriage *is*, but what it is popularly *imagined to be* in the West, and this understanding of marriage is meaning-generating insofar as it gives people reasons to desire to act in accordance with the norms of romantic love that it legitimizes. However, allowing LGBT people's entry to marriage only *after* they demonstrate their sameness to heteronormative conceptions of intimacy and family is the approach this research rejects. What is required instead is a shift in the dominant shared Western social imaginary. LGBT people ought to have the option to access the same institutions as heterosexuals while nonetheless allowing for the cultivation of different lifestyle choices and identities. But what does it mean to say that LGBT people should be entitled to cultivate and foster difference(s)? What do LGBT identities involve?

LGBT identities do not simply consist of an 'alternative' sexual orientation overlaid on a 'normal' human identity. Being an LGBT person does not amount to being the same as a heterosexual with a sexual orientation twist. Moreover, it is important *not* to consider LGBT people in this way, since such an approach implies that heterosexuality is normal and homosexuality is aberrant. It implies that the existing standards we have for talking about 'normal' humanity (plus or minus a few differences) is adequate for comprehending difference. But this is simply not the case. Sexual identity is not a mere add-on to a base component of normalcy, it is entirely bound up with and inextricable from one's subjectivity. 'Cultivating difference' and 'fostering LGBT identities' should be interpreted as recognizing, endorsing, and legitimizing alternative subjectivities in their own right. Thus, these subjectivities need to be rethought outside of the phallocentric logic which has heretofore designated them as 'Other'. Moreover, undertaking this task also allows for the cultivation of a 'heterosexuality done differently', insofar as these diverse identities and lifestyles may gain further visibility and acceptance.

The question at hand is whether LGBT people can endorse and claim a right to marriage—an institution which still offers a number of legal advantages and obligations—without endorsing this institution as the morally superior structure for intimate relationships or framing LGBT subjectivities as poor copies of the normal human subject. I argue that this is possible, but only if same-sex marriage is regarded as one option among a plurality of personal intimacies which need to be promoted and legally protected. Furthermore, it is crucial that the shift I propose—respect for difference and for a plurality of possible personal intimacies—gains uptake in the dominant shared Western social imaginary. To this end I propose a feminist human rights framework which weaves together insights from Rainer Forst's intersubjective justification theory and Luce Irigaray's politics of sexuate difference.[20] I will argue that this 'combined approach' can justify same-sex marriage without requiring assimilation and can also challenge the characterization of homosexuality as immoral. Indeed, what I claim is that this feminist human rights framework can provide a stronger and more transformative vision for the ultimate goal of equal regard than standard rights-based justifications of same-sex marriage.

The combined approach is a constructivist account of rights which holds that all people are entitled to give and receive reciprocally and generally acceptable justifications for the norms and rules which govern their lives. All men and women are to be acknowledged as potentially differing persons who exist intersubjectively, and this demands a revised understanding of, and encounter with, difference. As a constructivist theory, this argument denies the *intrinsic* status of marriage as a prepolitical, hierarchically, and morally superior form of union. It holds instead that traditional and nontraditional features of caring relationships may be deemed useful or valuable to the state and its citizens, and the state ought to recognize several unions as horizontally valuable. As such it attempts to provide a new meaning-generating story: the narrative of caring-love. The narrative of caring-love acknowledges that all persons at all stages of their life require, desire, and/or deliver care, and that care is fundamental to our flourishing as intersubjective individuals. A new narrative which seeks to value multiple forms of intimacies and families is fitting with the demand for respect for difference, then.

This approach also shifts the onus of proof onto those who oppose same-sex marriage. In other words, the combined approach demands that the opponents of same-sex marriage provide acceptable reasons for this state of affairs. It is not upon LGBT people to prove their likeness to heteronormative couples in order to justify why they are worthy of entry to the institution, it is on those who would maintain the status quo to justify inaction while acknowledging the following: there is a basic commitment to all people as having equal status *qua* members of the human community, there is a general recognition that a potential for difference exists between us, and there is a history of LGBT discrimination in the West stemming from a designation of LGBT people as Other. I will argue that no acceptable justification to prevent same-sex marriage can be provided, and that change is necessary on this basis.

The structure of this book is as follows: Chapter 1 looks at the status of same-sex marriage in the West. In particular, it focuses on the formulation of the claim to same-sex marriage as a matter of human rights, on the pattern of small legal changes which precedes its introduction, and on the emerging transnational soft law norm of same-sex relationship recognition. An analysis of these factors shows that the dominant strategies that have been employed to gain access to marriage are largely assimilative in character.

Chapter 2 further addresses assimilative arguments in favour of same-sex marriage. In particular, it provides an analysis of the personhood account of human rights, which attempts to justify same-sex marriage on the ground of liberty. The 'personhood account' of human rights has been called 'arguably the most significant philosophical meditation on human rights to emerge in the human rights–intoxicated era'.[21] It holds that same-sex couples face a paucity of options where they are unable to participate in marriage, and, because marriage plays a central role in most people's conceptions of the good life, this option ought to be made available. However, the personhood account implicitly holds some commitment to marriage as an intrinsically valuable institution. It also assumes the 'sameness' of same-sex relationships to different-sex relationships. The personhood account therefore seems likely to continue to stigmatize 'bad' LGBT people (and possibly stigmatize 'bad' heterosexuals), where to be 'bad' is to be other than heteronormative. What this chapter demonstrates is that not all justifications in favour of same-sex marriage are likely to lead to the nondiscrimination of LGBTs as a collective. However, from this analysis of the personhood account we can glean what a desirable theory of human rights would do: it would (a) oblige those who are able to introduce same-sex marriage to undertake this task, irrespective of their personal inclinations; (b) not assume that marriage is an intrinsically worthy institution worthy of reproduction; (c) have a socially comparative element balanced by a critical component; and (d) take into account the history of LGBT discrimination.

Importantly, it is critical to assess whether *any* account of human rights has the capacity to fulfil these functions, for rights are arguably ineffective tools for securing social justice for certain sorts of persons, resulting in paradoxical consequences. The task of chapter 3 is to investigate these paradoxes and to assess whether they are inherently irresolvable. The paradoxes of rights are as follows: (a) when rights are explicitly specified for certain sorts of persons (for example, 'Women's rights' or 'LGBT rights') these persons can have their subordinate status reinforced by being marked as different; however, (b) if rights are neutral in nonneutral contexts, this can enhance the privilege of some and eclipse the needs of others. In addition, (c) advocating for group rights involves presenting a united front, and this often means certain group members are not adequately acknowledged; however, (d) advocating for more and more highly specific rights means that the basis of group identity is likely to be lost. Ultimately, I argue that the paradoxes of rights can be avoided by reconceiving the notion of difference that informs identity recognition. Thus, an acceptable theory of human rights must also involve a reconception of difference at its core.

In order to attempt the challenge of developing a theory of rights that meets the criteria outlined, chapter 4 turns to discursive constructivism. In particular, it looks to Rainer Forst's intersubjective justification theory. The intersubjective justification theory holds that one fundamental human right lies behind all other rights claims: the basic right to justification. The basic right to justification is the primary right of all people to give and receive justifications for the norms that they are each to live by. The criteria that determine a moral norm's legitimacy are 'reciprocity' and 'generality' in the first instance. In addition, one must consider the historically situated context in which specific rights claims arise and give weight to empirical considerations. That is to say, one must pay attention to any history of privilege/exclusion, and this will inform the legitimacy of norms and their justifications. However, the intersubjective justification theory does not meet each of the aforementioned criteria. While it is socially comparative, Forst's version does not offer a strong enough critical component. More pressing is that Forst's intersubjective justification theory does not explicitly involve a reconception of difference. A final issue is the recommendation that same-sex marriage be tolerated, which does not imply equal regard.

Thus, in chapter 5 I supplement Forst's intersubjective justification theory with insights from sexual difference feminism. In particular, I look to Irigaray's philosophy of sexuate difference. Irigaray develops an alternative method for recognizing difference—as thinking (through) two. While I stress that Irigaray's focus is on the two of sexuate difference (men and women), I also demonstrate that Irigaray's philosophy is not heterosexist and that Irigaray only finds an approach beginning with two to be useful insofar as it can teach people how to re-cognize and reimagine difference itself. Once this figuration of difference is adopted, a deeper critique of one's sociopolitical and legal circumstances is made possible. From this, we are also able to see that there is nothing legitimately objectionable about LGBTs and their practices, which means that tolerance should be repudiated in favour of promoting respect. It is at this point that I elaborate fully the structure of the combined approach that I ultimately endorse.

In chapter 6, I put this combined theory to the test against Cheshire Calhoun's assessment of the 'better' argument for same-sex marriage. She claims that the better argument for same-sex marriage is the one which will offer LGBT people some kind of positive moral esteem. She also thinks that this esteem will come specifically from the belief that LGBT people are fit to participate in *normatively ideal* forms of marriage and the family. This perspective is problematic if what is 'normatively ideal' does not shift from its present conception in the dominant shared Western social imaginary. Fortunately, the combined approach can create multiple possible ideals for structuring one's intimacies and familial life, since a reconceptualization of difference is at its core. Thus, I argue that the combined approach must be endorsed. It must be endorsed so that it can become a primary influence in the dominant shared Western social imaginary—so that it will, in other words, provide a new dominant meaning-generating narrative of caring-love. While such a theory perhaps appears *too* utopian to be considered a pragmatic goal for the LGBT community, I nonetheless hold that utopian visions are necessary and that the power of the human imagination to prompt social change should not be underestimated.

Finally, in anticipation of a critical reading of my argument, there is one further point I must address. It may be asked why LGBT people cannot simply play the heteronormative game in order to obtain legal access to marriage and then work from the inside out to shift the symbolic dominance of traditional marriage. That is, why not strategically assimilate? This seems like a plausible strategy which could effect the same kinds of changes I endorse. Furthermore, assimilative arguments are the *politically expedient* arguments.[22] This proposal, I believe, depends in part on matters of material access. If LGBT people do not even have minimal access to certain legal protections and benefits because those protections and benefits are restricted to heterosexual marriage, then the expedient method may have some merit in a pragmatic sense. However, in admitting this, it is important to point out that such a response does not answer the question of *why* married-couple families should have access to certain rights which are not afforded to other family forms.[23]

In addition, I have two further responses to the proposal of strategic assimilation. The first is that this revolution from the inside out does not seem to be occurring in those countries which have already legalized same-sex marriage. Intolerance of LGBT people is still common, and LGBT people regularly face bullying in schools, have a higher rate of mental illness and suicide as a result of the prejudice they face, and so on.[24] Heinz Paetzold considers the Netherlands, which was the first country to legalize same-sex marriage. He argues, 'In recent time, however, we notice, for instance, in the liberal Netherlands a growing aversion of young men against homosexuals.'[25] More recently, the French protests against the introduction of same-sex marriage demonstrate that homophobia is still common. The *Daily Mail* reports that the first three months of 2013 saw homophobic attacks triple in

France when compared to the same period of 2012.[26] In other words, the strategy of assimilation appears to be having little real social effect.

Secondly, like Irigaray, I seek to defend the impossible.[27] This is important since, as Marcel Stoetzler and Nira Yuval-Davis note, 'social agency . . . regularly changes society to the effect that what used to be an impossibility becomes a possibility. The (largely imaginary) status of a goal or value might change from impossible to possible, from 'utopian' via feasible to matter of fact.'[28] Thus, I ask, why should one endorse an argument for same-sex marriage that only implicitly criticizes the institutionalised heterosexuality that has made LGBT people out to be inferior? Employing such a method is dangerous insofar as it risks *strengthening* the heteronormative meaning-generating story of traditional marriage and the nuclear family in the dominant shared Western social imaginary. This, in turn, may incline people against a revolution from the inside. The combined approach, on the other hand, has the benefit of justifying same-sex marriage in present conditions, while encouraging us to reflect on and reconstruct our shared commitments—which is surely better for the goal of LGBT equal regard.

NOTES

1. Simone de Beauvoir, *The Second Sex*, 1949, trans. C. Borde and S. Malovany-Chevallier (London: Vintage Books, 2009), 507.
2. Ibid., 521.
3. Elizabeth Brake, *Minimizing Marriage: Marriage, Morality and the Law* (Oxford: Oxford University Press, 2012), chap. 5; Claudia Card, 'Against Marriage and Motherhood', *Hypatia* 11, no. 3 (1996): 1–23.
4. Brake, *Minimizing Marriage*, chap. 5.
5. Inspiration for these demands is found in Diane Richardson, 'Sexuality and Citizenship', *Sociology* 32 (1998): 83–100.
6. Elizabeth Cole et al., 'Against Nature: How Arguments about the Naturalness of Marriage Privilege Heterosexuality', *Journal of Social Issues* 68, no. 1 (2012): 46–62; Cheshire Calhoun, *Feminism, the Family, and the Politics of the Closet: Lesbian and Gay Displacement* (Oxford: Oxford University Press, 2000), chap. 5.
7. Adrienne Rich, 'Compulsory Heterosexuality and Lesbian Existence (1980)', *Journal of Women's History* 15, no. 3 (2003): 11–48.
8. Georgia Warnke, *After Identity* (Cambridge: Cambridge University Press, 2007), 164–65.
9. Leena-Maija Rossi, '"Happy" and "Unhappy" Performatives: Images and Norms of Heterosexuality', *Australian Feminist Studies* 26, no. 67 (2011): 17.
10. Kathy Miriam, 'Toward a Phenomenology of Sex-Right: Reviving Radical Feminist Theory of Compulsory Heterosexuality', *Hypatia* 22, no. 1 (2007): 211.
11. Adrienne Rich, 'Reflections on "Compulsory Heterosexuality"', *Journal of Women's History* 16, no. 1 (2004): 10.
12. Rosemarie Buikema, 'Monumental Dresses: Coming to Terms with Racial Oppression', in *Teaching Race with a Gendered Edge*, ed. B. Hipfl and K. Loftsdóttir (Budapest and New York: Central European University Press, 2012), 56.
13. Elizabeth Grosz, *Sexual Subversions: Three French Feminists* (New South Wales, Aus.: Allen & Unwin, 1989), xx; see also Luce Irigaray, *An Ethics of Sexual Difference*, trans. C. Burke and G. Gill (London: Continuum, 2004), chap. 1.
14. Richardson, 'Sexuality and Citizenship', 92; emphasis added.

15. Calhoun, *Feminism, the Family*, 110.

16. Moira Gatens, 'Can Human Rights Accommodate Women's Rights? Towards an Embodied Account of Social Norms, Social Meaning, and Cultural Change', *Contemporary Political Theory* 3, no. 3 (2004): 282–83.

17. Moira Gatens, *Imaginary Bodies: Ethics, Power and Corporeality* (London: Routledge, 1996), preface.

18. Gatens, 'Can Human Rights Accommodate Women's Rights?' 284.

19. Warnke, *After Identity*, chap. 5.

20. A shift in terminology has occurred in Irigaray's work from *sexual difference* to *sexuate difference*. For the purposes of consistency, earlier works that employ the term *sexual difference* will be edited to align with this shift. The term *sexuate* is intended to reflect an ontological difference between women and men without denying that multiple forms of diversity exist among and between women and men.

21. James Tasioulas, 'Taking Rights out of Human Rights', *Ethics* 120, no. 4 (2010): 647.

22. Cheshire Calhoun, 'Who's Afraid of Polygamous Marriage? Lessons for Same-Sex Marriage Advocacy from the History of Polygamy', *San Diego Law Review* 42 (2005): 1023–42.

23. See Nancy Polikoff, *Beyond (Straight and Gay) Marriage: Valuing All Families under the Law* (Boston: Beacon Press, 2011).

24. European Union Agency for Fundamental Rights (FRA), *EU LGBT Survey: European Union Lesbian, Gay, Bisexual and Transgender Survey—Results at a Glance* (Luxembourg: Publications Office of the European Union, 2013), 1–31, accessed November 14, 2014, http://fra.europa.eu/sites/default/files/eu-lgbt-survey-results-at-a-glance_en.pdf.

25. Heinz Paetzold, 'Respect and Toleration Reconsidered (Under Consideration: Rainer Forst's *Toleranz im Konflikt: Geschichte, Gehalt, und Gegenwart eines umstrittenen Begriffs*)', *Philosophy & Social Criticism* 34, no. 8 (2008): 953.

26. Amanda Williams, '"This Is the True Face of Homophobia": Gay Man Viciously Beaten in Paris Posts Picture of His Injuries to Facebook in Protest Move That Has Now Gone Viral', *Daily Mail*, May 27, 2013, accessed May 28, 2013, http://www.dailymail.co.uk/news/article-2307288/Paris-gay-attack-victim-Wilfred-Bruijns-Facebook-injuries-picture-goes-viral.html#ixzz2UZH3Bjz1.

27. Luce Irigaray, *I Love to You*, trans. Alison Martin (New York: Routledge, 1996), prologue.

28. Marcel Stoetzler and Nira Yuval-Davis, 'Standpoint Theory, Situated Knowledge and the Situated Imagination', *Feminist Theory* 3, no. 3 (2002): 326–27.

Chapter One

Rights, Norms, and Small Change

Same-sex relationship recognition first started gaining momentum in the 1980s and has achieved rapid political uptake. Rights discourse has become the dominant discourse surrounding LGBT issues, surpassing the rhetoric of gay liberation that formerly characterized the movement.[1] Certainly, it is politically expedient to frame one's complaints in accordance with an already established and largely accepted transnational framework. Moreover, there is an emerging transnational soft law norm of same-sex relationship recognition. To say that same-sex relationship recognition is emerging as a transnational soft law norm means that the dominant Western social imaginary has shifted to incorporate the belief that same-sex couples *ought* to have their relationships legally recognized (or that to legally recognize these relationships is *appropriate*, to the extent that this can be characterized as a guiding rule). Of course, this does not mean that same-sex *marriage* is normative. It is far more common for countries to (initially) introduce some form of civil union scheme, which, depending on its laws, may be more or less similar to marriage.[2] In other words, it is not yet seen as entirely appropriate to amend marriage *itself* so as to include same-sex couples; but popular opinion is slowly changing.

The introduction of civil unions and de facto status are common variations of same-sex relationship recognition, but LGBT activists often argue that this type of recognition is inadequate; they continue to demand access to marriage itself. For example, Kees Waaldijk, reporting on the Dutch registered partnership scheme, notes that 'after the 1998 reforms relating to parenting, the number of legal reasons why a same-sex couple could prefer marriage to registered partnership became almost zero. . . . However, this did not silence the call for the opening up of marriage. On the contrary, the social and political pressure increased.'[3] Similar evidence is displayed transnationally. In 2000, the Canadian government allowed same-sex couples to enter into common law partnerships. This victory also stimulated activists to call for full marriage rights. One policy activist responded that 'marriage still has meaning' beyond the pale of material benefits.[4] Presently, activists in the United States and Australia put forward arguments which claim that the ban on same-sex marriage disadvantages all same-sex attracted people by 'send[ing] out the message that discrimination on the grounds of sexual orientation is acceptable',[5] and that 'marriage says "We are family" in a way that no other word does'.[6]

The continued demand for access to marriage—rather than some form of civil union scheme—indicates that formal legal equality is not all that is at stake in the demand for equal marriage rights. And the activism works. Several countries, including Canada and the Netherlands, as well as Demark, Belgium, Norway, Sweden, the United Kingdom, and New Zealand, among others, have progressed from civil union or de facto schemes to marriage equality. Marriage itself may soon become the norm for same-sex relationship recognition.

This progression can be attributed to what Waaldijk calls the 'law of small change', where LGBT law reform occurs by building one small legislative change upon another, according to a certain pattern. It starts with '(1) decriminalisation . . . after which (2) anti-discrimination legislation can be introduced, before the process is finished with (3) legislation recognising same-sex partnership'.[7] The law of small change also dictates that the actualization of this pattern typically possesses a linear trajectory. But a simple focus on legal reform largely overlooks the social situation of LGBTs. In the introduction, I proposed that what is at stake in the same-sex marriage debate is the *equal regard* of LGBT people. What matters, in other words, is LGBT people coming to be respected as sexual citizens.[8] The question, then, is this: once formal legal equality is achieved, will matters of social discrimination also be resolved? Data from the recent European Union (EU) LGBT survey suggests not. For example, although the Netherlands was the first country to introduce same-sex marriage (2001), 30 percent of Dutch respondents reported feeling discriminated against or harassed in the previous twelve months based on their sexual orientation.[9]

Why is legal equality not translating into equal regard? This must be investigated. Since one aspect of access to the institution of marriage is socially symbolic, any account arguing for same-sex marriage and seeking the end of LGBT discrimination ought to consider what marriage equality will mean on this level. It is also imperative to investigate the difficulties that arise in framing same-sex marriage as a matter of human rights. There are two such difficulties: First, appealing to human rights need not imply an explicit challenge to the characterization of homosexuality as *immoral*. Second, appealing to human rights may be assimilative in character. Again, it bears repeating, this matters because *in principle* LGBT people ought not to be required to match heteronormative standards of acceptability in order to be treated with dignity. Thus, for any justification of same-sex marriage to be acceptable, it must circumvent these difficulties.

Throughout this book I will argue that a feminist human rights framework can provide a stronger and more transformative vision for the ultimate goal of equal regard than standard rights-based justifications of same-sex marriage. The aim of this chapter, then, is to give a brief characterization of the marriage equality movement in the West and to provisionally determine on what grounds same-sex marriage might legitimately be considered a matter of human rights. I will conclude that the same-sex marriage movement, as it stands, presents a bleak outlook for LGBT activists who seek equal regard. If LGBT acceptance is predicated on likeness to the heteronormative mainstream, and if law reform is only awarded in small, homogenizing, normative steps, then *at best* this approach will redraw the boundaries of acceptability to include only *some* LGBT people. This does not amount to equal regard.

I. SAME-SEX MARRIAGE AND HUMAN RIGHTS

While international LGBT organizations increased greatly beginning in the 1960s–1970s, it was not until the late 1980s–1990s that these organizations began to specifically frame their demands as matters of human rights. A particularly influential organization in this domain of LGBT law reform is the International Lesbian, Gay, Bisexual, Trans and Intersex Association (ILGA). The ILGA is a global organization split into six sectors, with ILGA-Europe its strongest and most influential branch. It is, therefore, unsurprising that same-sex relationship recognition began in Western Europe. The ILGA is credited with convincing already existing international human rights organizations, such as Human Rights Watch and Amnesty International, to recognize sexual orientation as a matter of human rights. This ongoing activism has influenced matters such as the inclusion of sexual orientation as a protected category in the Treaty of Amsterdam (1997), appeals from the European Parliament to allow same-sex marriage, and binding decisions from the European Court of Human Rights (ECHR) prohibiting LGBT discrimination. These, in turn, have reciprocally contributed to the definition of LGBT rights as ‘human rights’. Even the United Nations (UN) is a focus of LGBT rights campaigns.[10]

A human right, according to a commonsense definition, is a right that people are entitled to simply by the mere fact of being human.[11] When countries ratify declarations like the Universal Declaration of Human Rights 1948 (UDHR), or the covenants directly influenced by it—the International Covenant on Civil and Political Rights 1966 (ICCPR) and the International

Covenant on Economic, Social and Cultural Rights 1966 (ICESC)—the implication is that those particular countries deem the rights listed therein to be essential for any human life. On this basis, LGBT activists may claim that several of their rights are being violated due to the identity-based discrimination they face. Since the UDHR is the direct influence of the binding ICCPR and ICESC and forms the basis of many people's conceptions of what counts as a legitimate ground for human rights, I will consider the articles therein in order to determine whether same-sex couples can legitimately claim they have a right to marriage.

Taken together, articles 1 and 2 of the UDHR provide the grounds for interpreting the remaining articles within. Article 1 states: 'All human beings are born free and equal in dignity and rights. They are endowed with reason and conscience and should act towards one another in a spirit of brotherhood.' This article implies two things. It implies that if there is a denial of basic human *dignity*, then people have grounds for a complaint, and it implies that if basic *rights* are denied, then people have grounds for complaint. For it is in their *being human* that people are endowed with this equality. Thus, there must also be a corresponding duty binding all people to recognize the dignity and rights of others and to act in accordance with such duties; this is what it means to 'act toward one another in a spirit of brotherhood.'[12]

Article 2 states: 'Everyone is entitled to the rights and freedoms set forth in this Declaration, without distinction of any kind, such as race, colour, sex, language, religion, political or other opinion, national or social origin, property, birth or other status.' This article can be said to embody the *principle of nondiscrimination*: it is unjust to discriminate against a person or group of people on the ground of their identity. While sexual orientation is not mentioned specifically in article 2, the presence of the words 'such as' and 'other status' indicates that this is not a closed category of distinctions. This present interpretation is also justified by past events such as the inclusion of sexual orientation as a protected category in the Treaty of Amsterdam. Thus, it is plausible that sexual orientation ought to be considered under the principle of nondiscrimination for the purposes of the remaining articles.

Relevant to same-sex marriage are the following: articles 3, 12, and 16. These fall into the category of 'first generation rights', which refer to liberties, both civil and political. Article 3 states: 'Everyone has the right to life, liberty and security of person.' One may argue that where same-sex marriage is not legal, LGBT people are specifically lacking in liberty. Some activists have argued this point by drawing an analogy to miscegenation laws. On miscegenation laws, Hannah Arendt has argued:

> The right to marry whoever one wishes is an elementary human right. . . . Even political rights, like the right to vote . . . are secondary to the inalienable human rights to 'life, liberty and the pursuit of happiness' proclaimed in the

> [U.S.] Declaration of Independence; and to this category the right to home and marriage unquestionably belongs.[13]

This argument rests on the distinction Arendt draws between the private, social, and political realms.[14] In the instance of miscegenation laws, Arendt believes the political has overstepped its bounds into the private and that it cannot be justifiable to legally prevent one's free associations in this realm. Rodney Croome, national convenor of Australian Marriage Equality (AME), uses Arendt's argument to draw the analogy to same-sex marriage: just as blacks and whites were unfairly prevented from marrying one another, so too is it unfair to prevent two people of the same sex from marrying. This interferes with their liberties and fails to treat LGBTs as equals to heterosexuals.[15]

Another way to interpret the matter of individual liberty is to say that same-sex attracted people face a 'paucity of options'. According to James Griffin, there is a difference between a denial of liberty and a paucity of options; a denial of liberty typically involves constraint or compulsions, whereas a paucity of options involves an unnecessary narrowing of options. If a society finds itself in a position where it can allow further options to its citizens, and there is no good reason not to do so, then that society has a duty to create these alternatives.[16] On this basis, it seems as though one can make the case for same-sex marriage: if one group (different-sex couples) has legal opportunities available to them while another group (same-sex couples) has the very same legal opportunities *unreasonably* curtailed, such inequalities ought to be rectified. The obvious question is whether there is any justifiable reason to continue excluding same-sex couples from marriage. I will argue that there is no such justifiable reason. However, whether or not liberty-based justifications of same-sex marriage are suitable for endorsement is still an additional question.

On first blush, these responses seem compelling. Same-sex couples should be free to marry, regardless of whether LGBT people would actually choose to enter into a marriage. However, there are also reasons to be sceptical of this approach. If one *successfully* argues their case on the ground of liberty (that is, they do not rely upon assimilative justifications to make their case), this does not guarantee any change in the social reception of LGBTs. LGBTs may become legally equal and free to do as they please, but they are likely to continue to face identity-based discrimination.[17] These justifications have a strong appeal, but since what is at stake in the same-sex marriage debate is the *equal regard* of LGBT people, we will need to take care to ensure that equal regard is a likely consequence of such justifications.[18]

Article 12 pertains to privacy. It reads as follows: 'No one shall be subjected to arbitrary interference with his privacy, family, home or correspondence, nor to attacks upon his honour and reputation. Everyone has the right to the protection of the law against such interference or attacks.' Privacy has been commonly employed as a ground for LGBT law reform and was particularly influential in arguments seeking to decriminalize homo-sex,[19] given that 'sexual orientation' was not explicitly listed as an axis of discrimination until the Amsterdam treaty. For example, consider the Wolfenden Report (1957): the British Wolfenden Committee recommended that homo-sex between two consenting adults in private ought to be decriminalized. They found that 'it is not, in our view, the function of the law to intervene in the private lives of citizens'.[20] In other words, the committee was convinced that there is a realm where the arm of the law does not belong: the private realm. The justification for decriminalising homo-sex stood regardless of the fact that there was much social opposition to the practice at the time. Consider also a more recent example: In 1994 *Toonen v. Australia* came before the United Nations Human Rights Committee (UNHRC). Toonen claimed that his right to privacy, in accordance with article 17 of the ICCPR, was being violated by Tasmania's antisodomy laws.[21] Importantly, article 17 of the ICCPR reads exactly the same as article 12 of the UDHR and is the second schedule to the Australian Human Rights Commission Act 1986. The UNHRC found that 'in so far as article 17 is concerned, it is undisputed that adult consensual sexual activity in private is covered by the concept of "privacy"'.[22] Thus, given the success of privacy claims in other areas of LGBT law reform, privacy seems to be a plausible ground on which to claim the right to marry. This also recalls Arendt's claim about miscegenation laws: the political realm has overstepped its bounds into the private realm, but it cannot be justifiable to legally prevent one's free associations therein.

However, appeals for human rights based on the right to privacy can be troublesome for two reasons. First, even if marriage *were* a completely private association, these arguments, like the arguments for liberty, need not challenge the social perception of homosexuality as immoral and unnatural. This may increase the difficulty of fostering LGBT identities and cultivating difference(s). In the aforementioned cases, both recommendations were not primarily based on the belief that homo-sex is morally acceptable. That is an irrelevant consideration. What is relevant is that the right to privacy holds regardless of whether homo-sex is immoral; the moral status of homo-sex need not be challenged in order for the decisions to be justified.[23] Take the Wolfenden Committee's decision into account in particular: This decision was not based on changed social attitudes which judged homo-sex as legitimate, natural, and/or normal behaviour. Instead, the decision was based on whether public condemnation is sufficient to justify making an act into a crime. Ultimately, if it is agreed that there must be 'toleration of the maximum individual freedom that is consistent with the integrity of society', and if the performance of homo-sex in private will not harm the integrity of society, then the law has no business forbidding these acts.[24]

Problematically, dominant prejudices pertaining to that identity, which hold, for example, that homo-sex is against nature, perverted, and abnormal, are not necessarily challenged when a right is gained on the ground of privacy. Because such detrimental interpretations of homosexuals and homosexuality are not challenged head on, these stereotypes persist in the dominant shared Western social imaginary today. This is true despite the fact that *legally* steps have been made towards LGBT equality. Thus, if privacy is to be claimed as a ground for marriage, it will need to be teamed with a positive claim for the respect of LGBTs' identities. LGBTs do not require private permission; they require the right to a private *and* public existence.[25] They require legal change *with regard for* sexual orientation, not legal change *in spite of* sexual orientation. Recognition in spite of one's identity would ensure a legal right without endignifying sexual orientation, whereas recognition with regard for one's identity would both bestow a right and endignify sexual orientation.

Second, some feminist theorists have held critical perspectives on the privilege granted to privacy as a right since it masks from state intervention a realm where potential abuses against women can, and have, occurred. Kate Sheill claims that privacy in human rights law is a gendered concept. She argues that lesbians, being women, have a significantly different relationship to the home, the family, and the public expression of sexual identity. In other words, she is arguing that the lesbian experience of discrimination is intricately tied with sex and gender discrimination. Because of these sexed and gendered assumptions, and because of the prevalence of abuse and subjugation against women in the private realm, lesbians may have more of a resistance to using privacy as a justification for rights claims in general than gay men.[26] Claudia Card also raises concerns about the private realm and married life. She claims that the legal rights of access that married partners have to the other's person and property makes it difficult for a spouse to defend him- or herself or to be protected from violence by the other. She argues, 'Legal marriage thus enlists state support for conditions conducive to murder and mayhem.'[27] This is not to argue that all marriages are violent, but rather that the structure of the institution itself puts barriers in the way of protection in the private realm.

Others, such as Wendy Brown, do not wish to deny the value of privacy altogether, acknowledging that some matters of sexual freedom and welfare rights are strongly dependent on the concept of privacy. Nonetheless, she acknowledges that all too often the realm of privacy has served to depoliticize women's issues.[28] These concerns are accentuated when we consider that the legal and nonlegal discrimination faced by same-sex attracted men and same-sex attracted women has often differed. For example, legal criminalization of homo-sex frequently only stipulated a ban on sex between men.[29] In other cases, laws may have only been relevant to women, for example, with regard to their status and rights as 'mothers'.[30] These variances may well explain why same-sex attracted men may find the ground of privacy a more attractive justification than same-sex attracted women—gay men do not have the same history of abuses attributable to the law's noninterference. Thus, without denying the value of privacy altogether, one should be wary of endorsing a private sphere entirely out of reach of the law.

Finally, article 16 of the UDHR is crucial when considering the claim to same-sex marriage since it sets out what a right to marriage supposedly means. It consists of three parts, and reads as follows:

1. Men and women of full age, without any limitation due to race, nationality or religion, have the right to marry and to found a family. They are entitled to equal rights as to marriage, during marriage and at its dissolution.
2. Marriage shall be entered into only with the free and full consent of the intending spouses.
3. The family is the natural and fundamental group unit of society and is entitled to protection by society and the State.

The first thing to notice is that although section 1 specifically mentions men and women rather than individuals, it does not state explicitly that men must marry women and vice versa. Second, it is important to recall that this 'right' comes under the section of civil and political *liberties*, meaning men and women ought to have the freedom to marry. But this raises an important question: There may be many things that people ought to be able to freely choose to do, so why does marriage specifically warrant articulation as a right in the UDHR and subsequent covenants? Why isn't marriage merely an implied right under article 3 (as Arendt suggests)? A potential answer is to be found in the third section of article 16, which proclaims the 'family' to be the 'fundamental group unit of society', thus entitling it to state and society protection.[31] Yet this answer warrants further questioning: What structure must this so-called fundamental group unit take? Furthermore, why is a reference to 'the family' made when the article pertains to the right to *marriage*—are marriage and the family inextricably connected?

Cheshire Calhoun has argued that in Western culture marriage is thought to play a unique and foundational role in sustaining civil society. Marriage is a naturally occurring and intrinsically good unit. It produces and nurtures new citizens and so can be considered the bedrock of modern societies.[32] The Family Research Council (FRC), a conservative American organization, argues this very point: 'Marriage is not a creation of the law. Marriage is a fundamental human institution that predates the law and the Constitution. At its heart, it is an anthropological and sociological reality, not a legal one. Laws relating to marriage merely recognize and regulate an institution that already exists.'[33] It seems that the UDHR endorses this political myth; article 16, section 3 states that the family is the 'natural and fundamental group unit of society'. Thus, it is abundantly clear that, according to article 16, one's ability to marry is intimately tied up with one's status as a citizen. This is why LGBT activists often claim that being denied equal access to marriage sends the message that LGBTs are second-class citizens.[34] But, do LGBT activists have a valid claim for same-sex marriage under article 16?

One may seek to clarify what definition of marriage and the family the UDHR endorses as 'natural'. If LGBTs can show that they are structuring their relationships and families according to the intrinsic, or 'natural', requirements of marriage, then there appears to be no good reason why LGBTs should continue to be excluded. Thus, LGBT activists will often focus on the primordial aims of marriage. For example, AME argues: 'Allowing same-sex couples to marry will admit *many more couples* who seek to uphold the core values of marriage and are enthusiastic for the institution. . . . It will also prompt opposite-sex couples to re-value wedlock as an institution in which the over-arching values are love, devotion, and not least, social inclusion.'[35] Activists can therefore claim that 'marriage equality' is not a matter of redefining marriage as such but of discovering and upholding the true definition of marriage. To support this position (some) LGBTs have sought to (a) demonstrate that they *do* structure their relationships and familial lives according to the 'intrinsic requirements' of marriage, and/or (b) they emphasize the 'born this way' aspect of LGBT sexuality, refusing to situate their sexuality as an expression of lifestyle choice. They have, in other words, promoted the LGBT subject as a 'normal' and 'good' citizen.[36]

However, we should also be wary of this type of justification. Marriage is bound up with a political myth which naturalizes and privileges a particular style of relationship and family unit by presupposing, rather than justifying, its value. This focus perpetuates the primacy of marriage, and as such it excludes other, nonmarital relationships from consideration. And, importantly, if the value of a relationship stems from the links of generosity and care it develops, it makes no sense to presume that the marital union is the only or even the best union which will facilitate such links.[37] While this ideal can exist within the normative framework of a marriage, we can easily imagine multiple other forms of intimacy providing the same functions. Thus, even if LGBTs can successfully articulate their claim to marriage without overturning the political myth, doing so seems likely to have negative repercussions for those who do not mimic a heteronormative lifestyle but do sustain significant caring relationships (which is, notably, inclusive of some heterosexuals). When legal changes are predicated on LGBTs' assimilation to heteronormative relationship criteria, this can only achieve a sham of equality and the illusion of progress, while real instances of homophobia, discrimination, marginalization, and hostility towards LGBT people continue.[38] These concerns are of paramount importance, especially in consideration of the emerging soft law norm of same-sex relationship recognition and pattern of small change, each of which I will discuss in turn.

II. SMALL CHANGE AND THE TRANSNATIONAL SOFT LAW NORM OF RELATIONSHIP RECOGNITION

As stated previously, formal same-sex relationship recognition has rapidly increased in the West, beginning primarily with the Nordic countries. It is not surprising that the debate regarding same-sex relationship recognition has been voiced as a matter of human rights in Scandinavia, since human rights discourse is already well-established in these countries. In other words, human rights rhetoric already has normative force, and LGBTs are simply attempting to tap into it. What has resulted from the adoption of this rhetoric is the emergence of a *transnational soft law norm of relationship recognition.*[39]

It is important to characterize 'soft law' compared to 'hard law'. There are three criteria by which to judge a law's severity: obligation, precision, and delegation. According to Kelly Kollman, 'International legal institutions approach the ideal type of *hard law* when the rules contained in them are binding on states without exception, are precise and are enforced by an independent body, usually a tribunal or court.'[40] A 'soft law', on the other hand, is 'only moderately specific, largely non-obligatory, and not clearly enforceable by a single body'.[41] Thus, soft law can include shared informal notions of 'best practice', broadly held ethical beliefs, and nonbinding decisions or recommendations made by international bodies like the EU or the UN, for example. Kollman asserts that in already well-established Western democracies, the most efficient way of encouraging widespread legislative change is through dissemination of a soft law norm and persuading people of its legitimacy.[42] Waaldijk provides evidence for this claim, having identified the law of small change present in LGBT legal reform.

Throughout the history of LGBT rights gains, a distinct pattern can be identified. Since the Netherlands was the first country to introduce same-sex marriage, it is worth recounting the Dutch history of LGBTs' legal recognition and increased protections. Gradual realization of LGBT equality begins with the abolition of the criminal rule against homo-sex, allowing for sexual activity (in private) without fear of legal ramifications. Homo-sex was decriminalized in the Netherlands in 1811. The Napoleonic influence on the Netherlands can account for why decriminalization took place rather early compared to many other countries. In fact, it took the influence of the civil codifications of the Napoleonic Empire to abolish the criminal rule against homo-sex in several parts of Europe. France was the first country to decriminalize homo-sex permanently, and this legal change influenced Belgium,

Luxembourg, parts of Italy, Spain, Switzerland, and Turkey, in addition to the Netherlands. However, the British, German, Austrian, and Russian/Soviet empires, as well as the countries they imperially dominated, reinforced the criminal rule against homo-sex well into the twentieth century.[43]

The second step in LGBT law reform is the introduction of antidiscrimination protections. Despite the Netherlands' early decriminalization of homo-sex, it was not until 1983, with the insertion of article 1 into the Constitution of the Kingdom of the Netherlands 1983, that discrimination against people on the basis of sexual orientation was first *implicitly* legally prohibited. Article 1 of the Dutch Constitution reads: 'All persons in the Netherlands shall be treated equally in equal circumstances. Discrimination on the grounds of religion, belief, political opinion, race or sex or on any other grounds whatsoever shall not be permitted'. It was almost a full decade later (1992) that the penal code was amended to *explicitly* prohibit sexual orientation discrimination for the first time. Notably, this was three years after the world had seen the first example of formal same-sex relationship recognition, by way of registered partnership, in Denmark (1989). Then the Dutch General Equal Treatment Act of 1994 extended the range of remedies available to those people who had been discriminated against based on their sexual orientation.[44] This progress is unsurprising, as it aligns with the general emergence of LGBT claims as matters of human rights during the 1980s–1990s.

The final stage in LGBT law reform is the removal of the 'marriage rule', which holds that all marriages must be heterosexual. Relationship recognition was being formally considered in the Netherlands from the early 1990s. It was in 1992 that the Netherlands Advisory Commission for Legislation recommended registered partnerships for same-sex couples to be implemented. A partnership bill was introduced in 1994; however, it underwent significant amendments between then and when it was eventually passed into law. Initially, the 1994 Dutch bill had a provision that 'proposed to offer the possibility of partnership registration not only to same-sex couples, but also to close relatives who were not permitted to marry each other (like brother and sister, parent and child, grandparent and grandchild)'.[45] However, the bill was amended over the period of 1995–1996 so as to base registered partnerships on a more *marriage-like* model. This bill came into law in 1997 and became effective in 1998. At the time the Netherlands introduced this new model of registered partnership, Norway, Sweden, and Iceland had already introduced same-sex partnership recognition based on the original Danish model. The Dutch model of registered partnerships differed significantly from the prior examples of same-sex relationship recognition, however, in that it was the first implementation of a registered partnership scheme which allowed both same-sex and different-sex couples to participate.[46]

Alongside this progression towards the introduction of a registered partnership scheme in the Netherlands, the Dutch government established a further commission, the Commission on the Opening Up of Civil Marriage to Persons of the Same Sex (or the 'Kortmann Commission'), in 1996. The Kortmann Commission, reporting in 1997, found by a majority vote of five against three that same-sex couples ought to be able to marry. With an election set for May of 1998, the Lower House of Parliament passed new resolutions demanding legislation to open up marriage just one month prior. Following this, the bill which would eventually allow same-sex couples to marry was introduced by the Dutch government in July 1999, passing by the end of December 2000 and coming into force on 1 April 2001, making the Netherlands the first country to legally allow same-sex marriage.[47] Thus, the three key phases in the standard sequences of small change are: (1) decriminalization, (2) antidiscrimination legislation, and (3) legislation recognizing same-sex partnership.

Compare this to Australia, a Western country that has yet to legalize same-sex marriage. Primarily, homosexual law reform in Australia has occurred at the state level. The first state to decriminalize homo-sex was South Australia in 1972. This step was followed by the Australian Capital Territory in 1976, Victoria in 1980, the Northern Territory in 1983, New South Wales in 1984, Western Australian in 1989, Queensland in 1990, and lastly by Tasmania in 1997. This accounts for stage one of the standard sequence of LGBT law reform. Each individual state and territory has also explicitly prohibited discrimination on the basis of sexual orientation in each of their antidiscrimination acts, covering grounds such as employment and accommodation, as well as goods, services, and facilities, for example.[48] This accounts for stage two of the standard sequence of LGBT law reform.

In terms of relationship recognition in Australia, there has been movement at the state as well as the federal level. Although Tasmania was the last state to decriminalize homo-sex, it became the first state to introduce civil unions open to same-sex couples. Interestingly, Tasmania's Relationships Act of 2003 includes a provision for 'caring couples' as well as same-sex and different-sex couples, which is akin to the original proposition for registered partnerships in the Netherlands. A caring relationship is defined as a relationship characterized by emotional interdependence, domestic support, or personal care. Partners in a caring relationship are not sexually intimate, though they must not be otherwise married. The caring couple may or may not be related by family.[49]

However, this advancement of LGBT relationship recognition was resisted by the Howard government's 2004 reforms to the Marriage Act 1961. Here, section 5.1 was amended such that it currently states, '"Marriage" means the union of a man and a woman to the exclusion of all others, voluntarily entered into for life.' This amendment effectively prevents the possibility of same-sex marriage by definition. The Howard reforms also prevent same-sex marriages which are legally performed in other countries from being recognized in Australia, although same-sex couples may wed at the British consulate in Australia so long as at least one partner has British citizenship.

While these amendments have slowed LGBT law reform, progress has still been made. At the state level, the introduction of civil unions/registered partnerships was achieved in both the Australian Capital Territory and Victoria in 2008, followed by New South Wales in 2010 and Queensland in 2011. Tasmania also confirmed in 2010 that it would recognize same-sex marriages that have been performed overseas as though they were civil unions, without the couple having to perform another registration within Tasmania. In 2014, New South Wales passed a similar law. Otherwise, only residents of a state which offers civil unions to same-sex partners may enter into them at present. It is important to make it explicit that civil unions are not recognized by Australian states without such schemes, and, furthermore, a lack of uniformity can result in much confusion as to what benefits Australian same-sex couples are actually entitled to.

On the federal level, after a report from the Australian Human Rights Commission (AHRC) titled 'Same Sex: Same Entitlements', the Australian Labor government introduced a series of changes to federal laws so that same-sex couples and different-sex couples would receive equal de facto recognition. The laws that were amended cover areas such as 'taxation, social security, employment, Medicare, veteran's affairs, superannuation, worker's compensation and family law', and came into force between the end of 2008 and mid-2009.[50] Thus, same-sex de facto couples and their children are now recognized by commonwealth law in the exact same manner as de facto different-sex couples. In total, eighty-four federal laws had to be reformed in order to allow for this equal de facto status.

Despite this progress, Australia has not yet made the step to marriage reform. In 2009, the Australian Greens introduced the Marriage Equality Amendment Bill, which was defeated on its second reading. In a second attempt at achieving marriage equality, Greens senator Sarah Hanson-Young introduced the Marriage Equality Amendment Bill of 2010. This bill was referred to the Senate Legal and Constitutional Affairs Committee for review but was ultimately defeated. In 2012, two further bills for marriage equality were tabled in the House of Representatives. The Marriage Amendment Bill of 2012 was introduced by Labor MP Stephen Jones and was defeated that same year. The Marriage Equality Amendment Bill of 2012 was introduced by Greens MP Adam Bandt with the support of Independent MP Andrew Wilkie. It remains before the House of Representatives.[51] Attempts to introduce same-sex marriage at the state level also have not progressed. Same-sex marriage was briefly legal in the Australian Capital Territory before the High

Court of Australia ruled these marriages were inconsistent with the Marriage Act 1961 and, therefore, unconstitutional. Prior to this, Tasmania attempted to introduce state-based same-sex marriage laws, but the bill failed to pass a vote in the Senate.

Nonetheless, given this recent history, Australia does seem to be following the same general trajectory of homosexual law reform seen in the Netherlands. Reform first began with the abolition of the criminal rule, which happened on a state-to-state basis with homo-sex finally becoming officially decriminalized in 1997. States also introduced antidiscrimination legislation, which would allow same-sex oriented people legal recourse in matters of unfair dismissal, housing opportunities, and so forth. Australia has also begun step three by coming to recognize same-sex de facto couples federally. Furthermore, several of its states now allow for some form of registered partnership.

Importantly, this linear trajectory of LGBT law reform is common. Having undertaken more detailed observations of several European countries, including Belgium, Denmark, Norway, Sweden, Finland, Iceland, Germany, France, and others, Waaldijk identifies that 'different countries seem to be doing things in the same order. Therefore it seems likely that developments in other countries will be roughly along the same lines'.[52] It is this very pattern that has led Waaldijk to identify the law of small change, which can be understood as a 'soft law'. It holds that 'any legislative change advancing the recognition and acceptance of homosexuality will only be enacted [a] if that change is either perceived as small, or [b] if that change is sufficiently reduced in impact by some accompanying legislative "small change" that reinforces the condemnation of homosexuality'.[53]

Another way of phrasing this insight is to say the following: There are norms when it comes to LGBT law reform. LGBT law reform will only be perceived as acceptable if the legal change is small and so not a threat to the dominant heteronormative way of life or if it is accompanied by some other legal change which reinforces the superiority of the heteronormative way of life. Eventually, however, these legal changes accumulate. This results not only in a significant shift in the legal status of LGBTs over time but also in a shift of the normative status of LGBTs in society. Just how significant this normative shift will be depends on the arguments we circulate and the conceptions of homosexuality they assume.

The second clause to the law of small change is especially important; it acknowledges that sometimes countries appear to take steps 'backwards'. That is, they take steps which are contrary to the linear trajectory of LGBT law reform. But this does not halt the progress of reform overall. For example, the Howard reforms of 2004 imply a break in the linear trajectory of Australian LGBT law reform, but we have seen relationship recognition continue to grow despite these legal challenges. This is true of other countries, too. Consider the Defense of Marriage Act (DOMA) as a backwards step in the trend of homosexual law reform in the United States. DOMA purported to 'defend' marriage by defining it as taking place between one man and one woman and allowed individual states to refuse to recognize same-sex marriages performed elsewhere.[54] In 2013, DOMA was found to be unconstitutional by the Supreme Court of the United States in *United States v. Windsor*. At the time of writing, thirty-two American states recognize same-sex marriage. Consider also Great Britain's 1988 law which made it illegal for authorities to promote homosexuality. LGBT law reform has progressed here, too, and as of 2013, England and Wales legally recognize same-sex marriages. A similar example is Russia's 2013 law banning 'propaganda' regarding 'nontraditional' sexual relations to minors. Although Russia appears to be taking steps backwards, we may infer that LGBT rights will nonetheless progress, albeit at a slower pace. It is clear, then, that 'backwards' steps do not altogether halt the progress of LGBT law reform, they merely slow it down.

Another reason accounting for why some countries are quicker to accept LGBT law reform depends on particular nations' reception of European and international norms. In other words, the variance in legal uptake depends in part on whether a particular country gives weight to transnational norms as legitimate influences on their national policy.[55] Kollman gives two examples to demonstrate this point: one from within Western Europe (Austria) and one from outside Europe (the United States). In *Karner v. Austria* (2003), Karner argued that he was being discriminated against because he was unable to take over his long-term male partner's lease in the event of his partner's death, despite the fact that an unmarried heterosexual partner would legally be able to do so. The ECHR agreed that this was a case of discrimination and ruled that the Austrian government must grant same-sex cohabitants the same rights as unmarried, different-sex cohabitants. That is, Austria was effectively ordered to give legal de facto status to unmarried same-sex couples.

What is interesting about this legal decision regarding same-sex relationship rights is that, despite Austria being legally bound to change its laws regarding the de facto status of same-sex couples, the Austrian government only changed the wording of its tenancy laws. At that time it did not change any other laws which discriminated against same-sex couples in a would-be de facto relationship. Kollman speculates that one of the key reasons for Austria's noncompliance with this court ruling was due to the lack of influence European norms had in the Austrian political setting at that time. She argues that it is a state's conception of itself as obliged to and part of a transnational network that indicates how well it will internalize transnational soft law norms.[56] In other words, the national imaginary—encompassed in the dominant social imaginary—plays an important role with regard to the influence of transnational norms. That the legitimacy of European norms is questionable in this context can be attributed to the fact that Austria was a late comer to the European Union (in 1994). As such, 'neither the Austrian public nor its political elites feel as compelled to follow the lead of European institutions or other states'.[57] European norms were simply not as powerful in Austria as in other European countries and even in some other Western countries. This is not to say that the norm of same-sex relationship recognition has had no influence—Austria has recognized same-sex registered partnerships since 2010—it is merely to demonstrate that discrepancies in uptake can be attributed, in part, to a state's national imaginary.

Kollman's other example compares the progress of relationship recognition in the United States with that of Canada. The United States, we have seen, has been relatively slow to internalize the norm of same-sex relationship recognition. We have already considered the introduction of DOMA in 1996, which represents an active resistance to the transnational norm of same-sex relationship recognition. While DOMA has now been ruled unconstitutional, we may still question why there has been such divergence in uptake between the United States and neighbouring Canada. Kollman speculates that the United States has had a greater ability to resist the framing of same-sex relationship recognition as a human rights issue because its national imaginary is that of the 'reigning hegemon'.[58] She argues that 'regardless of the norm under consideration, some countries are simply less willing to learn from transnational networks and policy makers outside their own borders', and the United States is one such country.[59] To prove this point, consider the court ruling in *Lawrence v. Texas* (2003) where antisodomy laws were found to be unconstitutional. The majority opinion in *Lawrence* referenced a similar decision made by the ECHR, although it did not base the ruling on this decision. The mere mention of international law was enough to prompt the introduction of resolutions, in both the House of Representatives and the Senate, forbidding the use of foreign and international law in judicial decisions.[60] Kollman argues:

> There is a deep-seated antipathy to the use of international legal principles and precedents among many U.S. political elites and the public, a reluctance that is much less visible in Canada and Western Europe. The data suggest that Canada's citizens and, in particular, their policy makers are better integrated into these transnational networks and are more willing to let their domestic policy be influenced by them.[61]

In other words, it seems as though the United States perceives itself as a country which is not and does not want to be influenced by others. This accounts for much of the reason why the United States is significantly slower to implement same-sex relationship recognition than many other Western countries. The point to be made here regards the 'identity' of the United States and its willingness to internalize 'outsider' norms. The United States does not seem to view itself as *primarily accountable* to a transnational network of Western, liberal, democratic states. Canada, on the other hand, is much more willing to be influenced by transnational norms.

Thus, it seems to be true that because same-sex relationship recognition is a phenomenon occurring primarily in already well-established democratic countries, its success can be largely attributed to persuasion about the legitimacy of this soft law norm. This claim is rendered more convincing if we consider the law of small change, which helped to develop the present transnational norm of relationship recognition. The law of small change, on the face of it, looks like a good thing. The identification of a pattern that increases LGBT rights in small, sequential steps, culminating in marriage recognition, may be comforting news to the supporters of same-sex marriage. However, this does give rise to a significant question: What symbolic statement are LGBTs sending when they claim they desire to marry, or what symbolic statement is sent when LGBTs do marry?

III. THE LIKELIHOOD OF ASSIMILATION

So far we have only touched on the concern that seeking marriage rights is an assimilative move, the outcome of which sees the current institution of marriage accepted rather than critically reassessed. Ultimately, Kollman thinks that the homogenizing effect of the same-sex relationship recognition norm should not be exaggerated: due to domestic mediating factors—which we might call variations in different countries' national imaginaries—same-sex relationship recognition appears unlikely to take the same shape in all states.[62] However, an analysis of the pattern of small change, which has produced the transnational norm of same-sex relationship recognition, demonstrates that these changes *are* ultimately homogenizing, since marriage is the specific ideal end point of the third stage of LGBT law reform, and no critical analysis of marriage has managed to secure dominant uptake.

This indicates that serious assessment should be given to the symbolic weight of marriage in the dominant shared Western social imaginary, as well as the meanings attached to it as a normative institution which shapes and regulates behaviour. Kollman may believe that domestic mediating factors are enough to secure diversity in same-sex relationship recognition, but the pattern of small change and the dominant justifications which circulate in favour of same-sex marriage would suggest homogenization is quite likely. When the trifold process of homosexual law reform is considered, the outlook is bleak for LGBT activists who seek dignity with regard to their identity. If LGBT acceptance is predicated on likeness to the heteronormative mainstream, and if law reform is only awarded in small, homogenizing normative steps, it seems likely that LGBT identity as a political identity will be lost; the 'good' citizen will not challenge dominant oppressive social practices. Thus, if LGBTs need equal access to marriage in order to even be candidates for equal regard, it is imperative that the arguments we circulate in favour of same-sex marriage do not rely on assumptions of sameness. It is also imperative to explore whether rights rhetoric remains useful for this task—and, indeed, the ground of liberty remains intuitively compelling and so is worth additional exploration. Let us remember, though, that a successful human rights argument should hold that rights are owed to LGBT people *not* thanks to their assimilative capabilities but *qua* members of the human community with regard to (the potential for) difference(s).

NOTES

1. Kelly Kollman, 'Same-Sex Unions: The Globalisation of an Idea', *International Studies Quarterly* 51 (2007): 329–27; Kollman, 'European Institutions, Transnational Networks and National Same-Sex Unions Policy: When Soft Law Hits Harder', *Contemporary Politics* 15, no. 1 (2009): 37–53; Kay Lalor, 'Constituting Sexuality: Rights, Politics and Power in the Gay Rights Movement', *International Journal of Human Rights* 15, no. 5 (2011): 683–99.

2. Kees Waaldijk has undertaken a comparative study of several European countries, assessing how closely other recognised unions match marriage. The Netherlands' civil unions are the closest to marriage, rating at 96 percent equal. See Kees Waaldijk, *More or Less Together: Levels of Legal Consequences of Marriage, Cohabitation and Registered Partnership for Different-Sex and Same-Sex Partners: A Comparative Study of Nine European Countries* (Paris: Institut National d'Etudes Démographiques, 2005), 9.

3. Kees Waaldijk, 'Small Change: How the Road to Same-Sex Marriage Got Paved in the Netherlands', in *Legal Recognition of Same-Sex Partnership: A Study of National, European and International Law*, ed. R. Wintemute and M. Andenæs (Oxford: Hart Publishing, 2001), 446–47.

4. Kollman, 'Same-Sex Unions', 352.

5. '12 Reasons Why Marriage Equality Matters', Australian Marriage Equality, accessed 2 November 2014, www.australianmarriageequality.org/12-reasons-why-marriage-equality-matters/.

6. 'Why Marriage Matters', Freedom to Marry, accessed 2 November 2014, http://www.freedomtomarry.org/pages/why-marriage-matters.

7. Waaldijk, 'Small Change', 439–40.

8. Diane Richardson, 'Sexuality and Citizenship', *Sociology* 32 (1998): 83–100.

9. Discrimination is still reported among other European countries with same-sex marriage, including Denmark at 31 percent, Belgium and Sweden at 35 percent, Spain at 38 percent, France at 41 percent, the United Kingdom at 44 percent, and Portugal at 51 percent. See European Union Agency for Fundamental Rights (FRA), *EU LGBT Survey: European Union Lesbian, Gay, Bisexual and Transgender Survey—Results at a Glance* (Luxembourg: Publications Office of the European Union, 2013), accessed 2 November 2014, http://fra.europa.eu/sites/default/files/eu-lgbt-survey-results-at-a-glance_en.pdf, 15.

10. See Kollman, 'Same-Sex Unions'; Kollman, 'When Soft Law Hits Harder'; Kelly Kollman and Matthew Waites, 'The Global Politics of Lesbian, Gay, Bisexual and Transgender Human Rights: An Introduction', *Contemporary Politics* 15, no. 1 (2009): 1–17.

11. James Griffin, *On Human Rights* (Oxford: Oxford University Press, 2008), intro.

12. It is worthwhile to note that fraternity quite literally means for men to act in a spirit of brotherhood among themselves. This notably excludes women, and women's difficulty in gaining human rights recognition is well documented.

13. Hannah Arendt, 'Reflections on Little Rock', *Dissent* 6, no. 1 (1959): 49. Although Arendt refers to the U.S. Declaration of Independence and not the UDHR, she clearly states her

belief that 'life, liberty, and happiness' are *human* rights, and the overlap between the two is clear.

14. See Hannah Arendt, *The Human Condition*, 2nd ed. (Chicago and London: University of Chicago Press, 1998), chap. 2.

15. Rodney Croome, *Why vs Why: Gay Marriage. Yes* (New South Wales, Australia: Pantera Press, 2010).

16. Griffin, *On Human Rights*, chap. 9.

17. Consider the data cited in note 9 as evidence of this.

18. Because these liberty-based arguments are so compelling, it will be worthwhile to explore them in more detail. I will discuss the paucity of options argument in chapter 2.

19. *Homo-sex* should be taken to mean sex acts between either two men or two women, although the explicit legal ban on homo-sex has predominantly been directed at male-male sex acts.

20. Ronald Dworkin, 'Lord Devlin and the Enforcement of Morals', *Yale Law Journal* 75, no. 6 (1966): 988.

21. Michael Kirby, 'Same-Sex Relationships: An Australasian Perspective on a Global Issue', in *Legal Recognition of Same-Sex Partnerships: A Study of National, European and International Law*, ed. R. Wintemute and M. Andenæs (Oxford: Hart Publishing, 2001), 7–21.

22. United Nations Human Rights Committee (UNHRC), '*Toonen v. Australia*, Communication No. 488/1992, U.N. Doc CCPR/C/50/D/488/1992 (1994)', accessed 2 November 2014, http://www1.umn.edu/humanrts/undocs/html/vws488.htm.

23. As a matter of fact, the UNHRC did also challenge the moral status of homosexuality, unlike the Wolfenden Committee. The Wolfenden Report recommended the decriminalisation of homo-sex *in spite of* significant social disapproval, whereas the UNHRC found that since sexual orientation was already decriminalised in all other Australian states and the Tasmanian legal ban on homo-sex was not enforced, criminalisation of homo-sex could not be deemed essential to the protection of morals in Tasmania. That is to say, in *Toonen* it was recognised that there had been a shift in the public perception of the view that homo-sex posed a moral *threat* to Australian society. This was evidenced by the lack of enforcement of the legislation against homo-sex. It should be noted, however, that the reaction of the Tasmanian public to the ruling in *Toonen* remained grudging towards homosexuals. Not being seen as a direct threat is not the same as being accepted. See Lalor, 'Constituting Sexuality'.

24. Dworkin, 'The Enforcement of Morals', 986–89.

25. Diane Richardson, 'Locating Sexualities: From Here to Normality', *Sexualities* 7 (2004): 391–411.

26. Kate Sheill, 'Losing Out in the Intersections: Lesbians, Human Rights, Law and Activism', *Contemporary Politics* 15, no. 1 (2009): 55–71.

27. Claudia Card, 'Against Marriage and Motherhood', *Hypatia* 11, no. 3 (1996): 1–23.

28. Wendy Brown, 'Suffering Rights as Paradoxes', *Constellations* 7, no. 2 (2000): 208–29.

29. Note that this in no way implies that lesbian sex has always been legally or socially acceptable. This makes it hard to determine the level of discrimination LGBTs may actually face. For example, Waaldijk asks whether discrimination levels in Cyprus and Russia ought to have been ranked (in 1994) at the same level as Romania, where all gay sex was illegal, or whether they were more tolerant, akin to Italy and Switzerland, since lesbian sex was not forbidden. He concludes that 'we would need at least two rankings . . . one for women and one for men' in order to adequately assess the level of discrimination aimed at gays and lesbians. See Kees Waaldijk, 'Standard Sequences in the Legal Recognition of Homosexuality—Europe's Past, Present and Future', *Australian Gay and Lesbian Law Journal* 4 (1994): 50–51.

30. Ibid. See also Rebecca Jennings, 'Lesbian Mothers and Child Custody: Australian Debates in the 1970s', *Gender and History* 24, no. 2 (2012): 502–17.

31. My response to this question is, of course, only part of the story. There are instances where strong reasons for articulating rights about marriage exist—in order to prevent forced marriage and child marriage, for example, which is implied by section 2.

32. Cheshire Calhoun, *Feminism, the Family, and the Politics of the Closet: Lesbian and Gay Displacement* (Oxford: Oxford University Press, 2000), chap. 5.

33. 'Questions and Answers: What's Wrong with Letting Same-Sex Couples "Marry"?' Family Research Council (FRC), accessed 2 November 2014, http://www.frc.org/whats-wrong-with-letting-same-sex-couples-marry.
34. '12 Reasons'; '"A Failed Experiment": Why Civil Unions Are No Substitute for Marriage Equality', Australian Marriage Equality, accessed 2 November 2014, http://www.australianmarriageequality.org/wp-content/uploads/2010/12/A-failed-experiment.pdf.
35. '12 Reasons'; original emphasis.
36. Richardson, 'Locating Sexualities'.
37. Martha Albertson Fineman, 'Why Marriage?' in *Just Marriage*, ed. Mary Lyndon Shanley (Oxford: Oxford University Press, 2004), 46–51; Elizabeth Brake, *Minimizing Marriage: Marriage, Morality and the Law* (Oxford: Oxford University Press, 2012), intro.
38. Richardson, 'Locating Sexualities'.
39. Kollman, 'Same-Sex Unions'; Kollman, 'When Soft Law Hits Harder'.
40. Kollman, 'When Soft Law Hits Harder', 41; emphasis added.
41. Ibid.
42. Ibid.
43. Kees Waaldijk, 'Civil Developments: Patterns of Reform in the Legal Position of Same-Sex Partners in Europe', *Canadian Journal of Family Law* 17 (2000): 62–88.
44. Waaldijk, 'Small Change'; Kees Waaldijk, 'Others May Follow: The Introduction of Marriage, Quasi-Marriage and Semi-Marriage for Same-Sex Couples in European Countries', *Judicial Studies Institute Journal* 5 (2005): 104–24 .
45. Waaldijk, 'Small Change', 444.
46. Ibid.; Waaldijk, 'Others May Follow'.
47. Ibid., 'Small Changes' and 'Others'.
48. A full list of Australia's antidiscrimination acts, both federal and state, as well as the specific grounds, conduct, and areas they cover, are listed by the Australian Human Rights Commission (AHRC). See 'A Guide to Australia's Anti-Discrimination Laws', accessed 2 November 2014, http://humanrights.gov.au/info_for_employers/law/index.html.
49. 'Caring Couples', Relationships Tasmania, accessed 2 November 2014, http://www.relationshipstasmania.com/caringcouples.html.
50. 'Same Sex: Same Entitlements', AHRC, accessed 2 November 2014, http://www.humanrights.gov.au/human_rights/samesex/index.html.
51. See 'Same Sex: Same Entitlements'; Mary Anne Neilsen, 'Background Note: Same-Sex Marriage', *Parliament of Australia: Department of Parliamentary Services*, 10 February 2012, accessed 2 November 2014, http://parlinfo.aph.gov.au/parlInfo/download/library/prspub/1409734/upload_binary/1409734.pdf;fileType=applica%20tion/pdf, 1–30; Mary Anne Neilsen, 'Marriage Amendment Bill 2012 [and] Marriage Equality Amendment Bill 2012 [and] Marriage Equality Amendment Bill 2010," *Parliament of Australia: Parliamentary Business*, 18 June 2012, accessed 2 November 2014, http://www.aph.gov.au/Parliamentary_Business/Bills_Legislation/bd/bd1112a/12bd158.
52. Waaldijk, 'Standard Sequences', 65.
53. Waaldijk, 'Small Change', 440.
54. Calhoun, *Feminism, the Family*, chap. 5. The introduction of DOMA was in retaliation to the ruling in the Hawaiian case *Baehr v. Lewin* (1993). *Baehr* found the denial of marriage licenses to same-sex couples to be a potential violation of the Hawaii state constitution. Kathleen Hull argues, 'It was the Hawaii case that put same-sex marriage on the political and cultural radar screen, eventually prompting passage of the federal Defense of Marriage Act and similar legislation in more than thirty states.' See Kathleen Hull, 'The Political Limits of the Rights Frame: The Case of Same-Sex Marriage in Hawaii', *Sociological Perspectives* 44, no. 2 (2001): 207.
55. State religiosity plays a role, but the evidence would suggest that religiosity *alone* is not strong enough to determine the uptake of international norms. See Kollman, 'Same-Sex Unions'.
56. Kollman, 'When Soft Law Hits Harder'.
57. Ibid., 50.
58. Kollman, 'Same-Sex Unions', 343.

59. Ibid., 344.
60. Ibid.
61. Ibid., 346.
62. Kollman, 'When Soft Law Hits Harder'.

Chapter Two

Assimilative Justifications of Same-Sex Marriage

As discussed in the previous chapter, human rights discourse is the main discourse which LGBT activists employ to seek redress for the various forms of discrimination they face. A prime example of this is demonstrated by the International Lesbian, Gay, Bisexual, Trans and Intersex Association (ILGA), whose aim as an organization is to promote the universal observance of human rights for LGBT and intersex people. More specifically, they aim for the elimination of all forms of discrimination and the realization of specific provisions of various international human rights instruments.[1] And not only do advocates of same-sex marriage employ rights discourse, the dominant justifications circulated in favour of same-sex marriage are often implicitly or explicitly assimilative. That is, they seek to demonstrate that same-sex couples and different-sex couples are just the same for all relevant purposes and argue that marriage equality is justified on these grounds.

This chapter begins by outlining some of the popular justifications for same-sex marriage circulated online and in the media. It is important to reflect upon the narratives being circulated with regard to same-sex relationships, as media coverage affects the way the public 'learns, understands, and thinks about an issue'.[2] As Xigen Li and Xudong Liu point out, media coverage 'sets the public agenda' and leads to further discussion on same-sex marriage across other various mediums.[3] This chapter also examines the tendency of 'sameness' justifications to appear in academic scholarship favouring same-sex marriage. In particular, I will examine the paucity of options justification that was touched upon in chapter 1. The paucity of options justification is developed in James Griffin's personhood account of human rights. Although this justification sounds compelling on first blush, I will argue that the personhood account is unable to achieve the goal of equal regard for LGBT people because it implicitly endorses a thick conception of the necessities for the good life, unjustifiably privileging heteronormative practices and institutions. A critical analysis of the personhood account does, however, help us to identify what would be required for a successful justification of same-sex marriage. It must (a) oblige those who are able to introduce same-sex marriage to undertake this task, irrespective of their personal inclinations; (b) not assume that marriage is an intrinsically worthy institution worthy of reproduction; (c) have a socially comparative element balanced by a critical component; and (d) take into account the history of LGBT discrimination.

I. SAME-SEX RELATIONSHIPS IN THE MEDIA

A quick survey of the images of and arguments about same-sex couples circulating in the media and in dominant same-sex marriage campaigns demonstrates a particularly normative model of homosexuality. For example, Australian Marriage Equality (AME) has run several television advertising campaigns, which are readily accessible on YouTube. One such advertisement features Ivan Hinton, deputy director of AME, and his partner Chris. They are a young-adult, interracial gay couple who appear to be middle class. The ad opens with Ivan's parents and notes the length of their marriage—forty-five years. Ivan later claims that he wants to get married because he wants to be with Chris for life. These signals remind the viewer that marriage is supposed to be a lifelong commitment. The advertisement also focuses on Chris's parents, who claim that, thanks to their son's relationship, their family has now expanded. The ad cuts between segments of spoken opinion and shots of wedding rings, family time spent at dinner or in a park, and so on. At one point Ivan states, 'We're not activists; we're just people who want to get married, like everyone else.' This reiterates the 'normalcy' of the desire to marry in general, which is confirmed by Chris's statement when he says, 'It means that everyone would accept it. It's sort of like a normal . . . A sense of normality.' This ad positions same-sex couples as if they are all already normal, just like everyone else, and simply await recognition. It does not challenge the perception of what 'normal' is. Finally, the advertisement closes with the written statement: 'Marriage: It's about family. Everyone's family.' This advertisement thus draws connections between the legal institution of marriage and socially shared normative conceptions of familial life.[4]

Marriage Equality, an Irish organization, also has put out a public service advertisement in support of same-sex marriage. This ad features a young white man dressed in a suit, knocking at a door. A middle-aged man answers, and the young man asks him permission for Sinéad's hand in marriage. The older man grants this permission. Although less common today, many are familiar with the tradition of the groom asking the bride's father for permission to marry her. The young man then moves on to another door. This time a woman answers. Again, the young man asks permission for Sinéad's hand in marriage. The woman also grants permission. Then he moves on to the next door, and the next, and the next. Each time he asks permission for Sinéad's hand in marriage. The video cuts to text: 'How would you feel if you had to ask 4 million people for permission to get married?' followed by 'Lesbians and gay men are denied access to civil marriage in Ireland.' The ad cleverly points out an injustice: it is not just that same-sex couples are unable to wed, but that heterosexual people should have a say in whether this is so. The comparison is drawn by purposefully conjuring up the audience's notion of traditional marriage and likening same-sex relationships to this image.[5]

Finally, consider GetUp! Action for Australia's advertisement for same-sex marriage, which went 'viral' with over 15 million views on YouTube at the time of writing. This ad is shot from a first-person perspective where the camera is the eyes of the subject. It follows the blossoming of a relationship: from meeting a man on a boat to exchanging phone numbers, dating, attending social events with friends, sharing special occasions, meeting each other's families, sharing a home, caring for sick family members, and so forth, finally culminating in a proposal for marriage. Upon the proposal it is revealed that the couple consists of two young-adult, white, middle-class men. The purpose of this advertisement is to surprise the audience member, as the gay couple's relationship follows the same trajectory of what is typically expected in a heterosexual relationship. The effect, in turn, is to shock the audience member into recognizing that same-sex couples are just like different-sex couples. Hopefully, this will also serve to justify to the audience member that LGBT people deserve the same legal treatment as heterosexuals. The couple in this advertisement appear to be monogamous; their relationship seems to have blossomed over a length of time; they support each other's families, and the couple comes to share a home. Projecting images like these suggests that such aspects are the relevant features of marriage, which LGBT people enact 'just like everyone else'.[6]

Contemporary fictional representations of same-sex relationships are also presented in this light. For example, consider the relationship of Mitch and Cameron in the popular US sitcom *Modern Family*. Mitch and Cameron share a house, have an adopted daughter, and maintain a fairly traditional lifestyle where one partner works full time as a lawyer, while the other remains at home and is the primary caregiver for their daughter. Eventually, when their daughter, Lily, is older, Cameron returns to work. Their relationship is monogamous and long-term, and the couple marry in season five (in line with California's Proposition 8 ballot being overturned in 2013). These characters, too, are both white and appear to have a middle-class status. Similarly, the less successful US sitcom *The New Normal* features a white gay couple (one is Jewish) who share a home; are in a long-term, monogamous relationship; and who both have careers. This sitcom centres on this couple's decision to have a child and the life of the woman who decides to act as their surrogate. This couple are also financially well off.[7]

Alongside the aforementioned advertising campaigns, activist groups publish arguments in support of same-sex marriage on their organizational websites which aim to project this (hetero)normative image of the standard same-sex couple. Consider Freedom to Marry, an American organization, which argues the following:

> Marriage matters to gay people in similar ways that it matters to everyone. Gay and lesbian couples want to get married to make a lifetime commitment to the person they love and to protect their families. Marriage says, 'We are family' in a way that no other word does. Marriage is one of the few times where people make a public promise of love and responsibility for each other and ask our friends and family to hold us accountable. Gay and lesbian couples may seem different from straight couples, but we share similar values—like the importance of family and helping out our neighbors; worries—like making ends meet or the possibility of losing a job; and hopes and dreams—like finding that special someone to grow old with, and standing in front of friends and family to make a lifetime commitment.[8]

What we see here is a focus on the injustice of being unable to pursue the same lifestyle as normative heterosexual couples given the relevant similarities between the two. The rhetoric is one of commitment, love, family, and accountability/responsibility. Evan Wolfson, executive director of Freedom to Marry, argues further in a piece published in the *Portland Mercury* that the clarity, security, and dignity that come with the status of being married are 'precious and irreplaceable'.[9] He continues, 'Marriage is a commitment, an aspiration, a highly significant personal lived experience, a bundle of personal, social, and spiritual meanings, and, at its best, a strengthener of couples, children, kin, communities, and country.'[10] From this he argues, 'It makes no sense to exclude loving couples already doing the work of marriage in their daily lives from the legal structure intended to reinforce that dedication, those meanings, and, at its heart, commitment and love.'[11]

Consider also AME's argument, published on their website, that 'Australia's ban on same-sex marriages disadvantages same-sex attracted people by sending out the message that they are less capable of love and commitment than heterosexual people. It says their relationships are less stable, less resilient and of less value to the partners involved and their family and friends.'[12] The implication of this argument is that sending out this message to the general public is bad because the message is false: *same-sex couples and different-sex couples are just the same*. Moreover, AME claim that allowing same-sex couples to marry will admit more couples seeking to uphold the 'core values of marriage' and will prompt different-sex couples to 're-value wedlock as an institution in which the over-arching values are love, devotion, and not least, social inclusion'.[13] To this we can add AME's recent photo campaign 'Just Like You—Love Knows No Difference'. The aim of this campaign is to boost support for marriage equality by demonstrating in images how 'relatable' same-sex relationships are. Not only is this campaign easily accessible online, AME has also released a Just Like You 2015 calendar for purchase, with all funds supporting marriage equality campaigns.[14]

We see that both organizations stress the similarities between the relationships of same-sex couples and different-sex couples, while the differences between these two relationships (namely, the types of participants) are disregarded as irrelevant. Both types of relationship are equally capable of love, commitment, stability, and resilience. They are also equally valuable. The argument is that marriage equality is justified because like people should be treated alike. And importantly, it is *marriage* that matters, not simply some form of legal relationship recognition. As Kees Waaldijk argues, 'Attaching all consequences of marriage to either registered partnership or *de facto* cohabitation would leave the *marriage rule* on homosexuality unaffected. In law, that . . . rule would then be less important, but in social reality, it would continue its function of marginalizing same-sex love and same-sex lovers.'[15] If only civil unions are offered to same-sex couples instead of marriage, then, AME says, civil unions might '*actually encourage discrimination* against same-sex partners and downgrade the status of their relationships by entrenching a second-class status'.[16] This is an important insight because (perceived) differences between same-sex and different-sex couples are often taken as justificatory grounds for the denial of same-sex marriage. This is why many same-sex marriage activists have set out to prove that same-sex couples are the same as different-sex couples in the *relevant* way and that the sex of one's partner is *irrelevant* to marriage.

Importantly, this type of justification is not only limited to the activist realm. Scholars have advocated assimilative justifications in favour of same-sex marriage, too. Take William Eskridge Jr., who asks us to imagine ourselves seated in an aeroplane that is plummeting from the sky. What is going through the passengers' minds? 'For most of us', he contends, 'it would not be the great sex we have had, the property we have acquired, or the awards we have won. It would, instead, be the parents who nurtured us, the romances we have enjoyed, and the children we have raised.'[17] Eskridge proceeds to argue, 'Straights have no monopoly on such a desire for connection. Human relationship knows no sexual orientation. For the state to single out gay people and try to discourage their relational fulfilments epitomizes prejudice and discrimination.'[18] LGBTs have needs for emotionally fulfilling bonds, and again there is an undercurrent of presumed normative practice. For 'gay people are good role models and gay couples ought to receive state stamps of approval'.[19]

There are several other arguments which also emphasize the need for, or desirability of, assimilation. One reason to be in favour of same-sex marriage is that it supposedly encourages monogamy, which in turn encourages stability and lessens the risk of the spread of sexually transmitted infections, such as HIV/AIDS. For men in particular, marriage has the power to 'tame' or 'civilize'; since marriage is difficult to dissolve, couples will be more likely to work at their problems. Marriage is like an anchor, and it signals to the wider (heterosexual) community that same-sex relationships are just as worthy of respect as different-sex relationships; they are no better, no worse. Moreover, marriage is recognized as a 'stable, socially sanctioned, highly functional, and economically viable setting' in which to raise children, which will benefit same-sex couples with children, or who would like to have children.[20]

However, there is substantial disagreement about whether same-sex marriage is desirable from both activists and scholars alike. As argued in the previous chapter, some believe that when arguments are circulated which stress the 'sameness' of different-sex and same-sex couples, this can only achieve a sham of equality and the illusion of progress. Thus, some argue that true justice depends on accepting differences from mainstream culture, while some are in favour of the abolition of marriage altogether.[21] I do not seek the abolition of marriage as an institution—not because I think that marriage is necessarily an institution worth reproducing but because such a position is counterproductive for the goal of LGBT equal regard. If true respect for LGBTs' dignity can only be achieved by a combination of respect for difference *and* an undercutting of heterosexual privilege, then we need legal equivalence and a different approach to symbolism. Allowing for (the potential for) difference(s) is important because these alternatives may be more desirable and fulfilling on an interpersonal level than what is permitted by our socially shared (hetero)normative commitments. It is therefore imperative that the arguments we circulate in favour of same-sex marriage speak directly to the site of marriage's symbolism without reinforcing its privileged normative position. Thus, instead of rejecting arguments for same-sex marriage outright, it pays to subject them to a careful scrutiny.

On this note I return to the liberty-based justifications of same-sex marriage mentioned in chapter 1. Liberty-based justifications have intuitive appeal because they do not, on first blush, seem to endorse the normative worth of marriage. However, I will demonstrate that this cannot always be presumed to be the case by analysing the argument from a 'paucity of options'.

II. JAMES GRIFFIN AND THE PERSONHOOD ACCOUNT

The paucity of options argument stems from what has been called one of the 'most developed theories of human rights',[22] and 'arguably the most significant philosophical meditation on human rights to emerge in the human rights–intoxicated era'.[23] This is the personhood account of human rights. The personhood account takes a 'bottom-up' approach to determining what constitutes a human right. A bottom-up approach requires one to start with the historical evolution of human rights and from there to investigate which higher principles require endorsement in order to justify the weight of commonly agreed upon rights. In other words, an assessment of commonly agreed upon human rights takes place in order to discover from what general principles they have been derived. One can then reflectively endorse those higher principles. A bottom-up approach differs from top-down approaches to human rights, which begin with either a principle or set of principles, such as Kant's Categorical Imperative, or an authoritative decision-making procedure from which human rights are derived, such as Act or Rule Utilitarianism.[24]

The overall goal of the personhood account is to give human rights more determinate content and to restore, in today's understanding, the idea that human rights are 'grounded in natural facts about human beings'.[25] The 'indeterminateness' of human rights can be attributed to the gradual movement from theologically based 'natural rights' in the Middle Ages to the secular, reason-based understanding of 'human rights' in the Enlightenment, continuing on into modern history. Nothing has replaced the determinate theological content that was lost with the move to secularization. Griffin believes, however, that the indeterminateness of human rights can be remedied by adding to their little remaining evaluative content. In order to determine what specific content should be added to flesh out a notion of human rights, one must examine their current criteria for use. Although human rights have lost their theological content over time, they have not lost their ethical content and thus, even though the notion of human rights is incomplete, it is not completely empty.

To reiterate the argument thus far, then, the concept of human rights has *evaluative* content. Previously, that evaluative content consisted of *theological* content and *ethical* content. That is, a code of ethics and theological beliefs were used to determine and justify what there was a human right to and who could claim it. Today the concept of human rights has lost its *theological* content. Because of this loss, it is harder to assess and justify what there is a human right to and who has a right to it. But there is still ethical content, which can be used in this evaluation. The personhood account attempts to add to that ethical content (and thus to the evaluative content) in order to make the concept of human rights more determinate.

This is an ethically substantive account of human rights, then, and it holds the following to be true: 'We human beings have a conception of ourselves and of our past and future. We reflect and assess. We form pictures of what a good life would be—often, it is true, only on a small scale, but occasionally also on a large scale. And we try to realize these pictures. This is what we mean by a distinctively *human* existence.'[26] That is to say, a distinctively human existence will involve the conception and pursuit of 'the good life', and human rights are valuable insofar as they protect people's distinctively human existence. It therefore follows that protecting 'human rights' will mean protecting those capacities which allow humans to conceive of and pursue such conceptions of the good life, as well as ensuring that there are opportunities to exercise these capacities and, to an extent, succeed in this exercise. The definition of 'personhood' is thus purposefully conflated with 'normative agency'. To have one's personhood respected means to be able to deliberate, assess, choose, and act in a way that is congruent with one's own conception of the good life.[27]

Thus, human rights are primarily grounded in or justified in their weight by personhood, where personhood is understood as the acknowledgement of an individual's normative agency. Griffin believes that the generative capacities of the notion of personhood are quite great. That is to say, most current, commonly accepted human rights can be justified with reference to the notion of personhood. Personhood can be broken down into three components. To be a normative agent in the relevant way, one must have *autonomy*, *liberty*, and *minimum provision*. To be autonomous means to be able to choose for oneself one's own path in life; to have liberty means to be able to act upon one's choices, which also provides a constraint not to interfere with others' liberty; and finally, to have minimum provision means to have the basic resources and capabilities that it takes to enact one's autonomy and liberty. The 'personhood account' is also a teleological account: exercising personhood is about being able to repeatedly choose the pursuit of the good. Yet human rights do not guarantee each person will achieve their desired conception of a good life; rather, human rights are meant to ensure that the pursuit of this conception of the good life is not unfairly limited. There is no right to attainment of the good life as such, only to pursue some or other conception of it.[28]

To this end, human rights are designed to protect personhood; however, 'personhood' alone is still not determinate enough to adequately flesh out a conception of human rights. Relying on 'personhood' alone is problematic since a rights claim that remains too indeterminate cannot act as a conceptually effective, socially manageable claim on others. To solve this problem, Griffin postulates a second ground, termed *practicalities*, which will provide more determinate content for human rights. Practicalities 'are not tied to particular times or places. They are universal, as any existence condition for rights that one has simply in virtue of being human must be. Practicalities will be empirical information about . . . human nature and human societies, prominently about the limits of human understanding and motivation.'[29] It must be emphasized that 'practicalities' are understood as the actual, universal facts and circumstances pertaining to human nature and societies.[30] But, as it stands, the ground of practicalities is quite vague; Griffin does not elaborate on the nature of any of these universal facts and truths.[31]

Finally, it is important to articulate who bears the duties correlative to human rights. If any party may demand something on the ground of human rights, then some other agent must have a corresponding duty to supply it. To be held accountable as a duty-bearer on the personhood account he or she must have the *ability* to help. This is not ability *simpliciter*, however, but ability limited by other factors. Humans are partial by nature and 'cannot enter into and exit from all our particular commitments at will'.[32] As such, people are permitted to follow their own commitments to their idea of the good life, and this permission limits one's obligation. In other words, there is a permitted domain of partiality. A further limit to ability is granted since, in the world as it is, people tend to distribute burdens along membership lines. For example, if there is a failure of rights in one's local community and that community has the ability to ensure the right, then the duty falls on that community to do so, even if a further removed group also has the capacity to help. Thus, 'ability' is one key ground on which to fix the consideration of where duty lies, but 'ability' is permissibly limited by one's personal commitments as well as membership obligations. If such limitations were not permitted, especially with regard to positive rights, the duties demanded may become exceedingly burdensome.[33]

Altogether, then, a clear picture of the personhood account emerges: It is the possession of a capacity to identify and pursue the good life, which guarantees people the protection of human rights. To be able to deliberate on, assess, and pursue a conception of the good life means to have normative agency. Normative agency is thus the centre of personhood. Human rights are *instrumental* to the protection of personhood, and personhood dictates what higher abstract principles are to be endorsed. Three are of the utmost importance: autonomy, liberty, and minimum provision. However, considerations of these three criteria alone are not sufficient to determine the content of specific human rights, so practicalities must also be taken into account. This means that, as well as ensuring minimum provision, autonomy, and liberty, one must also take into account facts about human nature and human societies when fleshing out the content of human rights. Who will be obliged to ensure the human rights of others depends on ability. However, in order to prevent this duty from becoming too burdensome, people are permitted a domain of *partiality*. Furthermore, there is a higher burden of duty on 'members' compared with those who are 'nonmembers'. This does not mean that nonmembers are never obliged to assist in a human rights claim, but that the primary burden lies elsewhere.

III. JUSTIFYING SAME-SEX MARRIAGE

People hold three basic rights which correlate with the components of personhood: a right to autonomy, a right to liberty, and a right to minimum provision. These rights are required if a person is to be enabled as a 'normative agent'. However, such rights do not go unqualified. The right to liberty, for example, has both a material constraint and a formal constraint. The material constraint holds that an acceptable claim must bear upon whether or not one functions as a normative agent. That is, it must bear upon one's ability to deliberate on, assess, and pursue a conception of the good life. The formal constraint holds that if any normative agent has the right to liberty, then all normative agents do. That is, if some are free to pursue some conception of the good life, then all must be free to pursue some conception of the good life. There are also the enemies of liberty to consider: constraint, compelling, and paucity of options. If a person is constrained either physically or by a threatening presence, then he or she does not have true liberty; if a person is compelled by some group or individual to act in a certain way, he or she does not have true liberty; finally, if a person finds him- or herself in a situation where very few life options are available to him or her but many more are available to others, then there is a paucity of options, and he or she cannot be held to have true liberty.[34]

The matter of same-sex marriage is considered as constituting a 'paucity of options'. But before one can determine any legitimate application of the 'paucity of options' categorization, the matter of 'equal opportunity' must be addressed. Given the emergence of human rights claims alongside the growth of egalitarianism, it would make sense to assume that equality would be one ground, or even *the* ground, for human rights.[35] However, the personhood account does not take equality into account beyond the formal constraint and the principle of equal respect. This 'respect' regarding human rights claims only extends as far as the recognition of normative agency. It does not extend to some kind of positive respect for one's identity, like equal regard. In addition, the principle of equal respect is not a ground for human rights; it is simply the moral point of view. Furthermore, 'to identify the existence conditions for human rights, one would not look to the equality of our human status but to the human status itself.'[36] That is to say, liberty, autonomy, and minimum provision already capture this human status, and thus, there is no need to assume equal respect is a ground for human rights itself. This is not to argue that equality does not exist between human adults—it does, insofar as people can be identified as normative agents and pursue the good life.[37]

Rather, the concern is simply about where one would draw the line in determining human rights other than where the personhood account has already drawn it. Ultimately, then, equality is not held to be an adequate ground for determining the content of human rights on the personhood account.[38]

Moreover, with regard to equality of opportunity and paucity of options, 'society does not have an obligation to ensure equal opportunity in the *realization* of one's conception [of the good life].'[39] For example, if several people have their hearts set on becoming philosophers, but there are not enough jobs in philosophy to accommodate the realization of these people's versions of the good life, then society is by no means *obliged* to produce more jobs in philosophy. Griffin argues, 'In a society with an *ample* range of options, if one cannot realize one conception, there are others: other lives that one can also value and that can become fully worthwhile lives for one to live.'[40] Since one's conception of the good life should always be open to revision, if one has been unable to attain a job in philosophy, it is fair to ask that person to consider and pursue an alternative conception of the good life. Many people can find value in various industries. Thus, these people already have a type of 'equality of opportunity'—the opportunity to make a good life for oneself in general.[41]

However, there are 'exceptions' to accepting that people must build their lives from the options with which fortune has endowed them. Griffin holds that a society 'can and should sometimes enlarge the range of options, *even in a society with a large choice already*'.[42] But when should a society do this? What options does society have an obligation to expand? Here, Griffin introduces same-sex relationship recognition as an example:

> If there are same-sex couples who want to form some sort of union and raise children—who want, that is, to have the rich, stable, recognized, respected relations that are at the heart of most people's conceptions of a worthwhile life—and, because of our ethical traditions, there are no social institutions to allow it, then we should create one or other form of them. This too, I believe, is an issue of liberty. No matter how many options there are already, this one, because of its centrality to characteristic human conceptions of a worthwhile life, must be added.[43]

Keep in mind the several people with their hearts set on employment as philosophers, although there are not enough jobs for all. Recall, also, that what supposedly matters is having the equal opportunity to *pursue* a good life, not an equal opportunity to actually achieve that conception. Does the case for same-sex relationship recognition differ significantly from the case of the aspiring philosophers? If society has no obligation to create more jobs in philosophy in order to accommodate the aspiring philosophers' specific dream of employment, then why would society have an obligation to create one or other form of legal union to fulfil *one* possible conception of the good life by same-sex couples?

Recall that the material constraint dictates that an acceptable claim must bear upon whether or not one functions as a normative agent. Could same-sex couples still act as normative agents without the option to get married? Griffin does not seem to think so. Marriage is 'central to characteristic human conceptions of a worthwhile life' and as such, 'no matter how many options there are already', this option must be made available. In considering why we cannot 'return to the social conditions of a century ago',[44] he argues:

> What is at stake for same-sex couples are *several of the most important components of a good life* available to human beings. Most same-sex couples could not have rich and deep personal relations in the conditions of a hundred years ago. Their affection would be stifled. They would not have, or raise, children, which for most of us, homosexual or not, is our best chance of accomplishing something important with our lives. Unless one is exceptionally talented . . . raising one's children well is probably the only great accomplishment available to us. Some persons could no doubt rise gloriously above the restrictions of a hundred years ago; some persons do not want deep personal relations or to raise children. But the great majority of us do, and the restrictions of a hundred years ago would deny same-sex couples some of the greatest, most widely distributed, most deeply embedded—sometimes even genetically embedded—least easily substituted ends of human life that there are. *And although these claims about the conditions of a hundred years ago apply less strongly to same-sex couples today, they apply strongly enough to support the same conclusions.*[45]

Not only would the conditions of one hundred years ago prevent almost all LGBT people from attaining a worthwhile life, these concerns still apply strongly enough to warrant the same conclusion today. But in some sense, it seems that the problem in the case of same-sex marriage is not so much a matter of a *paucity* of options as it is a matter of being denied the possibility to pursue something inherently valuable. We have already seen it argued that a society can be obliged to expand its options even when it presently provides a large spectrum of choice. Griffin clearly acknowledges that LGBTs do have a wider spectrum of choice today than in the conditions of one hundred years ago, so it is either the case that these choices are still not numerous enough or else he means to say that irrespective of these diverse choices some goods are so central to a worthwhile life that they simply must be available for all to pursue. Based on the above statement, that these are 'some of the greatest, most widely distributed, most deeply embedded—sometimes even genetically embedded—least easily substituted ends of human life that there are', the latter interpretation seems more plausible. To strengthen this interpretation, consider that 'a society will accept a person's claim to the protection of liberty only if the claim meets the material constraint that what is at stake is indeed conceivable as mattering to whether or not we function as normative agents.'[46] Since relationship recognition is Griffin's own example of a paucity of options, we must infer that he believes it to matter for normative agency.

However, it is not so obvious that LGBTs are prevented from acting as normative agents in the West at present. Same-sex couples *can* have rich, stable, and recognized relationships for the most part, even if they are only recognized by their family and friends. That is to say, it seems to be the case that LGBT people are capable of living worthwhile lives even in the face of exclusion from the institution of marriage or other recognized unions. If this assessment is correct, then this exclusion cannot be legitimately characterized as constituting a paucity of options and, as such, there is no right to it.

IV. EVALUATING THE ARGUMENT

There are two initial points to be made. The first regards the strength of the notion of personhood (or normative agency); the second regards the implicit endorsement of certain normative conditions as intrinsically valuable. Recall that normative agency involves the ability to deliberate on, assess, and pursue a conception of the good life. This can be interpreted in both a thick and thin sense. The thin notion would see personhood as 'the bare capacity for intentional action together with some measure of its successful exercise'.[47] Such an austere interpretation of personhood could allow people to be recognized as normative agents while simultaneously leading lives that might intuitively be said to be lacking some component of personhood. An extreme example that demonstrates this point is that of the slave. A slave can have the capacity for intentional action and some measure of successful exercise, but can the slave really be said to be a normative agent? This thin interpretation of personhood runs against the widely shared notion that slavery is antithetical to human rights.

It is also important to point out that given an austere interpretation of personhood, the LGBT person may well be considered a normative agent even in the conditions of one hundred years ago. Thus, if one wants to argue that an LGBT person's existence does not involve normative agency in the conditions of one hundred years ago, one needs to build content into the notion of what personhood itself requires. That is, the notion of personhood must be taken from an austere one and transformed into a thicker notion. The question is: how thick can this interpretation legitimately be? Certainly, it appears that same-sex couples can achieve a worthwhile life, *at least* in the conditions of the West today. As such, it remains unclear how same-sex couples are different from the example of the aspiring philosophers. Although same-sex couples will not receive the same legal benefits and obligations as different-sex couples, they will still be able to pursue some *other* conception of the good life. This good life can still involve relationships and childrearing if they so choose (in the form of civil unions or de facto status, for example); it will just be different in structure to heteronormatively understood marriage and the family. While this outcome might not seem 'fair' to some LGBTs, it is not necessarily a violation of human rights according to the personhood account. If it were to be a violation of human rights on the personhood account, then one must offer a stronger claim: same-sex couples cannot lead a worthwhile life under conditions which refuse same-sex relationships the possibility of legal recognition as marriages.

It is clear that personhood is not meant to be understood as an austere notion; personhood is a normative conception, and it seems to require 'the presence of a diverse array of *genuinely valuable* options from which to choose in shaping the direction of one's own life, and enough liberty and material wherewithal to make one's choices effective'.[48] That is to say, convergence on the justifications for specific human rights involves a direct agreement on a 'particularly deep conception of agency', which must be shared as a core value.[49] On the personhood account, refusing same-sex marriage constitutes a paucity of options because marriage and the family contain some of the most crucial aspects of a worthwhile life. The problem with holding a thicker conception of personhood, though, is specifying and justifying a plausible and sufficiently determinate threshold for identifying that this is genuinely valuable and worthy of protection or endorsement. For it to be the case that marriage could be conceived of as a necessary element in the protection of normative agency, one must commit to and justify some thick normative interpretation of what is genuinely valuable for a good life. But the personhood account does not supply any such justification. One may expect to call upon the second ground of human rights—practicalities—to make the content more determinate. However, there has been little elaboration on practicalities such that they may effectively serve as an indeterminacy-reducing factor.[50] Furthermore, at least *some* claims about the so-called facts of human nature and societies, if made explicit, are likely to be contentious and legitimately contestable.

This implicit endorsement of certain normative conditions as intrinsically valuable is the second issue. Griffin heavily relies on the *values* of deep personal relations and the accomplishments which eventuate from childrearing in justifying same-sex marriage, judging them to be necessary for the pursuit of a worthwhile life. The personhood account is ultimately problematic since endorsement of these values exists *prior* to the endorsement of the personhood account.[51] This is reminiscent of the critique aimed at article 16 of the Universal Declaration of Human Rights 1948 (UDHR) in chapter 1. Article 16 endorses the political myth that the family is the natural and fundamental group unit of society, and this is why marriage is entitled to state protection and explicit coverage in the UDHR. Similarly, although Griffin justifies same-sex marriage by saying there is a paucity of options, which societies ought to rectify, what precedes this argument is an implicit commitment to marriage as intrinsically valuable and a necessary element of the human good.

The thick assumption that Griffin is making indicates that he is making a moral rather than principled argument for marriage. Cheshire Calhoun argues, 'Understood morally, marriage is not simply one among many intimate relationships that people can voluntarily enter into. It is *the* normative ideal for how sexuality, companionship, affection, personal economics, and child rearing should be organized.'[52] The marriage-as-normative-ideal position finds that marriage is something people ought to have a right to because committed, monogamous, sexually faithful relationships contribute to personal and social flourishing.[53] They are, as Griffin said, 'some of the greatest, most widely distributed, most deeply embedded—sometimes even genetically embedded—least easily substituted ends of human life that there are'. The moral conception of marriage exists prior to its legal institutionalization. These values, then, are goods which the state has reason to protect.

Now, it is worth reiterating that Griffin has remained vague in his argument for same-sex marriage. He can be generously interpreted as promoting legal unions or narrowly interpreted as promoting marriage specifically. A charitable reading of Griffin's argument would claim that recognition for marriage-like relationships is sufficient. However, Griffin does explicitly describe his argument as pertaining to same-sex *marriage* as the text progresses. Specifically, he asks the reader to 'recall the example of same-sex marriage'.[54] This indicates that Griffin believes the greatest and least easily substituted ends of human life that there are belong specifically to the marital dynamic. But regardless of interpretation, what is clear is that for his paucity of options argument to stand, Griffin must endorse the notion that the ability to enter into these unions is central to one's ability to act as a normative agent *at all*. The relationships that Griffin imagines as being central to most people's conceptions of the good life are those which are rich, stable, recognized, and respected in a particular way. They also appear to be the appropriate framework for raising children, since Griffin later conflates intimate relationships with parenting.

As previously mentioned, promoting just one normative structure of intimacy as ideal can be problematic. Indeed, Allen Buchanan argues, 'There is no reason to believe that the liberty to engage in same-sex marriage is a *necessary* element of a satisfactory package of liberties from the standpoint of protecting normative agency',[55] and if there *were* something intrinsically valuable about marriage, one may question why other networks of care ought not to be considered equally intrinsically valuable. If it is claimed that LGBTs ought to have access to marriage because marriage encompasses several of the most basic human goods, including having a family, then positioning it hierarchically as the ideal way to structure one's intimate and familial life may encourage social coercion into marriage rather than allow diversified family structures to flourish. Moreover, the legalization of same-sex marriage does not necessarily remedy heteropatriarchal privilege or prevent discrimination from taking another unacceptable form. This argument for same-sex marriage is likely to endorse specific practices and behaviours, positioning them as crucial to the good life, and such a result goes against the goal of LGBT equal regard. It endorses a position which will see *some* LGBTs tolerated at the expense of 'bad' LGBTs. Griffin, of course, never commits to the position that all people *must* get married in order to have what they would consider a worthwhile life; but he does appear to commit to the position that all people must have the *option* to get married if they are to be able to have a worthwhile life. This should make us question what Griffin is implicitly endorsing.

Allow me to summarize this criticism against the personhood account. As stated above, when it comes to assessing whether or not a person has a legitimate claim under liberty, it must be determined whether that person's claim matters to the pursuit of a worthwhile life in general. This is the material constraint. The only way that same-sex relationship recognition can be justified as a 'paucity of options' is if this option is deemed to matter for whether or not a person can function as a normative agent at all. Since same-sex relationships are Griffin's own example of a 'paucity of options', we can infer that Griffin believes same-sex relationship recognition passes the material constraint. However, as stated, Griffin offers no justification for holding this position. He presumes the value of the institution prior to the endorsement of personhood. The only way to assert the validity of this commitment would be to refer to practicalities—facts about human nature and human societies—but such a justification is never explicitly undertaken and would likely be contentious since there is reason to presume that various networks of care can result in one's living a worthwhile life.

But let us hypothetically accept, for the sake of the argument, that the ability to have this kind of relationship recognized is fundamental to normative agency. It would then follow that same-sex couples do suffer from a paucity of options. That is to say, if one accepts that an inability to have one's relationship legally recognized as a marriage is a significant impediment to the bare pursuit of the good life (in a way that one's inability to pursue a career in philosophy is *not* an impediment to the pursuit of the good life), then LGBTs do suffer from a paucity of options. If same-sex couples desire to marry and raise children—to have rich, stable, recognized, respected relationships—and their society has the capacity to open this option to same-sex couples but refuses, then same-sex couples do not have full liberty.

Now, a paucity of options produces positive rights which can result in particularly burdensome obligations. Recall, though, that partiality to one's family, chosen aims, and institutions is permitted; people can choose *not* to fulfil an impartial positive duty, even if it is a claim of human rights. Thus, Griffin asks, 'Do I, then, as things stand now, have a duty to work for the introduction of same-sex marriage?'[56] The answer he gives to this question is 'no'. Since Griffin is impartial to the claim, as will be any other person who has no vested interest in seeing same-sex marriage legalized, there is no duty upon him to ensure the introduction of same-sex marriage. What is needed instead is 'for *some* people to work for the introduction of same-sex marriage; not all are needed. And some of the most directly interested parties are, in the form of gay-rights organizations, already at work to that end. It is natural to leave much of the job, if they will do it, to those with the greatest motivation.'[57] Thus, what the personhood account of human rights ultimately claims is this: same-sex marriage ought to be legal, since not to have this option prevents people from fully exercising their normative agency. However, since positive duties can be especially burdensome, partiality in remedying injustices is permissible. Therefore, the duty falls on those with a vested interest in seeing same-sex marriage legalized to remedy this injustice. In other words, those without an interest in the legalization of same-sex marriage are not at fault in choosing to refrain from aiding in its introduction, for they have a permitted domain of partiality.[58]

It is fair to say that this characterization of 'duty' would be largely unsatisfactory for the LGBT activist. This characterization of duty delegates the fight for same-sex marriage only to those who have a vested interest in seeing it legalized. LGBTs, however, are a minority group. Of course, it is true that some heterosexuals may have a vested interest in seeing same-sex marriage legalized if, for example, they have family or friends who are LGBTs and they find it unfair that LGBTs are restricted from this social institution arbitrarily. But if people are permitted this domain of partiality, and the human right that is owed is unpopular to the majority, the likelihood of change will be stifled. If saying that someone has a right to something is to say that they have an enforceable moral claim to it, then a desirable level of duty would hold people morally accountable for change even if to do so was not in their own personal interest.[59] Thus, even if the personhood account were thought to provide an adequate justification of same-sex marriage, it nonetheless fails to compel people to introduce a positive human right.

A final point regards the status of 'equality' in the personhood account. The personhood account is a bottom-up account of human rights and as such it is important that the account reasonably fits with what most people understand human rights to protect. When one considers human rights as they are understood in international legal doctrine and practice, it appears that 'human dignity' is the core of what human rights are designed to protect.[60] This accords with article 1 of the UDHR, which states that all human beings are born free and equal in dignity and rights. Typically, to say that human rights ought to protect dignity implies that dignity is an inherent human *status* to be respected. However, dignity as articulated under the personhood account is conflated with normative agency. In other words, protecting human dignity means protecting the factors which allow people the capacity to pursue the good life. In this sense, human rights do not protect a status so much as they act as instruments for achieving some desirable state of affairs or human well-being.

A failure to focus on equal status as the marker of dignity means that the personhood account is not a reasonable fit with the shared social understanding and application of international human rights. Moreover, the principle of nondiscrimination that characterizes article 2 of the UDHR rests on an endorsement of this equality of status. That is, all are entitled to the protection of human rights without distinction of any kind, 'such as race, colour, sex, language, religion, political or other opinion, national or social origin, property, birth or other status'. If we consider the exclusion of LGBTs from marriage, 'explaining the matter in terms of liberty seems less intuitive than appealing to the notion of equal status.'[61] That is to say, it seems to be a 'better fit' if the wrong of marriage inequality is explained with reference to one's treatment as inferior rather than in terms of a violation of one's liberty. Indeed, the wrong of discrimination is not based *primarily* on a perversion of one's liberty, even though it is true that LGBTs are not free to marry. For 'to judge a person's most intimate relationships and commitments inferior is not to make a judgment simply about what [he or] she does but also about what [he or] she is.'[62] This is essentially a point about the injustice of heterosexual privilege. It seems that the personhood account must reject discrimination by showing that it somehow undermines normative agency; but someone can be subjected to a great deal of discrimination and still be able to exercise his or her normative agency depending upon the threshold of 'personhood'. Moreover, this type of justification does not speak to heterosexual privilege in any way.

To summarize this argument: The exclusion of LGBTs from certain public institutions like marriage can be reasonably viewed as a result of the social perception of LGBTs as inferior in their human status. The primary wrong is not in their being denied access to marriage but in their being denied status as equal in dignity. This seems to be a better fit with real-world human rights claims. We saw that the personhood account excludes equality as a ground of human rights because it was thought to be too contentless a ground upon which to build human rights. But equality is not lacking in content if one considers a group's history of discrimination and uses some measure of social comparison.[63] It is possible to take into account the way that LGBTs have been constructed as what I will call 'marked persons' throughout history in order to demonstrate how this identity has been used as a marker of inferiority and to demonstrate how LGBTs have been wronged. One can then use this historical knowledge to add content to the notion of equality. This is what an approach striving for equal regard must seek to do. In order to successfully utilize social-comparison, one must also examine the construction of difference according to binary logic. This will open up an opportunity to rebuild an understanding of what it means to be different and to be held with equal regard. If assimilation is to be avoided, those striving for equal regard *must* take a critical eye towards the standards of comparison themselves and question whether they are something which ought to be matched. This project will be undertaken in chapter 3.

Thus, judging LGBTs as inferior and denying them their equal status in dignity should not be reduced to a 'violation of personhood', but rather it should act as its own grounding of human rights claims.[64] By limiting equal respect to normative agency, one is only able to account for the injustice of social discrimination if one endorses a thicker conception of personhood; if equality were endorsed as a ground of human rights, this would not be necessary. As such, we can conclude that a human rights account that is worth endorsing must do the following: it must (a) oblige those who are able to introduce same-sex marriage to undertake this task, irrespective of their personal inclinations; (b) not assume that marriage is an intrinsically worthy institution worthy of reproduction; (c) have a socially comparative element balanced by a critical component; and (d) take into account the history of LGBT discrimination.

NOTES

1. These include the International Covenant on Civil and Political Rights 1966 (ICCPR), the International Covenant on Economic, Social and Cultural Rights 1966 (ICESC), the International Convention on the Elimination of All Forms of Racial Discrimination, the Convention on the Elimination of All Forms of Discrimination against Women, the Convention on the Rights of the Child, the Convention on the Rights of Persons with Disabilities, and the United Nations Declaration on the Rights of Indigenous Peoples. See 'ILGA Constitution', section C3.1.2, accessed 3 November 2014, http://old.ilga.org/documents/ENG-ILGA%20Constitution-Nov08.pdf.

2. Xigen Li and Xudong Liu, 'Framing and Coverage of Same-Sex Marriage in U.S. Newspapers', *Howard Journal of Communications* 21, no. 1 (2010): 73.

3. Ibid.

4. Australian Marriage Equality, 'The Hintons, a Family That Supports Marriage Equality', YouTube, 20 August 2012, accessed 3 November 2014, https://www.youtube.com/watch?v=M7hwFD4Ii3E.

5. Marriage Equality, 'Sinéad's Hand', YouTube, 19 August 2009, accessed 18 October 2014, https://www.youtube.com/watch?v=6ULdaSrYGLQ.

6. GetUp! Action for Australia, 'It's Time', YouTube, 24 November 2012, accessed 3 November 2014, https://www.youtube.com/watch?v=_TBd-UCwVAY .

7. Something that is interesting to note about all of these media representations is that they rarely, if ever, show same-sex couples engaging in sexual behaviour, such as kissing, which is

standard for general representations of romantically involved different-sex couples. Deemphasizing the sexual nature of same-sex relationships is strategic, given that LGBTs have frequently been discriminated against because of the sex they have. But, importantly, ignoring this difference (the type of sexual behaviours likely to be involved and the sexes of the participants) cannot address this site of exclusion.

8. 'Marriage 101', Freedom to Marry, accessed 2 November 2014, http://www.freedomtomarry.org/pages/marriage-101#faq1.

9. Evan Wolfson, 'Marriage Makes a Word of Difference: Why We Can't Call It Something Else', *Portland Mercury*, 14 June 2007, accessed 3 November 2014, http://www.portlandmercury.com/portland/marriage-makes-a-word-of-difference/Content?oid=344646.

10. Wolfson, 'A Word of Difference'.

11. Ibid.

12. '12 Reasons'.

13. Ibid.; original emphasis.

14. 'Just Like You—Love Knows No Difference', Australian Marriage Equality, 2014, accessed 3 November 2014, http://www.australianmarriageequality.org/just-like-you/.

15. Kees Waaldijk, 'Civil Developments: Patterns of Reform in the Legal Position of Same-Sex Partners in Europe', *Canadian Journal of Family Law* 17 (2000): 85.

16. '12 Reasons'; original emphasis.

17. William N. Eskridge Jr., *Gaylaw: Challenging the Apartheid of the Closet* (Cambridge, MA: Harvard University Press, 1999), 286.

18. Ibid.

19. Ibid.

20. Gust A. Yep, Karen E. Lovaas, and John P. Elia, 'A Critical Appraisal of Assimilationist and Radical Ideologies Underlying Same-Sex Marriage in LGBT Communities in the United States', *Journal of Homosexuality* 45, no. 1 (2003): 51–52.

21. For criticisms of the same-sex marriage movement see Diane Richardson, 'Locating Sexualities: From Here to Normality', *Sexualities* 7 (2004): 391–411, and Richardson, 'Sexuality and Citizenship', *Sociology* 32 (1998): 83–100; Claudia Card, 'Against Marriage and Motherhood', *Hypatia* 11, no. 3 (1996): 1–23; Elizabeth Brake, 'Minimal Marriage: What Political Liberalism Implies for Marriage Law', *Ethics* 120, no. 2 (2010): 302–37, and Brake, *Minimizing Marriage: Marriage, Morality and the Law* (Oxford: Oxford University Press, 2012); Nancy Polikoff, 'We Will Get What We Ask For: Why Legalizing Gay and Lesbian Marriage Will Not "Dismantle the Legal Structure of Gender in Every Marriage"', *Virginia Law Review* 79, no. 7 (1993): 1535–50, and Polikoff, *Beyond (Straight and Gay) Marriage: Valuing All Families Under the Law* (Boston: Beacon Press, 2011); Michael Warner, *The Trouble with Normal: Sex, Politics, and the Ethics of Queer Life* (Cambridge, MA: Harvard University Press, 1999); and 'Beyond Same-Sex Marriage: A New Strategic Vision for All Our Families and Relationships', Beyond Marriage Allied Activists, accessed 3 November 2014, http://www.beyondmarriage.org/BeyondMarriage.pdf.

22. Allen Buchanan, 'The Egalitarianism of Human Rights', *Ethics* 120, no. 4 (2010): 706.

23. James Tasioulas, 'Taking Rights Out of Human Rights', *Ethics* 120, no. 4 (2010): 647.

24. James Griffin, *On Human Rights* (Oxford: Oxford University Press, 2008), chap. 2.

25. Ibid., 36.

26. Ibid., 32.

27. Ibid., chap. 2.

28. Ibid.

29. Ibid., 38.

30. Ibid., chap. 2.

31. Both James Tasioulas ('Taking Rights') and Allen Buchanan ('Egalitarianism of Human Rights') criticise Griffin for not elaborating more fully on the content of practicalities.

32. Griffin, *On Human Rights*, 98.

33. Ibid., chap. 5.

34. Ibid., chap. 9.

35. Buchanan, 'Egalitarianism of Human Rights'.

36. Griffin, *On Human Rights*, 40.

37. Griffin dedicates a chapter to discussing what kinds of people can rightly claim 'human rights'. See Griffin, *On Human Rights*, chap. 4.
38. Ibid., chap. 2.
39. Ibid., 162; emphasis added.
40. Ibid.
41. Ibid., chap. 9. Griffin seems to reject the notion that a person could be so bent on becoming a professional philosopher that they will accept nothing else as a valuable form of life.
42. Ibid., 163; emphasis added.
43. Ibid.
44. Ibid.
45. Ibid., 163–64; emphasis added.
46. Ibid., 167.
47. Tasioulas, 'Taking Rights', 660.
48. Ibid.; emphasis added. There is some similarity here to Joseph Raz's thought on autonomy. He argues that 'to be autonomous a person must not only be given a choice but he must be given an adequate range of choices.' See Joseph Raz, *The Morality of Freedom* (New York: Oxford University Press, 1988), 373.
49. Griffin, *On Human Rights*, intro. and chap. 1.
50. Tasioulas, 'Taking Rights'.
51. Ibid.
52. Cheshire Calhoun, *Feminism, the Family, and the Politics of the Closet: Lesbian and Gay Displacement* (Oxford: Oxford University Press, 2000), 110.
53. Ibid., chap. 5.
54. Griffin, *On Human Rights*, 169.
55. Buchanan, 'Egalitarianism of Human Rights', 697; emphasis added.
56. Griffin, *On Human Rights*, 169.
57. Ibid.; original emphasis.
58. Ibid., chap. 9.
59. See Duncan Ivison, *Rights* (Stocksfield, UK: Acumen Publishing, 2008) intro. This is also something that Tasioulas recognizes: the duties that emerge from rights claims are supposed to be categorical, meaning that they are held to be absolute, morally enforceable claims. Griffin's duties, however, do not appear to be categorical. See Tasioulas, 'Taking Rights'.
60. Griffin, *On Human Rights*, chap. 2.
61. Buchanan, 'Egalitarianism of Human Rights', 697.
62. Ibid., 710.
63. Ibid.
64. Ibid.

Chapter Three

Feminist Criticisms of Human Rights

Is rights rhetoric a useful tool for achieving LGBT equal regard? Some believe that it is not. This is because rights are 'conduits'; that is to say, while rights can be used to criticize existing relations of power, they also sit within these existing relations of power in various ways. Rights presuppose various conceptions of the person, practices, and institutions. Rights are also shaped by and help underpin social and political norms.[1] In this chapter, I argue that LGBTs are 'marked persons' and, as such, encounter paradoxes when they adopt rights discourse. A marked person is someone who belongs to a group that is systematically discriminated against. These people are marked insofar as they are explicitly 'named' by the trait that is stigmatized. This marking occurs thanks to a process of comparison with an implicit standard of 'normalcy' attributed to the hypothetical human subject. It is why we have 'sex' and 'gay sex'; 'athletes' and 'female athletes'; 'skin colour' bandages that are always coloured beige; the 'Special' Olympics, and so on. The standard of the hypothetical human subject is frequently presumed to be neutral and therefore valid. However, this unspoken yardstick of measure is highly biased in favour of a particular type of individual: the male, masculine, rational, heterosexual, adult, white, Western/Eurocentric, able-bodied public actor and property owner.[2]

In law, Margaret Thornton calls this figure the 'benchmark man'.[3] The existence of a benchmark man explains why LGBTs face paradoxes when they adopt rights discourse. LGBT rights claims are judged in comparison to the rights claims of the 'normal' human subject—an implicitly biased figure. The question at hand, then, is whether legal discourse can deal with the 'ontological complexity that is inherent to sexuality'.[4] Wendy Brown believes that rights are something we cannot *not* want, but she characterizes these paradoxes as irresolvable.[5] I will argue that the law has the capacity to deal with this ontological complexity provided we undertake a process of reconceiving difference outside of the binary schema which has heretofore characterized identity-based rights claims. I will, therefore, argue that these paradoxes are not inherently irresolvable and, as such, I will claim that rights discourse can be amiable to the goal of equal regard.

I. CONSTRUCTING 'MARKED PERSONS'

Western discourses of philosophy and law have been constructed around the premise of a singular human subject, as above described. Although it has become more important to recognize the diversity of people over time, the fundamental model of the human subject has remained unchanged. Diversity is conceived of and experienced hierarchically, and Others who do not entirely match the standard set by this subject are subordinate to him. Certain people, such as LGBTs, become 'marked persons' thanks to their supposed inadequacies in relation to this ideal; they are 'lacking' in terms of their sex, race, sexual orientation, age, ability, and so forth. That is, their inadequacies mark their identity as Other.

Take an example from Simone de Beauvoir's *The Second Sex* to demonstrate marked identity. She states, 'If I want to define myself, I first have to say, "I am a woman"; all other assertions will arise from this basic truth. A man never begins by positing himself as an individual of a certain sex: that he is a man is obvious.'[6] Thus, unless one asserts otherwise, humanity is assumed to be male—this 'truth' is so obvious that it goes unspoken. Being a man is not a particularity, like being a woman; rather, it is the norm. In this way, a woman is marked by her sex. Similarly, one will have to state they are 'queer', for 'heterosexuality is rarely acknowledged in accounts of social life, it is simply presumed. Indeed, it is precisely because of its naturalized, normative status, that it becomes invisible as an organizing principle of social organization and personal identity.'[7] Heterosexuality, too, is so obvious that it goes unspoken.

One key way in which Otherness and lack is ascribed to certain kinds of people is thanks to the implementation of logical dichotomies in the construction of social and political identities. The logical rules implied by dichotomous thought play a significant role in constructing a biased conception of the human subject. They are the principle of identity, the principle of contradiction, and the principle of the excluded middle. That is, if anything is A, it is A; nothing can be both A and not-A; and everything must be either A or not-A. The leading terms (A) are always accorded primacy, whereas their partners (not-A) are perceived as weaker and/or derivative. The use of dichotomous categories of thought can be traced back to ancient Greek philosophy. This is not bad or oppressive in itself, but 'it can covertly promote social and political values by presenting a conceptual division as if it were a factual or natural division'.[8] Indeed, we have seen these principles accord primacy to being 'invariably White, heterosexual, able-bodied, politically conservative, and middle class'.[9]

While the use of binary logic to define and categorize sex and gender has been frequently highlighted in feminist theory, analyzing binary relations is equally vital to considerations of LGBT discrimination. This is because the 'need' to dichotomize sexual differences in philosophical and political discourse 'contributes to anxiety about and stigmatization of homosexuality'.[10] This binary logic is clearly reflected in what Michael Warner calls hierarchies of shame. The left side of the table below lists the primary terms (A), while the right side lists the weaker and/or derivative partners (not-A):

Good, Normal, Natural	*Bad, Abnormal, Unnatural*
Heterosexual	Homosexual
Married	Unmarried
Monogamous	Promiscuous
Procreative	Nonprocreative
Noncommercial	Commercial
In pairs	Alone or in groups
In a relationship	Casual
Same generation	Cross-generational
In private	In public
No pornography	Pornography
Bodies only	With manufactured objects
Vanilla	Sadomasochistic[11]

This can be understood as a hierarchy of *shame* specifically because transgressions of social norms deeply engage people's emotions. Transgression is likely to result in feelings of guilt and indignity on the part of the transgressor and disgust, rage, and/or horror on the part of the norm-endorser.[12] The feeling of shame discloses a prereflexive consciousness of inferiority, even despite conscious endorsement of more egalitarian beliefs. Shame is, in other words, a 'pre-reflexive mode of knowing that consists in the self's "recognition" of how she or he is seen by an Other. . . . One's "recognition" does not imply one's overt "identification" with, much less affirmation of, the self-as-seen-by-the-Other. Yet without the recognition of this self . . . there would be no shame.'[13] Thus, it is those who align with the weaker side of the binary that become stigmatized to a greater or lesser extent.

Importantly, the 'distinctions between good sex and bad do not necessarily come as whole packages'.[14] People embody and practice traits that fall on both sides of the hierarchies of shame. As Warner points out, 'The main thing the different distinctions have in common is the simple fact that each is a hierarchy, and if you are on the wrong side of the hierarchy you will be stigmatized in a way that could entail real damage.'[15] From this we gather that nonnormative heterosexuals may also be shamed; different transgressions have different levels of severity, as well as greater or lesser social and material costs, and these levels are in constant flux. However, it is important to recognize that LGBT people have been repositories for the undesirable traits that both homosexuals and heterosexuals exhibit. In other words, homosexuals and heterosexuals are thought to be different in *kind* rather than *degree*. LGBTs are presumed to exhibit or strive towards the features on the right side of the table unless proven otherwise, whereas heterosexuals are presumed to exhibit or strive towards the features on the left of the table unless proven otherwise. Thus, while there is a continual shift between which acts normatively count as more or less devious (and where to draw the line), when LGBT people transgress norms it is a reflection of *who they are*, not what they do. Therefore, the shame felt by LGBTs is a direct result of their (prereflexive awareness of their) construction as lacking in certain ways, given their perceived and/or presumed failure to match certain social norms.

This construction of LGBT identities as abnormal and shame-worthy is apparent at the level of legal and social discourse, and institutions and practices have developed around these Othered identities. For example, homosexuality was historically pathologized as a perversion, as a mental illness, and as abnormal in contrast to natural, good, normative heterosexuality.[16] In the legal sphere, the construction and perception of subjectivity according to a hierarchical standard creates difficulties for marked persons attempting to employ rights discourse. Ngaire Naffine notes that legal personality is a cluster of rights and duties which varies greatly depending on one's age, sex, natural ability, and so on. Although the unstable concept of legal personhood allows all human beings to be persons for some purposes, 'some human beings are far more effective legal actors than others'.[17] As it so happens, the 'healthiest' legal person possesses the attributes of the 'normal' human subject. This is the individual unencumbered by family ties and community obligations: the rational, autonomous, self-determining subject. This benchmark man sets the status quo in the legal sphere.[18] This observation is crucially important when considering the politico-legal claims of LGBT people since the power to determine what is/can be normative is overwhelmingly claimed by the benchmark man.

Having now established how certain people come to be marked—by reference to the assumed traits of the normal subject, which they are (thought to be) lacking—it is now possible to consider what it might mean for LGBTs and Others to demand equality.

II. DEMANDING EQUALITY

In chapter 2, it was argued that a bottom-up approach to human rights ought to strive for a 'best fit' with current understandings of international human rights practice. As such, it seems that equality must be one, if not *the* ground for determining whether a human rights violation has occurred. When considering LGBT people's claims to equal rights, the first question is: what is the measure of equality? I will consider three interpretations: formal equality, substantive equality, and equal regard. As discussed in the introduction, equal regard is the version of equality that I endorse. There it was defined as respect for people as equivalent in dignity with regard to (the potential for) difference(s). It can therefore allow a space to cultivate difference(s) and foster LGBT identities, as I will emphasize below.

Formal equality means that each person has the exact same legal rights as any other person. For example, if it is a country's law to charge each person a flat tax, then all citizens are formally equal in this respect. However, the rich will be less burdened by such a flat tax than the poor, and, thus, it can be said that an inequality remains between the citizens. Formal equality alone is infrequently the best conception to endorse if one's aim is ending instances of social discrimination and disadvantage since it ignores the relevant differences (in this example, differences in economic status) that exist between people. Importantly, formal equality does not itself always present an injustice. It seems as though same-sex marriage is an instance of formal equality where the outcome would be just: all couples will be formally equal under the law. However, even if opening up marriage would not result in any injustice, formally equal laws alone are not enough to resolve instances of discrimination against LGBTs. If it were, we would not see empirical evidence reporting that 30–51 percent of LGBTs surveyed have faced discrimination in the last year due to their perceived sexual orientation/identity, despite living in countries where same-sex marriage is legal.[19] As such, it pays to be cautious about arguments championing formal equality.

Equality can also be interpreted substantively. While formal equality demands equal laws only, substantive equality appeals to social comparison. This form of social comparison involves assessing the relevant degrees of sameness between different types of persons and then arguing that the law should be structured to enable the disadvantaged to participate equally with the advantaged. It ultimately involves matching a predetermined standard. This conception of equality is common in justifications for same-sex marriage, as seen in chapter 2. The message behind these popular justifications of same-sex marriage is that *same-sex couples and different-sex couples are just the same.* Both types of relationship are equally capable of love, commitment, stability, and resilience. They are also equally valuable. Thus, marriage equality is justified because like people should be treated alike. It is worthwhile to explore further what it means for same-sex marriage advocates to appeal to substantive equality. Here it is heteronormative behaviours and structures that are associated with the legal institution of marriage which set the standard that is to be equalled. Such conditions are typically taken to include commitment, stability, monogamy, sharing a home, parenting, shared financial commitments, sexual intimacy, romantic love, shared interests and activities, the public acknowledgement of said relationship, long-term endurance, and so forth. These are all features of the previously discussed 'normative ideal of marriage'.[20]

One reason for opposition to same-sex marriage is that the normative ideal of marriage hides the fact that what it presents as normal is only one of many possible conceptions of 'normalcy'.[21] For example, the US collective Beyond Marriage argues that access to a flexible set of economic benefits and options regardless of sexual orientation, race, gender identity, class, or citizenship status would be more desirable than marriage equality. They seek instead to 'reflect and honor the diverse ways in which people find and practice love, form relationships, create communities and networks of caring and support, establish households, bring families into being, and build innovative structures to support and sustain community'.[22] The problem with appealing to substantive equality, then, is that the heterosexual mainstream determines the limits of what is permissible (and therefore tolerable), while dominant justifications of same-sex marriage disregard other equally legitimate systems of care and intimacy. LGBT men and women will be judged as acceptable based on how well they live up to the shared, imagined standards of 'normal' intimate life as imagined by the heterosexual mainstream. Thus, the power of these heteronorms contributes to the production of notions of the 'good' homosexual and the 'bad' homosexual.[23] Good homosexuals will deviate from 'normal' intimacies only insofar as they are same-sex attracted.

Same-sex couples who strive to display that they structure their relationships in much the same way that 'normal heterosexuals' are perceived to do ultimately position these same-sex relationships as more socially acceptable or legitimate than others as a result. When LGBT people seek entry to certain institutions like marriage on these grounds, they are unlikely to challenge the primacy of these institutions, nor are they likely to challenge heterosexual privilege. Moreover, this LGBT 'equality' is artificial because even good LGBT people can never fully exhibit all of the traits of the normal human subject. There is *at least* one difference to a heterosexual pairing: the sexes of the partners. Other differences may include (but are not limited to) the sexual activity one engages in and whether and in what way one becomes a parent.

As such, LGBT people can only become *normal enough* to be tolerable. This does not amount to equality. It is because these hierarchical commitments produce unjustified internalizations of shame and feelings of inferiority that the call for equal regard emerges.

So far we have explored the way that certain people become marked in relation to the standards of an implicitly biased subject or 'benchmark man'. We have also seen that demanding equality may take several forms. Both formal equality and substantive equality have downfalls. Formal equality fails to take context into account. This means that even if formal equality is just, it alone is unlikely to resolve or prevent instances of discrimination. Substantive equality is problematic insofar as, in striving to prove the similarities between same-sex and different-sex couples, it concedes that the heteronormative way of life is ideal. Since LGBTs can never completely match the heteronormative ideal, this leaves them in a situation of perpetually having to prove they are 'good' homosexuals. Equal regard, on the other hand, would seek to advocate for same-sex marriage while simultaneously challenging the normative worth of this very institution. Equal regard means to be equally recognized as a rights-bearing member of society while being simultaneously recognized as (potentially) different. It requires symbolic presence and visibility, endignifying representations, the cultivation and fostering of identities, and cultivation of alternative lifestyles. It avoids assimilation and marginalization. LGBT people cannot be said to be equal according to this position until they are respected *as LGBT people*, rather than treated as tolerable if and only if they sufficiently ape heteronorms.

Yet the question remains, can rights discourse secure equal regard? As mentioned above, Brown believes that rights are paradoxical for Others, but that they are something people cannot not want. I will endeavour to show that while rights discourse runs the risk of reinforcing LGBT discrimination, we need not conclude that rights present irresolvable paradoxes for marked persons.

III. WENDY BROWN AND THE PARADOXES OF RIGHTS

According to Brown, because rights are paradoxical they mitigate rather than resolve injustices. Although obtaining a right may weaken the subordination that marked persons face, the right/s obtained by these marked persons can ultimately do nothing to dismantle the mechanisms that reproduce those injustices.[24] Brown argues that rights are paradoxical for women, specifically. However, I will consider each of these paradoxes in order to show that LGBTs, as marked persons, face these same difficulties.

i. The Difficulty of Claiming Difference

The first paradox is the following: given that women have historically suffered legal, social, and political disadvantages based on 'natural' differences between women and men, specific rights *for women* have needed to be developed in order to remedy this situation. However, Brown finds that 'the more highly specified rights are *as rights for women*, the more likely they are to encode a definition of women premised upon [their] subordination in the transhistorical discourse of liberal jurisprudence'.[25] In other words, the fact that women have been *named* as a group who require different rights from men contributes to the entrenchment of women's subordinate status. This comes about since elaborating specific rights for women serves to 'prove' the stereotype that they are in need of 'special' or 'additional' rights.

When a group is perceived as requiring 'special' or 'additional' rights, this is usually interpreted in one of two ways. First, if a group is seen as gaining additional rights *on top of* the regular amount of standard human rights, then this may result in resentment towards the marginalized group. In this instance, the nonmarginalized group may believe that they are being treated unjustly since the marginalized group appears to receive something extra rather than something different. Kate Sheill argues that it took the United Nations until 1993 to see women's rights as human rights, for example, 'and still activists are having to argue that claiming women's human rights is not about claiming 'extra' or 'special' rights for women, but about claiming women's fair entitlement to universal human rights'.[26] Second, if a marginalized group is seen as requiring 'special rights', the interpretation may be that the marginalized group is inferior or lacking in some way when compared with the normal human subject. They are thus seen to require special rights in order to attempt the achievement of substantive equality, that is, to be just *like* the normal subject. This second interpretation rests upon an implicit belief that the marginalized group is inferior, even though the nonmarginalized may themselves be actively seeking to instate substantive equality for the marginalized. By naming a particular group that requires 'special rights' compared to those of the 'normal' person, the subordinate status of this group is reinforced.

Take the case for same-sex marriage in order to demonstrate the first type of response to group-specific rights. Bill Muehlenberg makes the argument that there is no real inequality for LGBTs where same-sex marriage is illegal. This is because anyone can marry, if only they fulfil a certain set of criteria. One such criterion that must be met is that a marriage needs to involve one man and one woman. The Family Research Council (FRC) similarly argues that 'the fundamental "right to marry" is a right that rests with *individuals*, not with *couples*. Homosexual *individuals* already have exactly the same "right" to marry as anyone else.'[27] A person who identifies as a lesbian is not discriminated against because she *can* enter a marriage with a man (assuming she is of legal age and not married to anyone else). Muehlenberg claims, 'This is not unjust or arbitrary "discrimination"; it is simply encouraging everyone to play by the rules. Since homosexuals refuse to play by the rules of marriage, they should not complain about foregone rights.'[28] Essentially, the claim here is that LGBTs and heterosexuals are already formally equal, which means there is no reason to alter the law.

If one accepts this logic, it is easy to see how heterosexuals may come to perceive LGBTs as unjustly demanding 'additional' rights: the right to marry the same sex. But such an argument entirely misses the socially comparative element. LGBTs are seeking a justification for why their same-sex relationships should be excluded from legal recognition. They ask why the criteria of marriage should be limited to involving only one man and one woman. Many fail to note that opening up marriage would extend the entitlement to marry someone of the same sex to all persons equally—so heterosexuals would be gaining something 'extra' too. In fact, this is true for all arguments that seek to open up marriage in various ways.[29] Moreover, there seems to be no justification for retaining the marriage rule. One cannot justify the heterosexuality of marriage based on an appeal to a past history in which marriage has been defined as between one man and one woman, for example, as this would be tautological and therefore invalid.[30]

Parenting may be considered as an example of the second interpretation of LGBTs as different and therefore needing 'special rights'. Access to facilities such as in vitro fertilization (IVF), adoption, and surrogacy (where it is legal) for LGBTs may be of crucial importance since same-sex couples are usually unable to biologically conceive their own children. Legally, giving LGBTs access to these rights would largely take a similar route as that of access for different-sex couples. However, the narratives that draw focus in extending these rights are those that centre on the supposed biological limitations of reproduction for same-sex couples. Options such as IVF and adoption are often considered to be *alternatives* available to different-sex couples *if* they are unable to conceive their own children. This assumption is likely what influences some countries to establish laws ensuring that only married heterosexual couples may become adoptive parents. Extending such reproductive options to LGBTs, however, may occur primarily because LGBTs are perceived to *lack* the ability to produce children. This is how they are dissimilar to heterosexuals. So while adoption and IVF are alternative options for heterosexuals, giving access to LGBTs is a *special* right because they cannot reproduce like heterosexuals do. The perception of inferiority is built into the assumption itself, irrespective of whether one opposes or supports same-sex parenting.

Of course, biologically it is not true that LGBTs are unable to reproduce. This assumption merely reflects a narrow heteronormative perception of the production of families. Rather, it is the case that generally LGBTs do not *want* to reproduce like heterosexuals do. LGBTs are capable of engaging in heterosexual sex where the outcome may be pregnancy and/or some form of shared parenting agreement. Or, if one member of a same-sex union is transgender, the couple may be able to conceive 'naturally'. In 2008, Thomas Beatie became the first legal male and husband to give birth on record. Although Beatie's was a different-sex union, there is every reason to suppose that transgender people are in several instances (capable of) reproducing with their same-sex partners.

It is the endorsement of the fiction that LGBTs are incapable of reproduction that results in the interpretation of 'access to IVF/adoption' as a 'special right' for LGBTs. Biased norms are mistaken for neutral observations and 'need' is weighted according to different criteria. Therefore, the paradox is that although marked groups are recognized as genuinely *likely* to have different needs and requirements to other people, and although recognition of this fact may alleviate *some* injustices against the marked persons, when marked persons achieve rights as a marked group they can be simultaneously reaffirmed as subordinate to the very norm they struggle against.

ii. The Difficulty of Claiming Sameness

The reverse to this paradox is also problematic. Where marked groups seek neutrality *in an already biased context*, the rights obtained will not adequately assist in ending discrimination, either. Brown argues, 'The more gender-neutral or gender-blind a particular right (or any law or public policy) is, the more likely it is to enhance the privilege of men and eclipse the needs of the women as subordinates.'[31] The argument is that rights claims on the basis of neutrality in nonneutral contexts do not adequately deal with the systematic inequalities present in society.

This is one key reason why calls for formal and substantive equality as strategies for recognition of marginalized people have been criticized. As mentioned above, asking for formal equality means to request the exact same legal rights as another group of people. As we saw in relation to the example regarding same-sex marriage, formal equality alone is unlikely to alleviate the discrimination that marked persons face. This is because it does not investigate the causes of the original inequality. The approach of substantive equality is also often rejected because, frequently, in order to gain legitimacy for a rights claim, *sameness* will be used as a justification. Like appealing to formal equality, this does little or nothing to question the structures from which the inequality originated. These appeals also illustrate how an approach privileging social comparison can be dangerous: while social comparison is important and illuminating, it must always be balanced by an overarching critical evaluation of the social climate as it stands.

Several scholars and activists have argued against the approach from sameness. For example, Nancy Polikoff argues that to seek the right to marry is to attempt to mimic mainstream society, with the result that the aim of gay liberation and radical feminism is betrayed since true justice depends on accepting differences from mainstream culture. Claudia Card finds that although such formal inequality cannot be justified, the institution of marriage is unworthy of reproduction and inherently problematic. It is problematic for several reasons: (a) Marriage has been historically mandatory and oppressive for women; (b) same-sex marriage would delegitimize other forms of relationships further; (c) marriage has a number of economic and health care benefits unfairly attached to it, and thus marriage ought to be deregulated and these benefits made available to all; (d) the difficulty of divorce encourages people to remain married; and (e) the marital environment can be conducive to violence which is difficult for the state to prevent since it occurs in the private realm and gives spouses legal access to the other's person and property. Several of these points are reflected by the allied activists of Beyond Marriage, as outlined above.[32]

To add to these opinions, Diane Richardson acknowledges that, since the 'normal citizen' has largely been construed as heterosexual, the mimicry of heterosexual norms is the simplest way to be conceived of as a normal citizen; however, an assimilationist agenda based on 'sameness' serves to further marginalize nonconformists, whether they are different-sex or same-sex attracted. Warner shares similar opinions, noting that formal inequality cannot be justified but that to articulate same-sex marriage as an LGBT goal via this assimilationist strategy does not aid in challenging the interpretation of certain sex acts and relationship structures as good and others as bad, abnormal, perverse, and so on. Finally, Elizabeth Brake claims that a diverse liberal society must be committed to respecting the many views of the good therein without privileging one monogamous, central, amatonormative union.[33]

Thus, while formal and substantive equality may sometimes result in the *appearance* of equal regard, such as in the case of legalizing same-sex marriage, there may well be problematic consequences. Importantly, though, this does not mean that the socially comparative approach should be abandoned altogether. One can also use social comparison to examine the construction of difference according to binary logic. This would then open up an opportunity to rebuild an understanding of what it means to be different and to be held with equal regard. That is to say, gaining access to marriage is only a success if it is accompanied by other radical revisions to the dominant shared Western social imaginary. If legalizing same-sex marriage will create substantive equality between *some* LGBTs and normative heterosexuals, then heterosexual privilege will not be alleviated. Normative heterosexuality will still be taken as the hierarchical marker of normalcy, which LGBTs must attempt, but will always inevitably fail, to match. According to this measure, LGBTs can never be perfectly normal; they can only ever be 'normal enough' to be tolerable. What needs to be questioned are the standards which LGBTs must meet in order to be regarded as socially acceptable in the first place, given that these standards are uncritically accepted as legitimate norms or 'natural facts'. The validity of these standards is always implicitly assumed, never publicly justified. This is what must be challenged.

iii. The Difficulty of Adequate Intersectional Recognition

The third paradox involves the difficulties that marginalized groups face in presenting a united claim for recognition. Brown claims that feminist legal reformers have a tendency to inscribe in the law 'the experience and discursive truths of *some* women which is then held to represent all women'.[34] Such an outcome is problematic since it can result in minorities from within a marginalized group failing to receive adequate recognition, cover, and protection. In other words, there is a danger of establishing normative standards for 'woman' that defines certain women as outside of this category. The gains won by marked persons frequently do not account for the various instances of discrimination its individual members face given the fact of intersecting marginal identities.

To give an example, consider that women's rights are often articulated according to the needs of heterosexual women. This occurs because issues to do with sex and homosexuality are treated as two different bases of discrimination. As such, heterosexuality has come to be treated synonymously with sex/gender, especially under the law. In this instance, lesbians miss out on adequate recognition since the rights gained for women pertain predominantly to the needs of heterosexual women. Several feminist scholars have raised this criticism. Indeed, this problem was identified as early as 1980 when Adrienne Rich claimed that lesbian experience is forgotten or ignored given a bias of compulsory heterosexuality. Nadine Gartner has also assessed how women's human rights are problematic for lesbians, even suggesting the introduction of a 'convention on the elimination of all forms of discrimination against lesbians' as a specific document. Sheill has likewise noticed that women's human rights are considered almost exclusively under the assumption that women are heterosexual.[35]

Consider the difficulties faced by lesbian mothers in 1970s Australia as an example of the separation of one's being a woman *and* same-sex attracted. It was not only legal discourse which had difficulty reconciling these identities, but sociopolitical discourse as well. Rebecca Jennings argues, 'The notion of motherhood . . . did not fit comfortably into the models of lesbian identity being embraced by many lesbian communities in the 1970s and a number of women reported a pervasive belief that lesbians could not be mothers.'[36] The custody battles of the 1970s ultimately produced two new models of lesbian identity: 'The visible, political lesbian, whose sexuality rendered her a "bad" mother, and the discreet, respectable lesbian, whose maternal instincts triumphed over her sexuality, enabling her to be a "good" mother.'[37] If a woman was too queer, she would be deemed a bad mother; if she was imperceptibly queer, she would be tolerable as a mother. Thus, lesbians had to downplay their sexual identities and appeal to heteronormative ideals of motherhood in order to maintain custody of their children. Importantly, it had to be demonstrated that 'good' lesbian mothers would not flaunt their sexuality, and they were required to claim to believe that a homosexual orientation for their children would be undesirable. While this distinction sometimes worked to the advantage of lesbian mothers who played the system, it nonetheless demonstrates the law's self-imposed limitations.[38]

More contemporary examples include the stereotypes surrounding domestic violence and the law's stance on reproductive freedom. There is very little awareness about intimate partner violence between same-sex couples, and there is little understanding of how to assist the victims of such violence. Sandra Lundy argues that 'cultural and institutional homophobia has isolated its victims from the psychological, social, and legal support they need to safely leave the abusive relationships'.[39] Angela West discusses her own struggle with the stereotypes surrounding intimate partner violence ('Women aren't violent by nature. Women don't hurt other women in relationships—do they?'[40]) and argues that lesbians are 'often referred to as an "invisible" group' and that their 'lack of visibility is connected to both sexism and societal homophobia'.[41] Meanwhile, Brown points out that the heterosexism of the law is evident in the framing of reproductive freedom in terms of accidental and unwanted pregnancy—issues that are not commonly faced by lesbian women.[42] More relevant concerns may include access to IVF and adoption.

Moreover, lesbians also miss out on adequate recognition under LGBT rights claims. Rich argues, 'Lesbians have historically been deprived of a political existence through "inclusion" as female versions of male homosexuality. To equate lesbian existence with male homosexuality because each is stigmatized is to erase female reality once again.'[43] LGBT rights claims tend to take issues pertinent to gay discrimination as the core of its movement. A prime example of this is the LGBT movement's substantial focus on AIDS in the 1980s. More current examples of the LGBT movement's exclusionary capacities involve a failure to take into account forms of discrimination and violence more likely to be faced by transgender people and same-sex attracted women, such as uniform recognition of gender identity or corrective rape. Dean Spade is not convinced, for example, that the Californian LGBT rights movement is genuinely concerned with the plight of all queer and transgender people. '"If they were," he argues, "their top priority would have been to deal with the violence against queer and trans people, immigration detention in California, and the massive criminal punishment system in California"', rather than focus on marriage equality.[44] Similar critiques can be levelled at LGBT activism in the West more generally. Because the focus of LGBT politics is primarily on gay men's issues—and indeed, gay, white, middle-class men are the face of dominant same-sex marriage activism—the LBTs often find themselves inadequately covered by the rights gains in this domain. For example, consider the complaints levelled at the UK's Marriage (Same Sex) Act of 2013 for failing to adequately recognize transgender people's relationships.[45] An acknowledgement of the ways the differences of class, age, sex, race, ability, and so on, can contribute to various experiences of discrimination is lacking. What emerges instead is an essentialized characterization of a group's needs, with the result that others 'lose out' in the intersections.

This paradox is the central concern of intersectional analysis. Kimberlé Crenshaw, discussing the intersection of race and gender, found that in legal cases brought to combat discrimination there was a 'tendency to treat race and gender as mutually exclusive categories of experience and analysis'.[46] This tendency can be called a 'but-for' approach. A but-for minority is a person who, but-for their being black or but-for their being queer or but-for their being a woman, would not have been discriminated against in a particular context. To be a but-for minority is to have one's differences to the norm considered in singular, additive terms. In other words, this but-for tendency is 'perpetuated by a single-axis framework that is dominant in anti-discrimination law' and is problematic because it misses the unique experiences of the marginalized who sit between axes of discrimination.[47]

Discrimination is usually considered in terms of one axis of difference or another but not as both simultaneously. Thus, the single-axis framework treats gender and sexuality as two different bases of discrimination. Being a heterosexual white woman is *one* axis away from being the norm. Being a gay white man is *one* axis away from the norm. Being a white lesbian woman is *two* axes away from the norm, then. To make this position clearer, it is helpful to consider, again, the implicit features assumed of the normal human subject. Where a woman finds herself discriminated against, the test of measure is to ask, 'If this woman had been a man in the same context, would the discrimination have occurred?' Where a gay man finds himself discriminated against, the test of measure is to ask, 'If this gay man had been a heterosexual man in the same context, would the discrimination have occurred?' If the discrimination would not have occurred but-for these people's identities, then the discrimination is perceived as wrong.[48]

Drucilla Cornell has commented on this legal trend for determining discrimination. She argues that typically the wrong of discrimination is interpreted as the imposition of a universal stereotype on an individual who does not match that stereotype. This is a problematic way to understand discrimination since its basis is the norms of a particular society—norms that have not themselves been justified—which are taken as a valid standard of measurement. Contemporary stereotypes of the same-sex attracted person have always emerged in relation to the presumption of heterosexual attraction and cisgendered identity as normal. During the first-wave feminist movement, cultural perceptions of homosexuality were marked by feminist challenges to the gender structure of the family. As such, gender nonconformity itself was taken as evidence of homosexuality. The nonconformist feminist was automatically suspected of lesbianism, and the image of this nonconformist, masculinized, 'doomed' lesbian was used as a motivator for heterosexual women's compliance with traditional gender norms. In addition, the identities of the lesbian and the gay were pathologized by medical theorists, with homosexuals characterized as 'inverts'. During the 1930s–1960s, it was primarily men's sexuality, rather than women's gender conformity, that was under scrutiny. In this time period, 'gay men were depicted as violent child molesters and seducers of youth'.[49] Effectively, the gay man was construed as a sexual pervert whose sexuality was a threat to men and children alike, and these fears were reflected in the cinematic expressions of the time.[50]

While stereotypes of LGBT identities may conflict, they have nonetheless found traction in today's dominant shared Western social imaginary. Indeed, the various meanings of any particular identity are often 'cobbled together and likely to be inconsistent'.[51] For example, shared conceptions of gay men as overtly feminine in appearance and behaviour are present, while stereotypes of the dangerous, predatory homosexual exist simultaneously. Consider also pornographic stereotypes of attractive young lesbians who are only interested in other women until the 'main attraction' arrives, versus the stereotype of the butch lesbian who is 'trying to be a man'. The list of anomalous stereotypes goes on, but these inconsistent beliefs can be and are held concurrently. As Moira Gatens has remarked in another context, 'the surprising toleration for inconsistency in belief sets . . . is often the hallmark of worldviews that attempt to justify oppressive social, economic, and political relations'.[52] Given this fact, it is not surprising that inconsistent stereotypes of LGBTs exist. In fact, the maintenance of heterosexual privilege seems to rely on their continuation.

Let us examine how this is the case by considering the stereotype that homosexuals are a threat to the family:[53] If a homosexual person or couple could show that their lives posed no threat to the traditional family, but they were nonetheless discriminated against regarding familial life specifically because they are homosexual, this discrimination would be 'wrong' in that particular case. Thus, 'The wrong is not the imposition of stereotypes *per se*, but the imposition of stereotypes when they are not "true"'.[54] In this example, it would be wrong to discriminate against homosexuals on the grounds that 'homosexuality poses a threat to the traditional family', as the stereotype imposed is not true of that person/those particular people. This is exemplary of the single-axis approach: but-for the sexual orientation of a particular homosexual couple, there would not have been any discriminatory action. However, such a judgement does not render the stereotype false; rather, the LGBTs who can 'prove themselves' are *exceptions* to the stereotype. LGBTs continually have to prove themselves. This is how heterosexual privilege is maintained.

It should be stressed again that in cases of legal discrimination typically only one axis of difference is considered as the cause of that discriminatory treatment. Thus, marked persons separated by only one axis from the normal human subject are better able to remedy injustices than multiply burdened Others. This is why, as Naffine has said, some 'persons' are far more effective legal actors than others—they are more easily recognized and protected by the law in its present state.[55] People who face injustices due to more than one modality of social power working against them are usually overlooked. And importantly, even when LGBTs have been able to gain legal recognition, the ongoing comparison to the benchmark man means that stereotypes about LGBTs are not altogether uprooted. Rather, only *some* LGBTs prove that they do not fit the stereotype. Thus, a more nuanced and intersectional approach to nonheterosexual discrimination appears crucial.

iv. The Difficulty of Group Recognition

The metaphor of intersections is useful in order to explain the need to actively imagine multiple axes of difference simultaneously so as to combat discrimination. However, recognizing diversity within groups can lead to other equally problematic consequences for marked persons. How can marked persons maintain a group identity when the harms they face are so varied, given the fact of intersectional differences? If marked persons seek to include all aspects of identity difference and still retain their group identity, then the group will have to articulate their needs according to a very thin shareable notion in order for it to be applicable to all. But when harms are articulated abstractly, it is hard to see how they play out in a concrete fashion. Alternatively, the group would have to give up on their collective identity in favour of more and more highly specified recognition. But, as Warnke questions, 'if membership in these classes or clubs of men and women is oppressive, why will adding new clubs help? Will these new clubs not have their own set of membership rules and their own behavioural codes?'[56] In other words, it is hard to see how specifying more unique groups of people will avoid issues of inclusion and exclusion; it will eventually boil down simply to individual difference. *This* is the final of Brown's paradoxes. If LGBT people try to maintain their group identity *and* focus on their individual specificities, the group will have to articulate their examples of subordination so abstractly that the particulars of the inequality 'will vanish from the content and justification of the right'.[57] However, if the rights are more uniquely specified, the effort to secure a claim to rights shareable by all persons under a broader identity category will fail, 'because the details of [an individual's] suffering and the constraints that they face in overcoming [this suffering] will appear too particular, too individual, too personal and unique to count as instances of the (group) harms that the right was supposed to remedy'.[58]

Consider an example of the intersection of race and gender to illustrate this point. In the case of *Moore v. Hughes Helicopters, Inc.* (1983), Tommie Moore alleged that her employer practiced race and sex discrimination in promotions. There was a large disparity between men and women promoted and a lesser disparity between white and black people promoted. However, the district court refused to certify Moore as the representative in the sex discrimination complaint on behalf of all women at Hughes Helicopter because she claimed that she was discriminated against as a *black* woman. According to the Ninth Circuit, 'this raised serious doubts as to Moore's ability to adequately represent white female employees'.[59] It is clearly necessary to promote a united front in the battle against injustices for marked persons. Yet it remains unclear *how* one may do so in the face of so much diversity. Consider again the complaint that lesbian, bisexual, and transgender subordination is inadequately covered by the LGBT rights agenda. If the remedy to this was to articulate more and more highly specific rights—that is, rights for lesbians, rights for gay men, rights for bisexual women, rights for transmen, and so on—it would be unclear why we should retain the category 'LGBT' at all. The queer community have already been colloquially identified as the 'alphabet soup'. The title 'LGBT' reflects at least six distinguishable groups of people—lesbian, gay, bisexual, and transgender men and women—each presumably with their own unique experiences of discrimination. This is not to mention other groups, such as intersex people, who are often united with the queer community and who also face particular instances of discrimination.

One must face the possibility that rights discourse may simply be incompatible with an intersectional focus on difference. Consider again *Moore v. Hughes Helicopters, Inc.* Here the details of an individual's suffering were taken to be too specific to be able to count towards the group 'women' as a whole or even 'race' as a whole. But, as Crenshaw rightly points out, 'the absence of a racial referent does not necessarily mean that the claim being made is a more inclusive one. A white woman claiming discrimination against females may be in no better position to represent all women than a Black woman who claims discrimination as a Black female and wants to represent all females.'[60] For, indeed, there is no 'absence' of a racial component here but a presumption of whiteness as the marker of normal racial identity. Appealing to the law can unveil an identity, claim a space for that identity, and introduce a new conceptual language for thinking about belonging, but legal discourses can also create half-truths and fuel stereotypes.[61] How might we respond to this final paradox, then? What I propose is not to specify new 'clubs' *ad infinitum* but to revise our approach to (the possibility of) difference(s), blurring the limits of categorical identifications and remaining open to difference(s) not yet experienced.

IV. RESOLVING PARADOXES

As discussed above, Brown believes that rights are something we cannot *not* want because 'rights function to articulate a need, a condition of lack or injury, that cannot be fully redressed or transformed by rights, yet can be signified in no other way within existing political discourse'.[62] Thus, rights are both paradoxical and necessary for marked persons. A key feature of paradox, according to Brown, is its irresolvability. Paradox offers 'multiple yet incommensurable truths', or 'truths which undo even as they require each other'.[63] The situation of paradox seems fatal, and Brown notes that 'paradox appears endlessly self-cancelling, as a political condition of achievements perpetually undercut, a predicament of discourse in which every truth is crossed by a counter-truth, and hence a state in which political strategizing itself is paralysed'.[64]

Under a certain light, this view is particularly optimistic: for Brown, rights, as paradoxes, 'can challenge authority without displacing it . . . because they can embody and emphasize multiple but incommensurable truths'.[65] However, to accept this view of rights as inherently paradoxical—where to be paradoxical means to be irresolvable—reflects a 'disillusioned and disillusioning' conception of marked persons' place in liberal democracies.[66] There, marked persons 'are supposedly faced either with rewriting their injuries through rights, or of doing without rights altogether'.[67] Ultimately, if the situation of paradox is politically paralyzing, if the application of rights claims by marked persons is plagued by paradoxes, and if it appears that rights discourse will never fully achieve the goal of equal regard desired by LGBTs, then it seems that rights discourse ought *not* to be adopted in attempting such ends. It seems that LGBTs should be looking for a new normative discourse.

However, this conclusion is entirely dependent upon believing that paradoxes are, in their very nature, irresolvable. Both Gatens and Annabelle Lever disagree with Brown's characterization of rights as irresolvable paradoxes. Gatens argues:

> A paradox is 'a seemingly sound piece of reasoning based on seemingly true assumptions that leads to a contradiction (or other obviously false conclusion).

> A paradox reveals that either the principles of reasoning or the assumptions on which it is based are faulty. It is said to be solved when the mistaken principles or assumptions are clearly identified and rejected.'[68]

Thus, if rights for LGBT people result in paradoxical consequences, then we should believe that our reasoning is faulty or that such consequences have occurred based on the adoption of false assumptions. Moreover, given 'legal rights' is the avenue which marked persons have taken to represent their interests, analyzing how rights work *against* those interests is a concrete clue to the ways in which rights could be reconstructed in their form and substance.[69] Lever argues that this challenge is not served by an understanding of rights as paradoxical, where a paradox is defined by its irresolvability. 'Instead', she claims, 'it pays to see them as a more or less predictable result of, and guide to, the forms of inequality in our society—both the ones of which we are already aware, and those of which we still have to learn.'[70]

By putting these two perspectives together one can begin to see that although rights discourse is a currently flawed means through which to have one's interests recognized, such flaws may not necessarily be inherent to it. A paradox reveals that either the principles of reasoning or the assumptions on which it is based are faulty. By considering the way that marked persons are constructed—by comparison to the implicitly biased norm of the human subject—it appears that rights are delegated on a faulty system of recognition using a single-axis framework and but-for reasoning. Thus, exposing the limits of the law will work to expose the limits of the subject's hegemonic claim to universality.[71] It seems clear that since the accepted measure of the normal human subject is biased, this will be a significant contributing factor to the continued inequalities of marked persons. As such, the benchmark man should be rejected as a valid standard of legal measurement, and relationships of difference should be reconceived.

In other words, if *difference* is itself reconceived, these paradoxes may be avoided altogether. As seen above, the A/not-A dichotomous structure that is implicitly assumed in heteromasculine (or phallocentric) logic certainly plays a significant role in allowing such a biased conception of the human subject to stand as the benchmark. However, it is important to point out that not all distinctions need to take the form of the A/not-A dichotomous structure. The point is that this is the formulation that they *have* taken. An alternative, which has yet to be adequately applied to human identity, is an A/B distinction. A/B distinctions both have positive realities, and they are not all encompassing like A/not-A distinctions. A/B distinctions allow for the possibility of a third, fourth, fifth term, and so on.[72] This kind of distinction would be a more appropriate reflection of the reality of difference between the sexes, as well as other kinds of human differences. It is to be understood as truly different, not as the other of the same. Revising the structures by which human identity is perceived, then, is a challenge which must be undertaken in order to reconstruct the form and substance of rights.

If difference may be reconceived in this way, what becomes of our four paradoxes? The first was that naming marked persons as a group who require different rights contributes to the entrenchment of their subordinate status. By revealing the implicit norm which stands as the benchmark of normalcy, we can refuse the comparison. The justification for this benchmark man to continue to act as the signifier of 'normal' human needs would be tautological, and therefore invalid. This revelation also prevents us from falling into the second trap of claiming sameness, for we have seen that where marked groups seek neutrality *in an already biased context*, the rights obtained will not adequately assist in ending discrimination. Because the benchmark man is an inadequate reference point for the needs of humanity, marked persons need not demonstrate their similarities to him in order to have their claims heeded. Differences exist, and different people have different needs that should be met in different ways.

The same reasoning can apply in paradox three: there is no reason that heterosexual women's needs ought to stand in as the reference point of 'women's rights', nor is there a reason to presume gay male needs are the legitimate marker of 'LGBT rights'. We may take a leaf out of Crenshaw's book and argue that those who are disadvantaged by more than one axis of difference should be endowed with the ability to represent those who are disadvantaged by only one axis of difference.[73] If we were to allow multiply burdened group members to act as representatives for singularly disadvantaged group members, then marked persons 'might accept the possibility that there is more to gain by collectively challenging the hierarchy rather than by each discriminatee individually seeking to protect her source of privilege within the hierarchy'.[74] An intersectional approach to law reform is certainly warranted. However, the final problem of retaining a shared group identity remains, given the fact of unquantifiable human diversity. How might this be approached?

It is important to remember that what makes queers a collective is not the fact that they are discriminated against but the fact that they are same-sex attracted and gender diverse. We need not all face the same problem as individuals in order to remain unified as a group or to support our fellow group members in the face of discrimination. The fourth paradox, in other words, is actually a false dilemma. While concrete harms are different for same-sex attracted and gender-diverse individuals, nothing precludes these diverse individuals coming together to work towards nondiscrimination. What remains imperative is that multiply burdened group members are permitted to act as representatives for singularly disadvantaged group members. For example, collective efforts to restructure marriage may better benefit LGBTs overall if singularly disadvantaged LGBTs take into account the impact the fight for same-sex marriage will have (and has had) on single and nonnormative LGBTs and allow those voices to act as the dominant voices. Instead of seeking to redraw the boundaries of inclusion around those couples whose relationships more or less match the heteronormative paradigm, we might consider a broader scale reform that would recognize the diversity that exists among LGBTs (and nonnormative heterosexuals). It is imperative, then, that the human rights account I endorse has a reconception of difference at its core. For this project, I will turn to another bottom-up approach to human rights—discursive constructivism.

NOTES

1. Duncan Ivison, *Rights* (Stocksfield, UK: Acumen Publishing, 2008), 156.
2. Moira Gatens, *Feminism and Philosophy: Perspectives on Difference and Equality* (Cambridge: Polity Press, 1991), intro.; Luce Irigaray, *Democracy Begins between Two*, trans. K Anderson (New York: Routledge, 2000), chap. 9.
3. Margaret Thornton, *Dissonance and Distrust: Women in the Legal Profession* (Oxford: Oxford University Press, 1996), intro.
4. Kay Lalor, 'Constituting Sexuality: Rights, Politics and Power in the Gay Rights Movement', *International Journal of Human Rights* 15, no. 5 (2011): 685.
5. Wendy Brown, 'Suffering Rights as Paradoxes', *Constellations* 7.2 (2000): 208–29.
6. Simone de Beauvoir, *The Second Sex* (1949), trans. C. Borde and S. Malovany-Chevallier (London: Vintage Books, 2009), 5.
7. Diane Richardson, 'Locating Sexualities: From Here to Normality', *Sexualities* 7 (2004): 401–2.
8. Gatens, *Feminism and Philosophy*, 92.
9. Thornton, *Dissonance and Distrust*, 2. See also Gatens, *Feminism and Philosophy*, chap. 5; Nancy Jay, 'Gender and Dichotomy', *Feminist Studies* 7, no. 1 (1981): 38–56; Rebecca Hill, *The Interval* (New York: Fordham University Press, 2012), chap. 1; and Joan Scott, 'Deconstructing Equality-versus-Difference: Or, the Uses of Poststructuralist Theory for Feminism', *Feminist Studies* 14, no. 1 (1988): 32–50.
10. Susan Moller Okin, 'Sexual Orientation, Gender, and Families: Dichotomizing Differences', *Hypatia* 11, no. 1 (1996): 30.
11. Michael Warner, *The Trouble with Normal: Sex, Politics, and the Ethics of Queer Life* (Cambridge, MA: Harvard University Press, 1999), 25–26.
12. Moira Gatens, 'Can Human Rights Accommodate Women's Rights? Towards an Embodied Account of Social Norms, Social Meaning, and Cultural Change', *Contemporary Political Theory* 3, no. 3 (2004): 275–99.
13. Kathy Miriam, 'Toward a Phenomenology of Sex-Right: Reviving Radical Feminist Theory of Compulsory Heterosexuality', *Hypatia* 22, no. 1 (2007): 218.
14. Warner, *The Trouble with Normal*, 26.
15. Ibid.
16. See Georgia Warnke, *After Identity* (Cambridge: Cambridge University Press, 2007), chap. 3; Cheshire Calhoun, *Feminism, the Family, and the Politics of the Closet: Lesbian and Gay Displacement* (Oxford: Oxford University Press, 2000), chap. 6.
17. Ngaire Naffine, 'Can Women Be Legal Persons?' in *Visible Women: Essays on Feminist Legal Theory and Political Philosophy*, ed. Susan James and Stephanie Palmer (Oxford: Hart Publishing, 2002), 70.
18. Thornton, *Dissonance and Distrust*, intro.
19. See chapter 1, note 9.
20. Calhoun, *Feminism, the Family*, chap. 5.
21. Lalor, 'Constituting Sexuality'.

22. Beyond Marriage Allied Activists, 'Beyond Same-Sex Marriage: A New Strategic Vision for All Our Families and Relationships', accessed 3 November 2014, http://www.beyondmarriage.org/BeyondMarriage.pdf.

23. Lalor, 'Constituting Sexuality'.

24. Brown, 'Suffering Rights as Paradoxes'.

25. Ibid., 231; emphasis added.

26. Kate Sheill, 'Losing Out in the Intersections: Lesbians, Human Rights, Law and Activism', *Contemporary Politics* 15, no. 1 (2009): 57.

27. Family Research Council, 'Questions and Answers: What's Wrong with Letting Same-Sex Couples "Marry"?' accessed 2 November 2014, http://www.frc.org/whats-wrong-with-letting-same-sex-couples-marry.

28. Bill Muehlenberg, *Why vs Why: Gay Marriage. No* (New South Wales, Australia: Pantera Press, 2010), 33.

29. For example, Elizabeth Brake argues that political liberalism requires the disestablishment of monogamous, amatonormative marriage and that marriage should be opened up to allow recognition for multiple forms of caring relationships. Even here, these 'special rights' would extend to normative heterosexuals who would not alter their relationship structures even if they could. See Brake, *Minimizing Marriage: Marriage, Morality and the Law* (Oxford: Oxford University Press, 2012).

30. Even if this were a valid argument, it would be unsound insofar as it is untrue that marriages have always been heterosexual and monogamous. See Cheshire Calhoun, 'Who's Afraid of Polygamous Marriage? Lessons for Same-Sex Marriage Advocacy from the History of Polygamy', *San Diego Law Review* 42 (2005): 1023–42; John Boswell, *The Marriage of Likeness: Same-Sex Unions in Pre-modern Europe* (London: Fontana Press, 1995); and William N. Eskridge Jr., 'A History of Same-Sex Marriage', *Virginia Law Review* 79, no. 7 (1993): 1419–13.

31. Brown, 'Suffering Rights as Paradoxes', 231.

32. See Nancy Polikoff, *Beyond (Straight and Gay) Marriage: Valuing All Families under the Law* (Boston: Beacon Press, 2011); and Polikoff, 'We Will Get What We Ask For: Why Legalizing Gay and Lesbian Marriage Will Not "Dismantle the Legal Structure of Gender in Every Marriage"', *Virginia Law Review* 79, no. 7 (1993): 1535–50; Claudia Card, 'Against Marriage and Motherhood', *Hypatia* 11, no. 3 (1996): 1–23; and Beyond Marriage Allied Activists, 'Beyond Same-Sex Marriage'.

33. See Richardson, 'Locating Sexualities'; Warner, *The Trouble with Normal*, 108; Brake, *Minimizing Marriage*, chaps. 5–8.

34. Brown, 'Suffering Rights as Paradoxes', 232–33; original emphasis.

35. Ibid.; Adrienne Rich, 'Compulsory Heterosexuality and Lesbian Existence (1980)', *Journal of Women's History* 15, no. 3 (2003): 11–48; Nadine Gartner, 'Articulating Lesbian Human Rights: The Creation of a Convention on the Elimination of All Forms of Discrimination against Lesbians', *UCLA Women's Law Journal* 14 (2005): 61–87; and Sheill, 'Losing Out in the Intersections'.

36. Rebecca Jennings, 'Lesbian Mothers and Child Custody: Australian Debates in the 1970s', *Gender and History* 24, no. 2 (2012): 505.

37. Ibid., 503.

38. Jennings argues, 'Lesbian mothers adopted a range of stratagems in their attempt to construct themselves as respectable, discreet mothers in opposition to the courts' notion of the crusading radical lesbian. The importance of appearance in shaping judges' assumptions about lesbian mothers seems to have been clear to many women.' See ibid., 513.

39. Sandra Lundy, 'Abuse That Dare Not Speak Its Name: Assisting Victims of Lesbian and Gay Domestic Violence in Massachusetts', *New England Law Review* 28 (1993–1994): 274.

40. Angela West, 'Prosecutorial Activism: Confronting Heterosexism in a Lesbian Battering Case', *Harvard Women's Law Journal* 15 (1992): 256.

41. Ibid., 263.

42. Brown, 'Suffering Rights as Paradoxes'.

43. Rich, 'Compulsory Heterosexuality', 28.

44. Lisa Dettmer, 'Beyond Gay Marriage', *Race, Poverty & the Environment: Weaving the Threads* 17, no. 2 (2010), accessed 3 November 2014, http://reimaginerpe.org/node/5822. Original radio documentary available for download from http://www.reimaginerpe.org.

45. A number of blog posts reflect this criticism. See Kat Gupa, 'Why the Marriage (Same Sex) Act 2013 Does Not Bring Marriage Equality: The Case of Trans* People', *Inherently Human: Critical Perspectives on Law, Gender & Sexuality*, 31 July 2013, accessed 7 November 2014, http://inherentlyhuman.wordpress.com/2013/07/31/why-the-marriagesame-sex-act-2013-does-not-bring-marriage-equality-the-case-of-trans-people/; Zoe O'Connell, 'Where "Equal Marriage" Leaves Trans Folk," *Complicity*, 18 July 2013, accessed 7 November 2014, http://www.complicity.co.uk/blog/2013/07/where-equal-marriage-leaves-trans-folk/; Sarah Brown, 'Same Sex Marriage Bill—Transgender Implications', *Sarah Brown's Blog*, 25 January 2013, accessed7 November 2014, http://www.sarahlizzy.com/blog/?p=139.

46. Kimberlé Crenshaw, 'Demarginalizing the Intersection of Race and Sex: A Black Feminist Critique of Antidiscrimination Doctrine, Feminist Theory and Antiracist Politics', *University of Chicago Legal Forum* (1989), 139.

47. Ibid. See also Darren Rosenblum, 'Queer Intersectionality and the Failure of Recent Lesbian and Gay "Victories"', *Law & Sexuality* 4 (1994): 83–122.

48. Rosenblum, 'Queer Intersectionality', 83–122.

49. Calhoun, *Feminism, the Family*, 146.

50. See Calhoun, *Feminism, the Family*, chap. 6; Vito Russo, *The Celluloid Closet* (New York: Harper & Row, 1987), chap. 3.

51. Warnke, *After Identity*, 65.

52. Moira Gatens, 'Paradoxes of Liberal Politics: Contracts, Rights, and Consent', in *Illusion of Consent: Engaging with Carole Pateman*, ed. D. O'Neill, M. Shanley, and I. Young (University Park: Pennsylvania State University Press, 2008), 43.

53. See Richardson, 'Locating Sexualities', 396; Calhoun, *Feminism, the Family*, 132–60; Okin, 'Sexual Orientation, Gender, and Families', 37.

54. Drucilla Cornell, 'Gender, Sex, & Equivalent Rights', in *Feminists Theorize the Political*, ed. Judith Butler and Joan Wallach Scott (New York: Routledge, 1992), 283; emphasis added.

55. Naffine, 'Can Women Be Legal Persons?'

56. Warnke, *After Identity*, 162.

57. Annabelle Lever, 'The Politics of Paradox: A Response to Wendy Brown', *Constellations* 7, no. 2 (2000): 243.

58. Ibid.; see also Brown, 'Suffering Rights as Paradoxes'.

59. Crenshaw, 'Demarginalizing the Intersection', 144.

60. Ibid., 144.

61. Lalor, 'Constituting Sexuality'.

62. Brown, 'Suffering Rights as Paradoxes', 239.

63. Ibid., 238.

64. Ibid., 239.

65. Lever, 'The Politics of Paradox', 245.

66. Ibid.

67. Ibid., 245–46.

68. Gatens, 'Paradoxes of Liberal Politics', 43.

69. Lever, 'The Politics of Paradox'.

70. Ibid., 245.

71. Lalor, 'Constituting Sexuality'.

72. See Jay, 'Gender and Dichotomy'; and Gatens, *Feminism and Philosophy*, chap. 5.

73. Crenshaw, 'Demarginalizing the Intersection'.

74. Ibid., 145.

Chapter Four

Towards a Feminist Human Rights Framework

The Intersubjective Justification Theory

The starting point of this investigation has been the assertion that the justifications we use to secure legal changes affect the normative position of LGBTs. Thus, justifications which reduce attitudes and instances of discrimination towards LGBTs are worthy of endorsement above those which do not. In the previous chapters, I explored issues associated with assimilative justifications for same-sex marriage. Namely, because marriage is a normative union that shapes and regulates behaviour, people face pressure to conform to a certain model of intimacy. Not only does this prevent people from seeking out various forms of intimacy and care that may be more suitable for their own personal flourishing, but there is an additional effect: some LGBTs are recognized as 'good' queers, while others remain 'deviant'. This does not encourage respect for LGBT identities in and of themselves. Rather, LGBTs must prove they are *like* normative heterosexuals in order to be tolerated. Since the overall goal of LGBT rights should be the nondiscrimination of all of its members, better justifications must be circulated in a way that may bring about this outcome. The wider goal, then, is to provide a nonassimilative justification for same-sex marriage and to challenge the perception of LGBTs as immoral/unnatural.

By analyzing the problems with assimilative justifications for same-sex marriage and feminist criticisms of rights discourse it is possible to name some specific features that a successful justification must have. It should create an obligation on those with the capacity to secure the right, even if it is not in one's personal interest to do so. It should not presume that marriage is an intrinsically valuable institution or the only valuable structure of intersubjective care; rather, it should be concerned with the indignity stemming from exclusion. It should not solely rely on abstract principles but should take the history of LGBT discrimination into account. It also should be socially comparative, but this must be met with a critical component. Finally, it must have a revised understanding of difference at its core in order to encourage respect for (potentially) varying LGBT identities. As we learned in chapter 3, rights are currently delegated on a faulty system of recognition using a single-axis framework and but-for reasoning. Importantly, we can highlight comparative inequalities without endorsing or reinforcing the norm.

This chapter will argue that discursive constructivism is a useful tool for developing a feminist conception of human rights and justifying same-sex marriage. Constructivism holds that the principles we ought to endorse are those that agents would agree to if they were to engage in a process of rational deliberation. Perhaps the most famous constructivist account comes from John Rawls, who hypothesized about the rights people would be entitled to given a practical standpoint shared by citizens who accept liberal democratic values. This thought experiment famously takes place from behind a veil of ignorance, which excludes 'irrelevant information' in order to avoid bias.[1] However, much criticism has been aimed at this original position, claiming that not only is it impossible to completely free oneself of bias in the reasoning process but that the particular perspectives one can bring to the table based on one's partial identity and experiences may actually be of value to this deliberation.[2] Fortunately, not all constructivist accounts require this same level of abstraction.

One particularly compelling account is the intersubjective justification theory proposed by Rainer Forst. It contends that there is a basic right to justification which stands as the normative centre, or anchor, of every legitimate political community. That is to say, this basic moral right forms the core of all political rights. Specific rights are not *derived* from the basic right to justification; rather, they are *constructed* with recourse to the basic right to justification. Through a discursive process of providing justifications for the sociopolitical and legal contexts in which people find themselves, rights are developed 'by all moral persons in cooperation with one another'.[3] Forst places real emphasis on the fact that all human people have an intersubjective existence that requires communication and the establishment of agreements and shared meanings. Importantly, while all moral norms must be justified by the moral community, political norms need only be justified by the relevant political community. This means that it is possible for states to respect the basic right to justification while having structural differences. Thus, 'members do not strive to found a republic of rational beings; they fight for a more just society that is worthy of being recognized as *their own* society', however it may look.[4]

I will argue that this account provides a useful prototype from which to develop a feminist human rights framework. This is because it creates obligations; does not presume that marriage is intrinsically valuable; is concerned with the indignity stemming from exclusion, namely, in the form of being denied justifications; does not solely rely on abstract principles; and is socially comparative. However, this account is not wholly compelling. Although it is socially comparative, Forst's version does not offer a strong enough critical component. This is evidenced by his appeal to the relevant sameness of same-sex and different-sex couples. Fortunately, this assumption is not inherent to the theory. Furthermore, Forst refers to justified differences in legal recognition as 'special rights', recalling the first paradox discussed in chapter 3. This leads to a third difficulty, which is that the intersubjective justification theory does not explicitly involve a reconception of difference, which is necessary to promote equal regard for LGBTs. However, I will propose that the intersubjective justification theory is *compatible* with a reconception of difference and, if undertaken, this may resolve the problem of designating 'special rights' to others and enhance the necessary critical component.

Finally, it can be claimed that the intersubjective justification theory is too vague to adequately determine what one has a right to. It may be the case that reasonable rejectability is unavoidable. Forst's solution to this latter problem is to introduce provisions of tolerance in determining acceptable rights claims. Importantly, what is grossly irrational or an immoral prejudice *cannot* be grounds for objection. This is because once the irrationality and/or prejudice disappears, so too does the need for tolerance of the behaviour or lifestyle.[5] I will question whether LGBTs and same-sex marriage genuinely ought to be tolerated, which is to ask whether there really is a legitimate 'objection component' to LGBTs and their conduct. To say that there is an objection component to a lifestyle or behaviour is to say that, although it must be tolerated, the practice remains objectionable according to reasons which are sufficiently defensible. While the reasons for objection need not be universally shareable, they must nonetheless be intelligible to those people who do not share the same system of beliefs and practices. I will argue that same-sex marriage is not an appropriate candidate for tolerance.

I. RAINER FORST AND THE INTERSUBJECTIVE JUSTIFICATION THEORY

Like the personhood account, the intersubjective justification theory begins from the bottom up, assessing of the historical emergence of human rights. The polemical force behind the historical concept of a 'natural right' indicates that the basic concern which underscores political questions of freedom and justice is for people to become recognized as *beings who are owed reasons*. This concern remains at the core of rights claims today. People claim rights when they are subjected to oppressive and exploitative treatment. Rights claimants want legitimately acceptable reasons for why they ought to be subjected to particular forms of treatment, and if there are none, they want the situation to be remedied.[6]

The constructivist account, therefore, requires its participants to embody a basic level of moral autonomy, where moral autonomy is understood as having the capacity to give and receive justifying reasons. Through the exercise of this moral autonomy, that is, through participation in an intersubjective realm of ongoing justificatory dialogue and exchange, moral norms are established. The 'objectivity' of moral norms, then, does not lie in some form of objective moral realism but in the very action of being intersubjectively justified. These moral norms then act as the basis to build more specific rights that secure equal social status, personal liberties, and bodily security. It is these discursive procedures of justification that will establish the actual political norms and laws that people are to live by, though basic human rights may be realized in different ways depending on the context in which the claims arise.[7]

Thus, human rights claims ultimately emerge when individuals or groups are not treated as agents to whom reasons are owed and are simultaneously treated unequally. Recognition of moral autonomy is of vast importance; it allows people who have been repeatedly treated as irrelevant, inferior, or who have otherwise been ignored the opportunity to have their unjust situation rectified. From this, one fundamental human right can be taken to underscore all other rights claims. This is the basic right to justification. The basic right to justification is the primary right of all to give and receive justifications for the norms that they are to live by. A violation of dignity, then, consists of one's refusal to acknowledge another agent's moral autonomy. That is to say, when an agent refuses to acknowledge another's right to contribute to the shared norms of society that all are to live by, one fails to respect that person's dignity. In Forst's opinion, 'the insult of not even being seen as someone others owe reasons to is worst of all' because it is insulting to people's self-understanding and self-respect.[8] Thus, the main function of human rights is to guarantee each person's status as an equal given their basic right to justification, and the legal and political function of human rights is to make the basic right to justification socially effective.[9]

It has been said that norms will be taken as legitimate only insofar as they are suitably justified. The criteria that will determine a moral norm's legitimacy, and therefore establish a human right, are 'reciprocity' and 'generality'. For now it is sufficient to give a basic definition of these criteria so as to understand what may count as a moral norm, as well as act as a justifying ground for a basic human right. The criterion of generality holds that the reasons which can ground universal normative validity must be shareable by all people who have reciprocally legitimate interests or claims and that no one with such an interest should be arbitrarily excluded.[10] There are two aspects to the criterion of reciprocity. The first is that no one can make a claim that they would deny to others (reciprocity of content). The second aspect is that no one can impose upon another person his or her own 'perspective, evaluations, convictions, interests, or needs' (reciprocity of reasons).[11] In other words, one is not justified in imposing on another his or her beliefs, convictions, and so forth, since they are subjective and not universal.

It is also important to stress that claims for human rights have always occurred in situated contexts and have pertained to specific demands. As such, there are two levels of human rights claims: At one level, basic human rights are agreed upon in an abstract and general sense, according to their reciprocal and general justifiability; at the other level, these basic inhuman rights become specified and solidified according to the political and legal agreements established and endorsed by the citizens of a particular society. In other words, human rights cannot be realized unless they are locally guaranteed. So while an abstract list of human rights would be theoretically possible and generally valid, the guarantee of such rights may take different shapes in different communities. Thus, the goal of the second level of human rights is to more concretely secure people's status as agents with equal social standing. The action of the oppressed claiming sociopolitical recognition and legal rights, and demanding that their voices be heard and taken into account, permits an active role to the discriminated-against in ending their mistreatment; it offers them a chance at self-determination, a chance to cultivate their identities.[12]

From this we develop a more complete picture of human rights. They are 'those rights which cannot be rejected with reciprocally and generally valid reasons, and that requirement opens up the normative space for claims that secure a person's status as an agent with equal social standing. That implies rights against the violation of physical or psychological integrity as well as rights against social discrimination.'[13] The key purpose of human rights, then, is to ensure that no one is treated in such a way that this conduct could not be legitimately justified to him or her, given his or her social, political, and moral standing as equal to others. The security of a person's status as an agent with equal standing is encompassed in the recognition of a person's moral autonomy, as well as in actions and sociopolitical structures which reflect that status.

It is important to point out that what is at stake here is second-order appreciation.[14] First-order appreciation is characterized by personal positive regard of one's own identity. It essentially amounts to self-respect: 'When we respect ourselves we both think and feel our own worth as persons, and act with a sense of that worth. It also means that we believe we are worthy of consideration, of being treated decently at least, if not well, and of being taken seriously by others.'[15] Second-order appreciation, alternatively, is characterized by a general external positive regard for a person's identity. Recall the discussion on shame in chapter 3. It was argued that the feeling of shame is a prereflexive mode of knowing that consists in the self's recognition of how she or he is regarded by another. If one feels shame when they think of the self-as-seen-by-other, this indicates a general lack of second-order appreciation; however, the intersubjective justification theory can bring about second-order appreciation, and this is essential for equal regard.

II. JUSTIFYING SAME-SEX MARRIAGE: THE MORAL VERSUS THE ETHICAL

Forst takes pains to distinguish between the moral and the ethical, where the ethical pertains to personal prudential values, while the moral pertains to the regulation of behaviour between people. The key feature which ethical justifications of human rights share is their substantive focus on the notion of the good life for the individual, and their 'view of human rights as means to guaranteeing essential minimal conditions for such forms of human life'.[16] Ethical justifications focus on the importance of the human interests they are meant to protect. Thus, ethical accounts of rights are derived from the basic interests that all people supposedly have in realizing certain values. The problem with ethical theories is that conceptions of the good are reasonably contestable and therefore cannot stand as the grounds for universal norms. Only moral norms, in the Forstian sense, can count as universal norms.

Moral norms are discovered after the criteria of reciprocity and generality are applied, whereas ethical beliefs can be meaningful motivators in a person's life regardless of whether they pass these tests. Ethical values can answer questions about what is right or good *for me* or *for us* within a shared ethical community, and 'moral norms do not replace ethical values or political norms; rather, they enter into competition with them only where these ethical values or political norms become morally questionable, that is to say, where they deny persons basic recognition'.[17] People may be entitled to certain rights given their ethical commitments but only insofar as this would not impose upon others who do not share those beliefs. If a moral norm and an ethical belief conflict, then ethical convictions are not *necessarily* disqualified or devalued, rather they simply cannot stand as the rule universally. It is precisely because ethical beliefs are not universal that they cannot possibly count as a justification to deny a universal human rights claim.[18]

Given this distinction, the personhood account would be classified as an ethical theory of human rights.[19] Let us take a moment to reconsider the personhood account in light of Forst's distinction. It is worthwhile to note that there has been a terminological shift. In chapter 2, I argued that the thick assumptions James Griffin makes about personhood indicates that he is making a *moral* rather than *principled* argument for marriage. In that context, *moral* simply means a normative belief that a particular structure for sexuality, companionship, affection, personal economics, and childrearing is a central human good and a belief that people are entitled to rights on the ground that it is a good. Now, let us recall that the only way that same-sex relationship recognition can be justified on the personhood account is if 'lack of recognition' meets the material constraint. That is, same-sex relationship recognition must matter for whether a person can function as a normative agent *at all* if one is to be able to claim a right to it. Normative agency is the precondition for being able to choose and act upon one's own assessment of the good life (the core of personhood).

Griffin seems to believe that 'enjoying a particular form of social union and raising children within a marriage is a substantive human aim and generally characteristic of a "worthwhile life"'[20] and that LGBTs identify with, desire, and attempt to structure their lives in accordance with a marriage-like relationship. Both assumptions are contentious. The personhood account attempts to position the so-called basic interests of persons, which are subjective interests, as though they were fundamental and intersubjectively justifiable for all people. But to make the step from the subjective to the universal, mutual justifiability must be placed theoretically prior to personal conceptions of the good. That is, there must be a procedure of justification in place for this to be a valid move. Yet no such procedure is provided.[21]

Let us consider these points in more detail. First, the personhood account does not do justice to those people who do not (desire to) structure their intimacies/care networks according to the normative model of marriage. Nor does it account for those heterosexual couples and families who have deviated from the 'normal norms' demanded of traditional marriage.[22] This is a point that Forst pursues in *Contexts of Justice* against Michael Sandel. He states:

> [Sandel] attempts to justify tolerance toward homosexual partnership and sexual practices by referring to the values of marriage, which homosexual relationships share. . . . By presupposing that homosexual couples identify with and live according to the 'values' and 'virtues' of marriage as are current in society, he does not do justice to the self-understanding of those who do not see their form of life according to this model. And even homosexuals who advocate the legal recognition of a partnership as a marriage do not necessarily have to accept for themselves the traditional implications of this form of community.[23]

Similarly, Griffin positions a particular type of relational arrangement as being all but irreplaceable in people's perceptions of the good life. However, he does not adequately justify why this type of relationship should be seen as *so valuable* that the option to enter it must exist for all people, even if they do not choose it. The importance of marriage is largely contestable insofar as other relationships fulfil the roles of care and intimacy, so this is not a strong argument for the introduction of same-sex marriage.

Forst, we see, does not support equal access to marriage if the reason for doing so is because marriage is itself taken to be intrinsically valuable and thus worthy of protection. That is because the basic claim in the context of human rights regards one's active status as a justificatory equal—not the pursuit of, or ability to pursue, the good life. This leads to the second point, which holds that what is at stake in determining a conception of human rights is where to locate the normative anchor. Even if it were true that all LGBTs value the heteronorms of marriage and wish to emulate them, and even if it were incontestable that marriage is an intrinsic good, this point need not ever be raised in the justification of same-sex marriage. What matters in determining a human rights claim on the intersubjective justification theory is mutual justifiability all the way down. First and foremost, LGBTs are to be respected as agents deserving of and able to give justifying reasons. If LGBTs demand equal access to marriage, they need not reveal any information other than that which directly pertains to reciprocity and generality and the history of LGBT exclusion.[24]

Let us explore in more detail how the intersubjective justification theory justifies same-sex marriage, then. According to this theory, abstract general principles become concrete in particular contexts thanks to the specific claims raised by historically situated people. As such, reference to reciprocity and generality must come prior to any agreed upon substantive conditions. Recall that moral norms then act as the basis to build more specific rights which will secure equal social status, personal liberties, and bodily security. One should always recognize the history of privilege and exclusion that has arisen in particular concrete contexts and should not be neutral to this history when assessing justifications for norms. Now, when the claim for same-sex marriage is brought forward, the onus is primarily on those who would retain the status quo to provide legitimate reasons for this state of affairs. If the reasons against same-sex marriage fail to pass the tests of reciprocity and generality, then there is a right to participate in these unions.

It is crucially important to note that this argument does not presume that marriage is intrinsically valuable. To wit, this is a matter of social comparison. There would be no right to marriage in a society where marriage did not exist. Imagine a society where LGBTs were discriminated against, but no one, whether heterosexual or homosexual, participated in legally recognized relationships like marriage. In this scenario, it would be nonsensical for LGBTs to demand access to some kind of legally recognized union in order to reduce their inequality since such a request would not confront the sites of their discrimination. In this situation, the concrete realization of a human right would emerge in another form. Now this is not to say that normative marriage has *no* value whatsoever; simply, this is not the relevant point. The intersubjective justification theory returns the stress to equality, making it a good fit with commonly held beliefs about the function of human rights.

Importantly, Forst argues that objections to same-sex marriage cannot pass the criteria of reciprocity and generality. If one attempted to provide a justification against same-sex marriage, the reasons would 'refer to beliefs, either ethical (human nature, the will of God) or empirical (findings about proper conditions for raising children), which cannot stand scrutiny as the basis for generally binding legal regulations'.[25] Ethical beliefs, we know, are partial and cannot stand as universal norms. And although empirical reasons may count towards denying a particular claim in a particular context, there are no such reasons that would count against same-sex couples' right to marry. Thus, the intersubjective justification theory holds that 'a society where the institution of marriage is reserved for some couples and denied to others without reciprocally justifiable reasons violates the demands of reciprocity', which is unjust.[26] This claim pertaining to the social and legal standing of citizens cannot reasonably be denied. Thus, we see again that it is the social and legal standing of LGBTs that is of the utmost importance in the claim for same-sex marriage, not the 'intrinsic value' of marriage itself.

Not only this, but the *demand* for same-sex marriage meets the criteria of reciprocity and generality, too. Critics may attempt to claim that the call for same-sex marriage does not meet the criterion of reciprocity, but this objection will be unsuccessful. Recall that reciprocity of reasons demands that no one impose upon another his or her own perspective, evaluations, convictions, interests, or needs. Against reciprocity of reasons, critics may claim that same-sex couples are pushing particular interests, needs, and perspectives on others. However, it would have to be proved that the existence of same-sex marriage would prevent others from following their own conception of the good. There is no reason that different-sex couples would necessarily cease to structure their intimate partnerships on the normative marriage model *unless this accorded with their own desires*. The existence of same-sex marriage itself does not press upon others a particular form of intimacy. Creating a new marriage model does not interfere with different-sex couples' capacity to get married.[27]

Critics may also attempt to argue against reciprocity of content. Recall that reciprocity of content holds that no one can make a claim that they would deny to others. Critics may assert that same-sex marriage *does* involve the denial of rights to other comparable forms of life, for example, a long-term relationship of mutual care between siblings.[28] One may respond to this critique in several ways. The first would be to argue that these relationships of care are not relevantly similar to heterosexual marriage, unlike same-sex relationships. Demanding same-sex marriage, then, is to demand recognition that 'such partnerships can exhibit the same relevant quality of intimacy and loyalty as heterosexual relationships'.[29] However, given the issues that justifications based on sameness produce, this would not be an acceptable response given the goal of equal regard. Moreover, it is unclear that sibling relationships (and other networks of care) do not display the *relevant* quality of intimacy and loyalty. What work is the term *relevant* doing here? How is relevance determined? It is vague to assert that different-sex and same-sex relationships are relevantly similar while other caring relationships are not.

One may also respond by arguing that it is far from clear that LGBTs would want to gain access to marriage and simultaneously demand that other relationships of mutual care remain unrecognized. This is not to say that all caring relationships can be recognized as marriages, but this concession is likely to be a pragmatic consequence rather than a symbolic refusal. It may well turn out to be the case that the law does not have the capacity to recognize several distinct forms of unions under one institution. This is, of course, speculative, and to admit this is not the same as to argue that networks of care ought not to be entitled to legal recognition and protection as marriages. Same-sex couples need not demand that they be allowed to marry and simultaneously withhold this entitlement from various others.[30] Finally, one may respond by arguing that heterosexuals who reject same-sex marriage on these grounds are failing their own test of measure—it is *they* who are denying a particular claim to others while retaining this privilege for themselves. Postulating the superiority or special worth of a particular way of religious/ethical life *is* reasonably rejectable, but it is something which the LGBT activist is not guilty of.[31]

Problematically, Forst adopts the first line of response. He argues that the point of LGBT claims to equal treatment is to document that same-sex relationships are relevantly similar to different-sex relationships and that to deny this and maintain an unequal legal status is a form of discrimination.[32] We should note that this does not mean Forst is falling into the trap of presuming the intrinsic worth of marriage, but it does illustrate the cautious approach we should take towards social comparison. This right is historically situated. It is because marriage is and has been esteemed that LGBTs are bothering to fight for entry, and Forst thinks the point of this fight is to illustrate sameness. As we have seen, though, an appeal to sameness is not necessary in order to utilize the intersubjective justification theory. As such, I plan to utilize the intersubjective justification theory as a prototype for developing a feminist human rights framework that does not justify same-sex marriage via sameness. I am also willing to argue that familial mutual-care relationships or polyamorous relationships (for example) ought to be entitled to some equivalent legal protections as with relationships of a monogamous romantic nature.

To summarize the argument from the intersubjective justification theory, then: what matters in the case for same-sex marriage is that some citizens have demanded justifying reasons for why they are excluded from a certain institution. Because there is no reason to maintain LGBT inequality—with reference to the criteria of reciprocity and generality, and with reference to the history of inclusion and exclusion that has disadvantaged LGBTs—LGBTs are owed access to marriage as a matter of right. It does not matter if same-sex couples are like different-sex couples, it only matters that they do not press an ethical doctrine upon others or seek to deny privileges to others. On this account, marriage is owed because it is a concrete realization of the equality possessed by moral agents in a particular, historically situated climate and because there are no justifiable reasons to count against the request. Importantly, this argument does not rely on asserting the value of marriage, which lessens the likelihood of assimilative behaviour and expectations.

III. BENEFITS OF THE INTERSUBJECTIVE JUSTIFICATION THEORY

We have already seen that the intersubjective justification theory goes some way to fulfilling the requirements of a successful human rights justification of same-sex marriage. It is socially comparative and, moreover, does not presume that marriage is intrinsically valuable. It also does not rely solely upon abstract principles since each right must be made concrete according to agreed-upon substantive conditions relevant to one's historical and geographical location. There are three further advantages of the intersubjective justification theory. It produces weightier obligations; the onus of proof is doubled; and it 'fits' with common understandings of the purpose of human rights.

The intersubjective justification theory is concerned with the indignity stemming from exclusion, namely, in the form of being denied justifications. Because the intersubjective justification theory stresses equality, it speaks to the intuition that the primary wrong of marriage inequality is one's treatment as inferior. This addresses the concern of the injustice of heterosexual privilege. It is not just that same-sex relationships are illegitimately believed to be inferior to different-sex relationships (insofar as this is an ethical rather than moral belief and so cannot stand as a universal measure of justification); it is that those who have brought the claim for marriage equality are treated as if they do not count. This is a violation of their dignity. This strong insistence on equality is a better fit with typical conceptions about the purpose of human rights, and moreover, it is compatible with the goal of equal regard. To gain equal regard would be to gain recognition and acceptance as a sociopolitical, legal, and moral equal; *this* is the fundamental aim of the intersubjective justification theory. It is about status first and foremost.

But how are obligations determined in the intersubjective justification theory? The introduction of a human right ought not to depend on how one is ethically motivated. Human rights are not a means to an end (for example, to the pursuit of a good life); rather, they just are what people are owed qua members of the human community. That is to say, human rights are grounded in the *status* of human subjects, namely that they are equal members of the human community. If it can be demonstrated that there are no reciprocal or general reasons to justify some state of affairs, then *all* members of the community have an obligation to support some change. Though the primary political addressee is the state, it is the citizens who make up a state, and so there is joint responsibility. That is to say, it is the citizens who make up the state who have the obligation to interpret, institutionalize, guarantee, and realize human rights. Thus, even if some people personally object to same-sex marriage, they are nonetheless obliged to ensure that it exists.[33]

It may be asked how far these obligations go, and the answer is not wholly clear. In cases where one's own views and claims are rejected on legitimate grounds, one must accept this and abide by the 'democratic rules'. The democratic rules involve general normative commitments to equality and nondiscrimination.[34] Perhaps it is one's place in democratically effective institutions that determines their level of obligation. For example, someone who ethically objects to same-sex marriage but is a member of Parliament would surely be required to abide by these norms and push for a change in their party's policies. But it is unclear whether a teacher or a nurse, and so on, would be morally obliged to sign a petition in favour of same-sex marriage if they were ethically opposed to the change. A reasonable rule of thumb might be that the obligation extends only so far as one is involved with an institution which will have a role in bringing about the change (politicians, policy writers, marriage celebrants, and so on). Of course, these obligations, like the specifications of rights, are context dependent.

For the LGBT community and sympathizers, a heavily weighted moral obligation to ensure LGBT rights is desirable since it increases the likelihood of change. However, simply because a state is morally obliged to ensure human rights does not mean that it will. In these instances, it is legitimate to ask whether and/or how the state may be encouraged to guarantee and enforce these rights. One possibility is external compulsion, as we saw in *Karner v. Austria*. Recall that the European Court of Human Rights (ECHR) found in favour of Karner and ordered the Austrian government to grant same-sex cohabitants the same rights as unmarried, different-sex cohabitants. Certainly Forst does not exclude the possibility of something like a world-state.[35] However, such an extreme measure may not be necessary. Recall that the best way to promote change in already well-established democracies seems to be via soft law. Mere *recommendations* made by international bodies may be enough to incite change. For example, consider *Toonen v. Australia* once more. The ruling that Tasmania ought to decriminalize homo-sex was a nonbinding decision. Thus, the introduction of the Human Rights (Sexual Conduct) Act 1994 in response to this recommendation is telling of the power that the international community can have on individual states. We do have reason to be cautious about the homogenizing nature of soft law, though, as we saw in chapter 1. Importantly, reliance upon soft law to encourage changes in Western liberal democracies is only a legitimate move if we endorse a theory where 'the burden of proof, in such questions of sexual morality, lay on those who would want to impose their standard on someone else'.[36] This leads us to the final advantage of the intersubjective justification theory.

The intersubjective justification theory *does* place an onus of proof on those who would deny a human rights claim. Usually, in legal terms, only the person who brings a claim bears the onus of proof. It is therefore his or her obligation to provide enough evidence to substantiate his or her claim. The intersubjective justification theory applies this onus to both sides. That is to say, those who are calling for same-sex marriage must have a claim that is reciprocally and generally justifiable, while those who would deny the claim must also show that they have reciprocally and generally justifiable reasons for maintaining the status quo. If the onus of proof were to remain only on the supporters of same-sex marriage, then they would be more likely to rely on but-for reasoning.

As we know, typically, legal reform in favour of LGBT rights has been awarded to those '"but-for" queers, who, "but-for" their being lesbian or gay, would be "perfect citizens"',[37] where 'perfect citizens' relies on a false universal definition. However, these 'victories' have not significantly contributed to the prevention of social or juridical heterosexism. This is because those legal 'victories' were predicated on similarities between same-sex relationships and heteronormative relationships, with reference to features such as financial codependence, a 'traditional' marriage-like partnership structure (including monogamy and a nuclear family structure), and relatively imperceptible homosexuality in public. Problematically, decisions based on such factors have neglected to open a more diverse path towards liberation from discrimination for poor queers, queers of ethnic or religious minorities, sexually subversive queers, gender subversive queers, and so on.[38]

Shifting the onus of proof is important for the goal of equal regard, then. Since there are no reciprocally or generally justifiable reasons to maintain the status quo, those who would seek to preserve it must answer for this state of affairs. Same-sex marriage must be allowed, and because same-sex couples are able to state their case without relying on the similarities they share with different-sex couples, there is room for sexual variances to flourish. There may be a multitude of reasons why LGBTs desire access to marriage. Some LGBTs may truly endorse the values of traditional marriage and nuclear family structure; some may believe entry to marriage will allow them to reform the institution from the inside out; some may want access to marriage purely as a statement to prove they are deserving of formal equality; some may want access to marriage for pragmatic reasons; some may want access to marriage, even though they have no intention of getting married, simply because others do not want them to have this opportunity; and so on. What is encouraging about the intersubjective justification theory is that the reasons LGBTs want access are not necessarily relevant. Thus, it is appealing from a perspective which seeks LGBT acceptance regardless of one's ability to assimilate. It can avoid the need to present oneself in terms of 'sameness'. Removing the need to appeal to sameness, or rather, removing the need to prove that but-for their sexual orientation LGBTs would be just the same as heterosexuals, would better allow for a plurality of resistances to heterosexist domination.[39] The intersubjective justification theory may, therefore, be compatible with a plurality of resistances to heterosexist domination while simultaneously justifying same-sex marriage. This would align with the goals of activists who reject LGBT assimilation as a valid ground for receiving rights.

IV. DRAWBACKS OF THE INTERSUBJECTIVE JUSTIFICATION THEORY

Despite its several advantages, the Forstian intersubjective justification theory is not a perfect candidate for endorsement. Although it is socially comparative, Forst's version does not offer a strong enough critical component. As we saw above, Forst appeals to the 'relevant' similarities between same-sex and different-sex couples to show that the call for same-sex marriage passes the test of reciprocity. Fortunately, this assumption is not inherent to the theory, as the demand for same-sex marriage need not involve a simultaneous (albeit implicit) demand that other networks of care be denied legal recognition.

However, there are other drawbacks yet to be discussed. For one, Forst argues that depending on the particular context, it may be necessary to have special regulations guaranteeing equal rights dependent on one's identity. This reference to 'special' regulations recalls the first paradox of rights discussed in chapter 3. Specifically, Forst argues, 'The scars of a legal community, the history of exclusion of certain groups from political and social life, determine whether . . . to grant, at the price of violating formal equality, to members of these groups . . . preferential rights.'[40] He adds, 'By recognizing these rights claims, law recognizes persons as "special" and, at the same time, "equal".'[41] In this context, Forst is considering the legitimacy of 'quotas', as when, for example, places are reserved in universities for a certain number of women to be educated in a male-dominated field.

It is right to acknowledge that formal equality may not necessarily amount to equal social opportunities or eliminate discrimination. But we have seen that positioning such rights gains as 'special' or 'preferential' can lead to a further entrenchment of the perception that this group is subordinate and can increase hostility towards that group by positioning them as though they are taking more than their fair share of legal and social benefits.[42] Part of the difficulty, of course, is that the intersubjective justification theory does not involve any explicit reconception of difference. This is a further drawback, for reconceiving difference is necessary in order to promote equal regard. Fortunately, the intersubjective justification theory is compatible with such a reconception and, if undertaken, this can resolve the problem of articulating different rights as 'special rights'. This is a task to be undertaken in chapter 5.

Finally, it may be claimed that the criteria of reciprocity and generality are too vague to adequately determine what one has a right to. The problem is that one is unaware how he or she should progress from the highly formal idea of the basic right to justification to particular, determinate human rights.[43] It is true that the criteria of reciprocity and generality do not offer much in the way of definitive boundaries. Generality holds that the reasons offered as justifications must be shareable by all people who have reciprocally legitimate interests and that no one should be arbitrarily excluded. A difficulty with this criterion is determining who has a legitimate interest to what. Contexts can be shrunk to legal and political communities, but this does not account for intervention into human rights violations outside the borders of such communities. As we saw above with regard to obligations, it is unclear what responses are warranted for particular violations of human rights. Additional contextual justifications are presumably needed before one may intervene.

If one seeks a definitive list of human rights and an unchanging ground for their universal application, one will not see the appeal of the intersubjective justification theory. Of course, this weakness is simultaneously its strength. As Moira Gatens argues, 'If a universal right . . . is to be effective, it will need to be transformed, reinterpreted, and adapted, to each context.'[44] On this theory the possibility of what could count as a right remains perpetually open. The particular content of a human right is never fully fixed; it is determined by the generally affected members of a community. Moreover, rights and norms should be understood as 'engaged in an ongoing mutual exchange that constitutes the meaning of both as permanently open to negotiation and reconfiguration' rather than engaged in a clash where one or the other must give way.[45] It seems that the intersubjective justification theory is malleable enough to incorporate a reconception of difference legally and normatively, thereby producing equal regard.

However, there are other difficulties that emerge given the application of reciprocity and generality as normative criteria. As discussed above, the normative legitimacy of the intersubjective justification theory emerges only thanks to the objectivity of universalizable norms yielded by the criteria of reciprocity and generality. Yet if all agents must participate in the practice of discursive constructivism, it is reasonably contestable that said agents will reciprocally come to mutual agreements. *Reasonable* rejectability may not be avoidable. The question is this: 'If the reasons for objection as well as those for acceptance are identified as moral . . . how can [it] be morally right or even obligatory to tolerate what is morally wrong or bad?'[46] It may be tempting to claim that the criteria of reciprocity and generality are not enough to adequately determine what to do in such contexts.

However, Forst contends that the validity of the two criteria should not be called into question; instead, provisions of tolerance must be introduced. He argues, 'In cases in which the criteria of justification are not clearly violated, being tolerant means living with such differences and seeking the best possible solution, where the latter is subject to further revision.'[47] 'Tolerance' is said to be a 'normatively dependent concept' which is legitimated by the requirements of reciprocity and generality.[48] In other words, tolerance is owed since it protects reciprocity and generality, and reciprocity and generality are justified because they protect people's basic human status as equals who are entitled to reasons. Tolerance, then, can act as a nonrejectable guiding principle when reasonable rejectability cannot be avoided. Forst argues, 'This reciprocal toleration is required precisely because human beings are not machines for applying morality.'[49] However, this then raises the question of what human behaviours or beliefs must be tolerated, why, and how.

V. TOLERANCE

There are four types of tolerance that exist simultaneously in present-day societies. They are (a) the permission conception, (b) the coexistence conception, (c) the respect conception, and finally, (d) the esteem conception. The coexistence conception, which is characterized by two equally balanced differing groups living side by side and promising each other mutual tolerance, is not relevant for the topic of same-sex marriage. I will discuss each of the remaining conceptions in turn. First, the permission conception: this is characterized by a majority population deciding to tolerate a minority group within their society, although the majority retains the power to revoke this tolerance. In other words, the majority allows qualified permission for a minority group to live according to their beliefs, ideals, and so forth. The qualification is that this expression of difference remains a private matter. Furthermore, when this tolerance is granted it is *not* the case that the minority is able to claim an equal social and political status to the majority.[50] This is a unilateral form of tolerance; the majority endures a conviction or practice which is 'regarded as neither worthy nor deserving of equal treatment'.[51]

Next, the respect conception: this is characterized by a community who respect individuals as *morally* autonomous and as having equal rights prima facie. Specific *ethical* beliefs are viewed as private matters. This lines up with the aims of the intersubjective justification theory. Tolerance is owed given that all citizens should be entitled to live by norms that all can reasonably accept and which do not favour one particular ethical party. One can judge another's beliefs and practices as ethically wrong in one's own opinion but not in a broader sense as generally wrong since that interferes with the shared norms the society generally agrees to live by. The respect conception of tolerance stands since it is accepted that there is a kind of qualitative equality of equal respect and rights owed to people with different ethical-cultural identities. If a society endorses the basic right to justification and holds to the respect conception of tolerance, then the promotion of a particular ethical perspective over individual moral autonomy will be unjustifiable.[52]

Finally, the esteem conception: tolerance is characterized by a positive esteem of the Other, rather than a simple acknowledgement of his or her equal moral autonomy. This is a more demanding form of mutual recognition; the Other's moral autonomy is respected, and their ethical practices and convictions are esteemed. However, the convictions and practices of the Other are not perceived to be equivalent to one's own practices and convictions. While these alternative practices and convictions are estimable, they are not as estimable as one's own. That is to say, although another's ethical belief system has value, it is not deemed to be equally as good as, or better than, one's own belief system.

Additionally, an objection component and an acceptance component are common to each form of tolerance. It is essential that the tolerated beliefs or practices are considered to be objectionable and in an important sense wrong or bad by those doing the tolerating. Forst argues, 'If this *objection component* were missing, we would not speak of "toleration" but of "indifference" or "affirmation".'[53] The objection component is then balanced by the acceptance component. The acceptance component does not remove the negative judgements but gives certain positive reasons which trump the negative reasons in the relevant context. In other words, the objection retains its force, but the positive reasons nonetheless demand tolerance.

There is more to be said about what constitutes a legitimate objection component. Determining what legitimately counts as objectionable is tricky. Forst argues, 'It would be an exaggeration to demand that the reasons for objection should be "objective" or "capable of being generally shared", nevertheless certain criteria for a "rational" critique are indispensable.'[54] Although reasons for objection will be drawn from particular ethical belief systems, these reasons must nonetheless be intelligible to people who do not share that belief system. That is, the practice or conviction can only be deemed objectionable according to *reasons which are sufficiently defensible*. What must be excluded are grossly irrational and immoral prejudices. This is important; if prejudices are removed, the need for tolerance will also be removed, resulting in indifference or affirmation, as mentioned above. The same does not follow for legitimate objection components. It must remain sufficiently defensible 'why the convictions and practices of others are condemned'.[55] This means that I must be able to rationally accept your reasons for objection, even if I do not believe or endorse them personally.

A note should be made on the esteem conception of tolerance. One may claim that, unlike the others, the esteem conception of tolerance appears dangerously close to losing its objection component because on this account one actually esteems the other's ethical beliefs, practices, and so on. However, Forst insists that the objection component does remain. Esteem involves the comparison of our own worth with that of others. Insofar as one believes their own convictions and practices to be *better* than those of the other, the objection lies in the belief that the other's convictions and practices are not as ideal as they could be.[56]

Consider Forst's argument for the toleration of same-sex marriage, then: when the German government granted civil unions to same-sex couples, the change was met with opposition which claimed that the legal recognition of LGBT relationships goes beyond what the requirements of tolerance demand. According to this opposition, from the perspective of the permission conception, the limits of tolerance had been reached when the elements of traditional marriage were put into question. However, such a reaction to the introduction of civil unions and the possibility of same-sex marriage is unjustified. Forst claims:

> A 'mere toleration' of same-sex partnerships in accordance with the permission conception without equalization of legal status draws the limits of toleration too narrowly, for it enshrines an ethical objection in law that is not reciprocally and generally sustainable. . . . This toleration not only enshrines ethical values in law; *it also condemns the corresponding minorities to a condition of sociocultural, stigmatizing 'deviance'*.[57]

Equal respect and rights can call for a new or more comprehensive interpretation of existing social institutions, and marriage is an example of one such institution. While the argument for same-sex marriage is based on reciprocity, counterarguments rely on, for example, religious views, which *violate* the demand of reciprocity. Justice in this instance demands equal legal recognition, not simply permissive tolerance of that identity's existence.[58]

We may ask Forst, why not take one step further and endorse the esteem conception of tolerance? The answer is that the limits of tolerance need only be drawn in accordance with the principles of justice, and the respect conception of tolerance already meets these conditions. Indeed, Forst argues: 'To tolerate them out of respect is *not* to appreciate them or to have some kind of esteem for them. All that is required is the understanding that such a kind of ethical critique is not sufficient to draw the limits of toleration.'[59] 'Respect' in this context means recognizing the other person as being entitled to equal rights simply as an active member of the sociopolitical community and qua human; it does not mean respecting their personal identities or practices as such. The question which arises at this point, then, is whether tolerance is an appropriate response to same-sex marriage at all if the goal is to remove the stigmatization of LGBTs as deviant and render them equivalent to heterosexuals. Forst criticized the permission conception of tolerance because it condemns minorities to a condition of sociocultural, stigmatizing 'deviance', but is such criticism not true of each conception of tolerance?

i. The Paradox of the Tolerant Racist

It is questionable whether good reasons exist for people to oppose same-sex marriage. I reject the legitimacy of the objection component, and propose that opposition to LGBT identities and practices is either implicitly or explicitly prejudiced. Insofar as this is the case, tolerance is not an appropriate response to same-sex marriage and LGBTs. Rather, there is a duty to repudiate such prejudice when one encounters it. To illuminate this point I will make a comparison to Forst's own position on the paradox of the tolerant racist.

According to the paradox of the tolerant racist, 'someone with extreme racist antipathies would be described as tolerant (in the sense of a virtue) providing that he showed restraint in his actions (without changing his way of thinking)'.[60] However, to be tolerant in this scenario is not a virtue because objections to that person and his or her actions are based on prejudicial assumptions about his or her race. This outcome is unacceptable. The racist *should* change his or her way of thinking, and there is a duty upon others to promote this shift. Indeed, Forst argues, 'To call on a racist to be tolerant, therefore, is a mistake; what is required is instead that one should repudiate this prejudice and attempt to convince him [or her] of its groundlessness. Otherwise the demand for toleration would be in danger of exerting repressive effects by perpetuating social discrimination and baseless condemnations.'[61]

In this paradox, the tolerant racist is not directly committing any hate crime. He is described as tolerant because he shows restraint in his actions. Nonetheless, Forst supposes that this racist attitude will perpetuate social discrimination. The attitude itself condemns the corresponding minorities to a condition of sociocultural, stigmatizing 'deviance'. Thus, demanding tolerance can itself be oppressive by allowing people to maintain their prejudicial sets of beliefs. The question is: Why does Forst think someone with extreme racist antipathies should have to change his or her way of thinking but someone with extreme antipathies to same-sex marriage should not? These antipathies, too, are based on prejudicial assumptions: assumptions about sexual orientation and gender norms. So, if the demand for tolerance would be in danger of exerting repressive effects in the case of race, would this not also be true for LGBTs? Why is the former a case of prejudice and not the latter?

In fact, *both* are instances of prejudice. To state the issue bluntly: LGBTs have historically (in the West) been discriminated against due to the sex acts they engage in and for the subversion of traditional sex/gender norms supposedly resulting from this behaviour. However, the stigma attached to LGBT identities and the shame attached to their sex acts can only be justified by a comparison to 'normal' heterosexual identities and sex acts, which is problematic since these standards can only be considered normal by reference to a past history in which they have been construed as normal. Similarly, racial discrimination stems from the presumption of whiteness as the neutral marker of humanity, defined according to a binary schema based upon phallocentric logic. In critically reflecting on the biased model of the Subject—who has come to represent humanity within the dominant shared Western social imaginary—one can conclude that LGBTs, like those who are nonwhite, have been condemned and discriminated against for unjustifiable reasons. From this, it seems tolerance is not the appropriate response to same-sex marriage, and one should repudiate this prejudice and try to convince the bigot of why his or her beliefs are groundless.

It is useful to recall again what is at stake in the same-sex marriage debate: second-order appreciation leading to equal regard. There remains a significant lack of second-order appreciation for LGBTs in the West and, furthermore, of what second-order appreciation there is, it is usually predicated upon LGBTs' ability to present themselves as 'normal citizens'. As we have seen, 'citizenship is constituted through heterosexual norms and practices',[62] and thus, for LGBTs to be seen as normal they have had to present themselves as *like-(normative-)heterosexuals*. Importantly, while heterosexuals and homosexuals mix traits of 'acceptable' and 'unacceptable' sexual behaviour, deviance has been projected onto LGBTs in a way that is not projected onto heterosexuals. Because it is possible to suffer the stigma of an LGBT identity quite apart from the engagement in any homo-sex acts, it may seem appealing or politically expedient to demonstrate how otherwise alike

LGBTs are to normative heterosexuals in order for them to be seen as legitimate. But while LGBTs can often list many aspects of their identities which are comparative to normative heterosexuality, we have seen that such a strategy does not actively challenge the shaming of homo-sex or gender deviance. It is, therefore, crucial that we challenge both these characterizations—of homosexuality as deviant *and* of homo-sex as shameful. If discrimination against LGBTs is based on the sex that they have and the sex/gender norms they might disrupt along the way, then the only way to effectively deal with LGBT discrimination for all will be to recognize, accept, and value LGBT identities for what they involve.

Insofar as LGBTs continue to engage in homo-sex, they will always remain deviant to some extent, unless the hierarchy of sexual shame is dismantled. This can only be achieved by challenging the phallocentric system of order which sees marked persons compared to the 'normal' human subject and heteronormative standards of social organization. Thus, if LGBTs are to have equal regard, then the encounter with difference *must* be reconceived and engaged in anew. But how to reencounter (the potential for) difference(s) between marked persons without hierarchy? The philosophy of Luce Irigaray is useful to introduce at this point, since it seeks to dismantle phallocentrism—displacing it by reimagining difference through the lens of two. This in turn solidifies the interpretation that opposition to LGBTs and their practices ought to be understood as prejudiced. Thus, in the next chapter, I will propose that the intersubjective justification theory is compatible with an Irigarayan reconception of difference, allowing one to take a more critical perspective to socially comparative issues. This reconception of difference can also resolve the problem of designating 'special rights' to others. Finally, this reconception of difference will illustrate that LGBTs are rightly owed respect (or in the very least indifference). This reconception of difference centres on 'being two'.

NOTES

1. John Rawls, *A Theory of Justice* (Cambridge, MA: Belknap Press of Harvard University Press, 1971), chaps. 1 and 3.
2. For example, see Susan Moller Okin, *Justice, Gender, and the Family* (New York: Basic Books, 1989), chap. 5.
3. Rainer Forst, 'The Basic Right to Justification: Toward a Constructivist Conception of Human Rights', *Constellations* 6, no. 1 (1999): 45.
4. Ibid., 41. See also Rainer Forst, *Contexts of Justice*, trans. J. Farrell (Berkeley: University of California Press, 2002), chap. 5, and Forst, 'The Justification of Human Rights and the Basic Right to Justification: A Reflexive Approach', *Ethics* 120, no. 4 (2010): 711–40.
5. Rainer Forst, *Toleration in Conflict: Past and Present*, trans. Ciaran Cronin (Cambridge: Cambridge University Press, 2013), chap. 1.
6. Rainer Forst, 'First Things First: Redistribution, Recognition and Justification', *European Journal of Political Theory* 6, no. 3 (2007): 291–304, and Forst, 'The Justification of Human Rights'.

7. Forst, 'The Justification of Human Rights'.
8. Forst, 'First Things First', 302.
9. Ibid. See also Forst, 'The Justification of Human Rights'.
10. Forst, 'The Justification of Human Rights'.
11. Rainer Forst, 'The Ground of Critique: On the Concept of Human Dignity in Social Orders of Justification', *Philosophy & Social Criticism* 37, no. 9 (2011): 969.
12. See Forst, 'Basic Right to Justification'; Forst, 'The Justification of Human Rights'.
13. Forst, 'The Justification of Human Rights', 735.
14. Forst, *Contexts of Justice*, chap. 5. Note that Forst uses the language of 'second-order esteem'. I will argue below that the term *esteem* implies that another's practices and convictions are as worthy of respect as one's own. As such, the term *appreciation* seems to be a better fit with the meaning I interpret Forst to be expressing.
15. Marguerite La Caze, 'Seeing Oneself through the Eyes of the Other: Asymmetrical Reciprocity and Self-Respect', *Hypatia* 23, no. 3 (2008): 121–22.
16. Forst, 'The Justification of Human Rights', 713.
17. Forst, *Contexts of Justice*, 237–38.
18. Ibid., chaps. 2, 4, and 5; Heinz Paetzold, 'Respect and Toleration Reconsidered (Under Consideration: Rainer Forst's *Toleranz im Konflikt: Geschichte, Gehalt, und Gegenwart eines umstrittenen Begriffs*)', *Philosophy & Social Criticism* 34, no. 8 (2008): 941–54.
19. Forst, 'The Justification of Human Rights'.
20. Ibid., 725.
21. Ibid.
22. Forst, *Toleration in Conflict*, chap. 12.
23. Forst, *Contexts of Justice*, chap. 2.
24. Forst, 'The Justification of Human Rights'.
25. Ibid., 726.
26. Ibid., 725.
27. Forst, *Toleration in Conflict*, chap. 12.
28. Ibid.
29. Ibid., 566.
30. Ibid.
31. Ibid.
32. Ibid.
33. Forst, 'Basic Right to Justification'.
34. Forst, *Toleration in Conflict*, chap. 9.
35. Forst, 'Basic Right to Justification'.
36. Michael Warner, *The Trouble with Normal: Sex, Politics, and the Ethics of Queer Life* (Cambridge, MA: Harvard University Press, 1999), 5.
37. Darren Rosenblum, 'Queer Intersectionality and the Failure of Recent Lesbian and Gay "Victories"', *Law & Sexuality* 4 (1994): 85–86.
38. Ibid.
39. Ibid.
40. Forst, *Contexts of Justice*, chap. 2.
41. Ibid.
42. Notably, the intersubjective justification theory does not appear to be susceptible to the other paradoxes of rights. It does not advocate for formal equality alone and acknowledges the existence of a historically biased playing field. It need not be taken to advocate the interests of *some* LGBTs at the expense of others. Bringing a rights claim is not automatically to reject or ignore alternative claims brought by members of the same group. Finally, there does not appear to be a risk of losing group identity. Same-sex marriage does not need to be shown to be a relevant concern for every LGBT; rather, it only needs to be shown that there are no reciprocal or general reasons against the introduction of same-sex marriage.
43. See James Griffin, 'Human Rights: Questions of Aim and Approach', *Ethics* 120, no. 4 (2010): 741–60.

44. Moira Gatens, 'Can Human Rights Accommodate Women's Rights? Towards an Embodied Account of Social Norms, Social Meaning, and Cultural Change', *Contemporary Political Theory* 3, no. 3 (2004): 288.

45. Ibid.

46. Forst, *Toleration in Conflict*, 21.

47. Ibid., 465.

48. Forst claims that tolerance itself is not a value, but rather it is an attitude called for by other values or principles. See Rainer Forst, "The Limits of Toleration," *Constellations* 11, no. 3 (2004): 312–25.

49. Forst, *Toleration in Conflict*, 465.

50. Ibid., chap. 1; Forst, 'The Limits of Toleration'; Paetzold, 'Respect and Toleration Reconsidered'. Paetzold translates the 'esteem' conception from the original German text as 'appreciation' in English.

51. Forst, *Toleration in Conflict*, 28.

52. Ibid., chap. 1; Forst, 'The Limits of Toleration'.

53. Forst, 'The Limits of Toleration', 314–15.

54. Forst, *Toleration in Conflict*, 19.

55. Ibid., 20.

56. Ibid., chap. 1; Forst, 'The Limits of Toleration'.

57. Forst, *Toleration in Conflict*, 568; emphasis added.

58. Ibid., chap. 12; Forst, 'The Limits of Toleration'.

59. Forst, 'The Limits of Toleration', 319. See also Forst, *Toleration and Conflict*, chap. 12.

60. Forst, *Toleration in Conflict*, 19.

61. Ibid., 19–20.

62. Diane Richardson, 'Locating Sexualities: From Here to Normality', *Sexualities* 7 (2004): 391.

Chapter Five

Advancing the Intersubjective Justification Theory

The Politics of Sexuate Difference

In chapter 4, I argued that an intersubjective justification theory is a useful prototype for developing a feminist human rights framework that justifies same-sex marriage and strives for equal regard. Recall that such a feminist human rights framework aims for the following: It should create an obligation on those with the capacity to secure the right, even if it is not in one's personal interest to do so. It should not presume that marriage is an intrinsically valuable institution or the only valuable structure of intersubjective care; it should rather be concerned with the indignity stemming from exclusion. It should not rely solely upon abstract principles but should take the history of LGBT discrimination into account. It should also be socially comparative, but this must be met with a critical component. And finally, it must have a revised understanding of difference at its core.

The intersubjective justification theory, as elaborated by Rainer Forst, achieves some of these goals. Specifically, it creates obligations; does not presume that marriage is intrinsically valuable; is concerned with the indignity stemming from exclusion, namely, in the form of being denied justifications; does not rely solely on abstract principles; and is socially comparative. It also provides another compelling element which warrants endorsement: it places the onus of proof on those who would maintain the status quo, not only on those who have raised the claim. However, this account is not wholly compelling. Although it is socially comparative, Forst's version does not offer a strong enough critical component. This is evidenced by his appeal to the relevant sameness of same-sex and different-sex couples. Secondly, it refers to justified differences in legal recognition as 'special rights', which encourages attitudes of resentment or perceptions of inferiority and reveals a third difficulty: the intersubjective justification theory does not explicitly involve a reconception of difference. Moreover, Forst characterizes tolerance as the appropriate response to same-sex marriage, yet this seems likely to condemn minorities to a condition of sociocultural, stigmatizing deviance. LGBTs have historically been discriminated against based on the sex acts that they engage in and their subversion of traditional sex/gender norms, which supposedly results from this behaviour. Thus, it seems overwhelmingly likely that opposition to same-sex marriage is based on its potential disruption of marriage as a primary site for the reproduction of normative sex/gender roles and heterosexuality.

In this chapter, I will supplement the intersubjective justification theory with insights from sexual difference feminism. Specifically, I will focus on the politics of sexuate difference as elaborated by Luce Irigaray.[1] There are three central reasons for this inclusion. First, the politics of sexuate difference can provide the lens through which to reassess the 'paradoxes of rights' discussed in chapter 3. This is because Irigaray is striving to imagine difference through an A/B figuration, rather than A/not-A binary logic, by maintaining a position of openness to difference. From this we can encourage a shift from recognizing the Other as 'different-from' to recognizing Others as 'diverse-between'. Insofar as this shift occurs, same-sex couples may perform a coexistence in difference.

Second, it provides the necessary foundation for understanding the work of Irigaray's contemporaries. For example, Drucilla Cornell explores how an Irigarayan recognition of difference may be written into the law as 'equivalent rights'. Exploring the capacity to write difference into the law is important for determining the practicality of my justification of same-sex marriage. The capacity to write 'equivalent rights' into the law also moves away from the legal stipulation of 'special rights', which is important because articulating special rights for others encourages attitudes of resentment or perceptions of inferiority.

Third, the politics of sexuate difference is a useful supplement to the intersubjective justification theory because it demonstrates that 'tolerance' is an inappropriate response to LGBTs and same-sex marriage. Because the politics of sexuate difference begins with a reconfiguration of difference through an A/B schema, opposition to same-sex marriage is illuminated as being based on insupportable prejudices. By the light of Forst's own argument, what is an irrational prejudice cannot be grounds for tolerance. In other words, this reconception of difference provides the groundwork for a stronger critical component. This is important because this issue goes beyond a claim about what is politically just to one of what is morally right. If difference *itself* is radically reformulated in the dominant shared Western social imaginary, then LGBTs are likely to be regarded with dignity, which is the goal of all LGBT human rights claims. Thus, the project of re-cognizing and reimagining difference is necessary, not optional, and it begins with the practice of *respect for the Other.*[2] Of course, pragmatically it makes sense to maintain a requirement of tolerant practice by those people who refuse to change their ethical point of view that opposes same-sex marriage and/or homosexuality. Yet, this pragmatic consideration does not concede that such opposition is legitimate. What LGBTs are rightly owed is respect.

A final note must be made about the language I employ in this chapter. Recall that one of Forst's conceptions of tolerance is the 'respect conception'. I propose that we reject the naming of this conception. If an appropriate response to a person or their practices is 'tolerance', this means that something is genuinely objectionable about them or their practices (from the legitimacy of the objection component). If one holds this perspective, it seems intuitively wrong to call such an attitude respect. Although Forst seemingly intends the word *respect* to refer to 'respect for one's moral autonomy'—that is, as treating the Other as a morally autonomous end in him- or herself—the terminology nonetheless remains inappropriate. What it is to be respected or respectable is to be seen as good, correct, or acceptable, as well as to be treated as an end in oneself. Simply put, there is nothing about oneself or one's practices to be ashamed of. It is to acknowledge one's worth as a person, to believe them to be worthy of consideration and of being treated decently. It is to have both first-order and second-order appreciation. Such an understanding of respect goes beyond the minimal recognition of moral autonomy and encompasses what Forst calls *affirmation.* If I affirm something, then I state firmly or publicly that something is true or that I support it strongly. Surely it is this more robust understanding of 'respect' that LGBTs demand and to which they are entitled.

I. LUCE IRIGARAY AND THE POLITICS OF SEXUATE DIFFERENCE

A key concern of Irigaray's has been to promote sexuate difference as the cornerstone for social justice and ethical relations between people. Like other sexual difference feminists, she argues that patriarchal societies are organized on a *phallocentric symbolic system of the singular subject.* Recall that phallocentrism is a singular, unified conceptual order that is always marked by the heteromasculine. The typical subject of philosophical, political, legal, and psychoanalytical discourses thus remains a highly specified subject: male, singular, white, Western, capitalist, heterosexual, Eurocentric, and so forth, as discussed in chapter 3. Irigaray argues:

> Others were nothing but copies of the idea of man, a potentially perfect idea which all the more or less imperfect copies had to try to equal. These copies, moreover, were not defined in their own terms, in other words, according to a different subjectivity, but in those of an ideal subjectivity and as a function of their deficiencies with respect to it: age, race, culture, sex, etc. The model of the subject thus remained singular, and the '[O]thers' represented more or less good examples within the hierarchy established in relation to the singular subject.[3]

In other words, the phallocentric symbolic system of the singular subject utilizes the logic of A/not-A binary relations, and since the fundamental model of the human subject has remained unchanged (even as it has increased in importance to recognize diversity), marked persons have only been able to gain piecemeal recognition. This is insofar as they more or less match up to certain unspoken principles of social organization and personal identity.[4]

Now, there is a connection between Others' statuses in Western thought and their statuses in Western society given that the two domains share the same dominant Western imaginary. Importantly, this blurs the difference between the metaphorical and social reality.[5] In other words, an Other's divergence from the standards of the subject reflexively affects how he or she is *treated*, as well as how he or she is imagined and perceived. The category 'woman', for example, is conceptualized and defined with reference to and against 'man' in both the symbolic and social realms. Woman's status in each realm mutually feeds her status in the other. Thus, 'woman' (and so women) becomes *like-man*, and/or *not-man*. This means that women have been refused the possibility of recognition *as women* in their own right. Similarly, because the subject is conceptualized not only as male but also as heterosexual, LGBTs find it difficult to rectify the discrimination they face. This is because they continue to be defined (and increasingly define themselves) against this standard model of normalcy, rather than in their own right. They can only be *like-(normative-)heterosexuals* and/or *not-(normative-)heterosexuals*.

One of Irigaray's key goals, then, has been to expose and emphasize a difference that hegemonic cultural forces have been most invested in excluding: sexuate difference. A further goal is to modify signifying spaces and symbolic structures via critical analysis with the intention of remedying women's conceptual and actual disadvantaged positions. We can push these goals further to explore how the recognition of sexuate difference can produce a re-cognition of difference as such and explore the ways that this can contribute to LGBT nondiscrimination.[6]

i. Reconceiving Difference

As noted above, Irigaray is striving for the construction of a feminine identity that can see women as subjects in their own right rather than in terms of their sameness or lack to the ideal subject. As such, Irigaray rejects the strategy of 'equality feminism'. She argues: 'To demand equality as women is, it seems to me, a mistaken expression of a real objective. The demand to be equal presupposes a point of comparison. To whom or what do women want to be equalized? To men? To a salary? To a public office? To what standard? Why not to themselves?'[7] Equality feminism has been unable to resist being reabsorbed into the existing male-dominated order.[8] Similar reasons have been given for LGBTs to avoid 'equality' arguments, as they also presuppose a standard of comparison that is only able to reabsorb them into institutionalized heterosexuality, as we saw in chapter 3.

The way that Irigaray imagines women might attain their own identity is through a shift away from phallocentrism in the symbolic as well as politico-legal realms. Importantly, while Irigaray rejects a version of equality based on sameness to the subject, she does not reject the possibility of *equality in difference*. This type of equality is based on the recognition of and respect for (the potential for) difference(s) existing between people, starting with what Irigaray calls the most basic human reality: sexuate difference. Irigaray claims, 'Being *we* means being at least *two*, autonomous, different.'[9] In other words, Irigaray's thesis is that the relationship *between two* is what can combat the appeal to sameness. That is, humanity must be recognized as (at least) two, male and female, who are not reducible to the Other, but who are recognized as truly different. Here, the focus is on the respectful recognition of difference per se, specifically via the medium of the two of sexuate difference. In addition, respect for difference should be granted not only when difference does emerge but in anticipation of such an emergence. It is a respect for the *possibility* of difference.[10] Moreover, it is important to explicitly point out that 'difference does not have to remain always eternal in exactly the same form in which we first encounter it'.[11] This is particularly relevant in order to avoid any charges of essentialism.

I propose that we can extend these insights on difference beyond specific considerations of sexuate difference. However, it would be a mistake to simply alter Irigaray's philosophy such that it would seek recognition between *multiple* forms of difference as a theoretical starting point. While differences exist between men and men, women and women, it is paramount that one avoids the celebration of diversity and multiplicity in its present forms. This is because 'society is made up of two sexes, not of "men": youth, workers, the disabled, immigrants, the unemployed, women, etc.'[12] To rephrase this point: society is not made up of man (A: the positive reality) and youth, workers, the disabled, and so on (not-A: the negative reality). For our present understandings of multiplicity follow the binary logic of the 'singular model of the one and the many'.[13]

When the 'many' make claims of recognition against the 'one', they are not undermining the phallocentric system which has marked them as 'Other' in the first place. Instead, they continue to define themselves against the standards set by this conception of the neutral subject. Thus, 'This singular model can, at best, allow for an oscillation between the one and the many, but the one remains more or less obviously in charge of the hierarchy of the many: the singular is [the] unique and/but ideal, Man.'[14] Alison Martin summarizes Irigaray's position on the matter as follows: 'Irigaray has always been wary of any call to difference that implies an immediate celebration of multiplicity. For her, the one and the many, the singular and the multiple, are flip-sides of the same coin which needs to be displaced by going back through the question of sexual difference.'[15] This does not mean that Irigaray disavows the importance of other differences; in fact, the opposite is true. However, genuine cultural and symbolic change cannot occur without first *thinking (through) two*: 'If we are to get away from the omnipotent model of the one and the many, we have to move on to the *two*, a two which is not two times one itself, not even a bigger or a smaller one, but which would be made up of *two* which are really different.'[16] That is, we need to re-cognize and reimagine the two of sexuate difference and other differences through it. We cannot keep imagining difference through the A/not-A binary schema. It is necessary to abandon the neutral universal subject altogether if one is to attempt the transformation of the dominant symbolic order of an entire culture.

ii. Thinking (through) Two

But why begin with sexuate difference? It is the very prevalence of phallocentric perceptions of 'real' manhood and womanhood—defined as heterosexual according to masculine parameters—as well as the assumed normative connections between sex, gender, and sexual orientation, that warrant Irigaray's starting point at the two of sexuate difference. This theoretical starting point is also warranted since Western societies are historically and culturally situated societies that divide and organize themselves in terms of sex.[17] And although it has become increasingly common to discuss 'gender inequality' rather than sex in recent decades, *sex* should retain a primary focus since 'it is not masculinity *per se* that is valorized in our culture but the *masculine male*'.[18] In other words, because '"masculinity" and "femininity" correspond at the level of the imaginary body to "male" and "female" at the level of biology', it is still necessary to consider sex as a significant factor in systems of subordination.[19] Even though the use of gender as an explanatory category may appear to avoid essentialist discourse on female subordination, sex- and orientation-based discrimination can only be properly understood when the dominant normative connections between sex, gender, and sexual orientation are taken into account.

Thus, reconceiving the two of sexuate difference is significant for adequately recognizing LGBTs. Reconceiving the two of sexuate difference also provides an avenue for separating out and articulating more clearly instances of discrimination from within marked groups. By coming to acknowledge the sexuately different person as radically other to oneself, and by exposing phallocentrism's requirement of heterosexuality, it becomes possible to more adequately understand how and why discrimination against LGBTs has taken various forms and varies depending on one's sex. For 'sexuality, though said to be private, cannot possibly escape from social norms'.[20] Thus, the politics of sexuate difference can be interpreted as necessary for marked persons to become subjects *in their own right*. These insights allow one to ascertain the potential that this model of thinking (through) two has for promoting justice for marked persons more broadly: the politics of sexuate difference is best recognized as the foundation set 'to bring about a cultural change towards a culture of difference'.[21]

Importantly, then, the politics of sexuate difference should *not* be seen as claiming that various forms of difference are unimportant or unworthy of consideration. Thinking (through) two is the path which will eventually lead to respectful recognition of all other forms of difference. Irigaray argues, 'Recognizing the other—man or woman—is different from me, and accepting that his/her right to exist and to human dignity is *equivalent* to mine, leads to the recognition of other forms of diversity.'[22] The point is that difference *itself* needs to be reconceived theoretically prior to general identity recognition (i.e., we need to understand human difference as an A/B relationship), and this requires that we expose and distance ourselves from the phallocentric subject. Especially in Irigaray's later work, it is apparent that her model of thinking (through) two can only be seen as having importance if it can also adequately respect other differences alongside sexuate difference.[23] This becomes possible because the process of thinking (through) two who are radically different to each other causes subjects to recognize that their own subjectivity is limited. Thus, sexuate difference is only the most important difference to focus on 'if it is the difference that might better facilitate all other differences in our culture'.[24] As such, the model of thinking (through) two is a purposeful and strategic approach to relieving matters of unjustified social and political exclusion. It is a strategy that aims ultimately to recognize difference in the dominant shared Western social imaginary and tends towards the production of just civil relations of respect for Otherness.

iii. The 'Space Between'

What Irigaray is looking to achieve in her promotion of respect for (the potential for) difference(s), then, is a civil coexistence in difference, for 'difference is present everywhere, in us and between us', yet so frequently these differences (real or potential) have been denied, ignored, or disavowed.[25] So how do we come to re-cognize difference? The 'space between' or 'interval' is the location where the potential for difference lies, and so it is where the theoretical focus should be placed, for 'we are still lacking a culture of between-sexes, of between-races, of between-traditions, etc.'[26] To better understand this point it is useful to elaborate on the characterization of the space between.[27]

Irigaray distinguishes between the perception of being 'different-from' something and being 'diverse-between'. Irigaray believes the perception of being 'different-from' will likely give rise to further conflict; to be 'different-from' implies a resistance to the Other, it implies a barrier of inclusion/exclusion. It is the making of something 'unknown' known as 'not like me'. In this instance, 'the "other" is categorized in a particular way and can then be excluded or ignored. No attempt is made to interrogate differences, or explore avenues in which we may come to know the other.'[28] Instead, Irigaray claims there is a right and a duty to recognize others and ourselves as 'diverse-between'. 'Thus, not: "I'm different from you", but: "we differ amongst ourselves", which implies a continual give-and-take in the establishing of boundaries and relationships, without the one having greater authority over the other.'[29]

Being diverse-between means there is always some connection between us, even though we are not exactly similar. Our differences are not a reason to create a barrier of exclusion. Instead, we must acknowledge the space of difference that remains between us. We must neither cut it off nor attempt to surmount it. This does not mean that there can be no recognition of shared needs. I do not seek to deny that similarities can exist between normative heterosexuals and LGBTs, but rather, I hold that when differences emerge they need to be encountered in an alternative way. They should not be dismissed as irrelevant. What is important is that we do not reduce the recognition of identity to simply belonging 'inside' or 'outside' a presumed standard of normalcy. This cultivation of the space between encourages a new approach to the encounter with difference altogether. It is to approach difference with wonder and generosity, which are attitudes we can cultivate within ourselves. Wonder acknowledges difference and generosity acknowledges similarity, or equivalence.[30] Thus, perception of the Other and of their (potential for) difference is crucial for sexed subjects' coming into their own specific civil identity, as well as for promoting relationships of respect between others. This space between is a generative threshold for a nonhierarchical ethics in relations of alterity.[31]

iv. The Lesbian

I have argued that focusing on the two of sexuate difference can allow us to re-cognize difference as an A/B relation and so allow us to re-cognize all relationships of diversity. However, Irigaray's scholarship has frequently been met with the charge of heterosexism. But one need not conclude this about her work.[32] To further the argument that this re-cognition of difference is applicable beyond the scope of sexuate difference, it is worthwhile to acknowledge that multiple aspects of female identity have been considered in Irigaray's scholarship, including the figure of the lesbian. In fact, Irigaray's early writings, particularly on Freud, address how lesbian identity has itself been defined within phallocentric parameters and how such an identity could challenge those parameters.

According to Freud, subjectivity is constructed through reference to the penis, that is, possession or lack of the penis. Irigaray argues, 'In Freud, sexual pleasure boils down to being plus or minus one sex organ: the penis. And sexual "otherness" comes down to "not having it".'[33] Women's normal sexual development is, therefore, discovered only in juxtaposition with man's normal sexual development, not in its own terms. According to Freud, the little girl's sexuality is phallic (clitoral). The clitoris was perceived, in other words, as the 'little penis'. However, the little girl must transfer from active clitoral pleasure to passive vaginal pleasure if she is to develop normally—'a girl has to change . . . she is biologically *destined*'.[34]

Furthermore, Freud also reinforced the sexual norms of his day by endorsing 'an economy and ideology of (re)production'.[35] That is, he held the sexual *function* to consist entirely in the fact of heterosexual reproduction of humanity. According to Freud, the perverse aspects of human sexuality never disappear but are instead subsumed under the reproductive function so long as normal development occurs. From this reasoning, it is possible to infer that heterosexual sex for procreative purposes is the proper, correct, standard, and normal sexual act, which is to take place between normally sexually developed men and women. Thus, the normal, sexually developed man will be of the male sex, possess masculine traits, and have an active heterosexual orientation. The normal, sexually developed woman will be of the female sex, possess feminine traits, and have a passive heterosexual desire.[36]

The lesbian, however, does not complete normal sexual development. The lesbian, it is said, suffers from a masculinity complex. 'The female homosexual is thought to act *as a man*', and she also chooses 'a feminine love-object'.[37] Such a description of the female homosexual appears to confirm the stereotype that masculinity and femininity complement each other—this is why the lesbian desires a feminine love-object. On Freud's account, it seems that a simple misdirection has occurred from the lesbian's sex to her appropriate gender identity. The lesbian, therefore, desires a love-object of the same sex. In other words, the lesbian is female but possesses masculine traits and either fails or refuses to transfer from an active to a passive desire and pleasure. She is thus not a 'real' woman in the sense of being normally sexually developed.

This perception of the *female* homosexual, in particular, as failing to become a 'real woman' has been a widely shared stereotype. Of course, such figurations of homosexuality defined in terms of a failed heterosexuality and a misdirection between sex and gender are insufficient to account for the experience of being a queer person. Irigaray criticizes Freud, for example, for failing to consider 'the special nature of desire *between women*'.[38] Irigaray's opposition to such a characterization of men and women's 'normal' sexual development is apparent when she questions dryly, 'Is there any more obvious device or more explicit way of banishing the auto-erotic, homosexual, or indeed fetishistic character of the relationship of man to woman than to stress the production of a child?'[39] For one need not infer that reproduction is the sole or even primary function of hetero-sex. Sex could function primarily as a mode of social inclusion, for example.[40] It may also simply symbolize erotic affection. That is to say, an emphasis on reproduction as the function of sex simply serves to define reproductive heterosexual behaviour as necessary, natural, proper, and thus normative while dismissing other forms of sexual actions as improper, abnormal, and even pathological. The Freudian discourse is, in Irigaray's words, 'imperious, normative, [and] moralizing' with regard to proper sexual functioning and development.[41]

Importantly, for Irigaray, lesbian relationships 'figure not only the possibility but also the actual existence of another kind of exchange, another kind of desire, "without identifiable terms, without accounts, without end"'.[42] Indeed, queerness, like 'woman' herself, is always threatening since it exceeds the definition placed upon it according to phallocentric logic.[43] As such, an important Irigarayan figure for rethinking women's sexuality, both heterosexual and homosexual, is women's two lips. Women's genitals are formed of two lips in continuous contact. Thus, 'Woman "touches herself" all the time, and moreover no one can forbid her to do so.'[44] The very figuration of the lips itself suggest a morphology of woman as full and lacking nothing, directly in contrast to Freud's morphological description of women as castrated. For Freud, 'her sexual organ, which is not one organ, is counted as none'.[45] Promoting this image of the lips can thus be read as an attempt to unlink the notion of sexuate difference from normative heterosexuality and to give woman a positive identity. In other words, Irigaray's project should be properly understood as invested in dismantling the heteronormative assumptions which underscore constructions of sex and gender, and not only as invested in changing the relationship between men and women.[46]

II. A UTOPIAN RHETORICAL STRATEGY

Irigaray's philosophy is also frequently acknowledged as being utopian in character. However, 'utopia' has gained some pejorative connotations throughout the twentieth century, being either linked with totalitarian fantasies or else seen to promote implausible or unrealizable visions of a perfect future. As such, Margaret Whitford argues that it would be dangerous for Irigaray to be mistaken as a guru able to dictate the precise needs and wants of future men and women since this would hinder the possibility for political reflection and refiguration.[47] Similarly, Nicola Lacey criticizes Irigaray's work for her use of reformist language in promoting a utopian theoretical framework. Problematically, Irigaray may be perceived as simply shifting the emphasis from one universal onto two. This is especially troublesome if, thanks to Irigaray's appropriation of the language of institutional reform, her work is misconstrued as a *simple* reformist project rather than as a utopian strategy with an eye to social and legal reform.[48]

If Irigaray is read as promoting only a reformist project, she may obscure the full range of the violence that law does to subjects given her overwhelming focus on sexuate difference. Misrecognition is always a risk when a philosophical theory is utopian. Thus, Lacey ultimately argues against Irigaray's utopian rhetorical strategy of thinking (through) two, finding Irigaray's play on sexual stereotypes to be problematic already at the level of rhetoric and potentially disastrous if she is taken to be offering a program of reform. She concludes that in attempting to eradicate sociopolitical and legal injustices, a more pragmatic approach should be preferred.[49] However, while one can accept that if Irigaray's work is read as a literal program for reform it could have problematic consequences, this does not mean that her utopian strategy is unable to effect positive shifts at the symbolic and social levels *if it is recognized as such*. Lacey defines a 'utopian rhetorical strategy' as that which 'sets out to tap the resources of the imagination: to read and speak against the cultural grain, and hence to make possible the impossible task of thinking beyond the present towards a different future'.[50] Irigaray herself admits the utopian aspect of her work when she states, 'I defend the impossible.'[51] Thus, we need not dismiss the potential value of employing a utopian rhetorical strategy.

The point is not to formulate one final utopian ideal but to imagine and reimagine multiple desirable impossibilities into possibilities and actualities. Utopian strategies are thus necessary if one wants to create a shift in the dominant shared Western social imaginary. Moira Gatens shares a similar sentiment specifically regarding rights discourses, stating:

> I would be reluctant to underplay the aspirational aspects of rights discourses, even while acknowledging that such aspirations are all too often disappointed. Reserving some space on the political platform for the inspirational, indeed the imaginary, dimension of rights seems important. Political theory need not confine itself to descriptions of political ontology (conceived in terms of what 'is') but may also entertain what could or should be.[52]

Without some kind of conception of what a better society might look like, how might one begin to imagine and reimagine the impossible to the plausible to the possible? It is via this very process of imagining, reimagining, and generating controversy that meanings are able to shift over time. Indeed, each moment of change creates a new situation which then requires the imagination of a new and different response. Competition between dominant and subordinate imaginaries, which arise in this context thanks to Irigaray's radical reconceptualization of difference, generates contradictions and conflicts. It is the very conflicts and contradictions *between* shared imaginings that can act as the motors of sociopolitical change.[53] It is for this reason that Irigaray's philosophy should not be abandoned or deemed less favourable than a pragmatic approach dealing only with political ontology. While it is important to stay with the trouble, it is also important to think beyond it.

The utopian rhetorical strategy at play in the politics of sexuate difference attempts to make possible the task of thinking beyond the present towards an alternative future. The desirability of such an approach is not lessened even though such aspirations are all too often disappointed. It is important to think beyond political ontology to what sociopolitical relationships could become. Thus, I hold that utopianism, the theoretical focus on the 'space between', and Irigaray's insights on how to encounter difference *as difference* (i.e., outside of binary logic) can better ensure a just sociopolitical and legal standing for LGBTs and other excluded Others. This is what Irigarayan philosophy can offer to contemporary matters of sociopolitical inequality. It is a springboard for thinking about how we may re-cognize difference in our present sociopolitical context, and any proposal for change need not be interpreted as having to remain always eternal in exactly the same form in which it was introduced. That is the very point of both the politics of sexuate difference *and* the intersubjective justification theory.

III. INTRODUCING EQUIVALENT RIGHTS

It has been argued, thus far, that thinking through the two of sexuate difference is a useful strategy precisely because it can allow for a new encounter with multiple forms of difference. The point of thinking (through) two is to allow for recognition of the limits of one's own subjectivity and to cultivate alternative subjectivities. Irigaray has attempted to show how her utopian rhetorical strategy is able to motivate legal protections in her collaborations with Renzo Imbeni, former mayor of Bologna. Together, they produced a Draft Code of Citizenship for the European Union (EU). A version of this code of citizenship was then proposed by Imbeni to the European Parliament. Although it was not adopted, it is important to recognize that Irigaray's utopian rhetorical strategy can influence pragmatic legal strategies.[54] Changing the way we think about difference necessarily amounts to changing the way we conceive of rights.

Irigaray's contemporary, Drucilla Cornell, has also attempted to show how the philosophy of sexuate difference may be practically applicable and employed by other systematically discriminated-against people. Recall Irigaray's argument that recognizing that the Other is different from me and accepting that his or her right to human dignity is *equivalent* to mine can lead to the recognition of other forms of diversity. She claims that we should look for 'a way for a cohabitation or coexistence between subjects of different but equivalent worth'.[55] From this Cornell has argued for the need to consider people as being owed *equivalent* rather than *equal* rights. This, I propose, would be a practical method of ensuring equal regard. Moreover, this proposal can replace Forst's endorsement of 'special rights'. It is important to advocate for equivalent rather than equal rights precisely because of the problematic standards of sameness which Others must match in order to gain recognition and legal protections at present. Cornell specifically considers LGBTs' rights claims in terms of equivalence. She claims, 'I advocate *equivalent* rather than *equal* rights to recognize the difference of homosexuality, which should not have to match itself to heterosexual arrangements in order to justify itself.'[56] These insights are based on her exploration of the legal determination of instances of discrimination.

As discussed in chapter 3, typically the wrong of discrimination is interpreted as the imposition of a stereotype on an individual who does not match that stereotype. In that chapter, I considered the stereotype that 'homosexuals are an enemy of the traditional family'. The standard way of determining discrimination would be to ask whether a given same-sex couple actually presents a threat to the traditional family. If the answer is 'no', then the couple has been unfairly discriminated against. However, such judgements do not prove the detrimental stereotypes about LGBTs false; rather, LGBTs must prove that they are themselves exceptions to the stereotype. If the discriminated-against party is enough *like* the socially acceptable party for the purposes of a specific rights claim, then the discriminated-against party ought to be treated as such.

As I argued previously, this is a problematic way to understand discrimination, since its basis is the norms of a particular society that have not themselves been justified as a valid standard of measurement. This is to inadvertently concede that heteronormative lifestyles are, in fact, superior to queer alternatives. Discrimination, so understood, is based on an inherently comparative evaluation that implicitly assumes the validity of an already established social norm. Such a standard for measurement is problematic, then, because (a) it does not forcefully challenge any stereotypes about LGBT identities, rendering 'good' LGBTs the exceptions rather than the rule, and (b) it does not question the value placed upon the traditional family (which includes the institution of marriage), but accepts it blindly as a valid standard of measurement. LGBTs who choose to structure their intimate lives outside these dominant social norms are likely to continue to face discrimination, even if laws change to allow for the formally equal treatment of such persons. The very process of stereotyping itself can therefore be understood as wrong since it forecloses individual possibilities, forcing LGBTs to have to operate within an unsatisfactory binary system of acceptability/unacceptability which is inseparable from the sex/gender hierarchy.[57]

Difference needs to be affirmed as irreducible to the dominant stereotypes prominent within the gender hierarchy. As such, the basis for equivalent rights is 'respect for difference', which is able to be continually reimagined, for equivalence is defined 'as "of equal value," but not necessarily equal value because of likeness'.[58] Given historical contexts where identity-based discrimination exists, equivalent rights can be justified for the sake of ensuring human dignity overall. Irigaray argues, 'In any case, our need first and foremost is for a right to human dignity for everyone. That means we need laws that valorize difference. Not all subjects are the same, nor equal, and it wouldn't be right for them to [attempt to] be so.'[59] Equivalent rights ensure equal opportunity and regard for those who have been systematically discriminated against. Being same-sex attracted is a real difference, but it is also a difference that has historically been interpreted as 'abnormal' and 'perverse' in the face of 'normal' heterosexuality. Such a rigid designation of appropriate sexual behaviour for people unfairly curtails the possibility of a sexuality lived differently.[60]

The discourse of equivalent rights seeks to gain recognition and respect for historically discriminated-against Others by recognizing their dignity and noting that difference dictates that various rights are owed to people of varying identities. The starting point for a conception of equivalent rights needs to recognize that 'the human species *as currently constituted* is composed of two genres, irreducible to one another'.[61] But although sexuate difference is a worthy starting point for considering equivalent rights, it should not be the end point. Those marked persons who have been Othered due to phallocentric logic will also benefit from the employment of equivalent rights.

Regarding LGBT relationships, Cornell advocates one equivalent right in particular, stating, 'Homosexuals should be given the *equivalent right* to be left alone in their intimate associations, whether or not they choose to mimic the life patterns of traditional heterosexuals.'[62] This right goes some of the way to achieving respect for LGBTs, regardless of their differences to traditional heterosexuals. However, I suggest a reformulation of this equivalent right. This is because Cornell's articulation alludes to privacy as a justification. As I argued in chapter 1, appeals for human rights based on the right to privacy can be troublesome for two reasons. First, they need not necessarily challenge the social perception of homosexuality as immoral and unnatural, which may increase the difficulty of LGBTs in fostering their identities and cultivating difference(s). Second, privacy masks from state intervention a realm where potential abuses can occur and have historically occurred to women in particular.

I would reformulate this as two equivalent rights: first, 'LGBTs should be given the equivalent right to be recognized fully in those relationships which the state chooses to regulate', and second, 'those who do not choose to mimic the life patterns of traditional heterosexuals need not justify to anyone why this is the case'. A separate argument can be made about which kinds of relationships the state *ought* to recognize. (I propose that any such relationships should be of the caring variety.) The point of this equivalent right is to ensure that LGBTs are not interpreted as less deserving of equal regard simply because their relationships might not match the traditional heterosexual norm. The right is 'equivalent' since it does not require homosexuals to be formally the same as heterosexuals in order to be recognized as having equal moral worth and dignity. This is why it is important to fight for LGBT equality with the use of equivalent rights: equivalent rights seek to target and alter unjustified, biased perspectives regarding homosexuality. 'Equivalent rights stress the value of different lifestyles and forms of intimate association.'[63] Thus, equivalent rights attempt to target the very assumption of homosexuality as somehow 'morally' wrong.

Equivalent rights therefore seek to avoid reliance upon the sameness model to justify rights claims, which would again lead to the elaboration of but-for justifications. Adopting the approach and language of equivalent rights is also largely compatible with Forst's theory, especially insofar as Forst has shifted the onus of proof. Thanks to the demands of Forst's theory, which requires justifications from those who *oppose* certain rights claims, the people who demand equal recognition can side-step the sameness trap. When LGBTs want to claim a human right which is to be realized through concrete sociopolitical and legal specifications, they do not have to prove their likeness via a but-for approach in order to be recognized. Furthermore, the language shift to 'equivalent rights' does not have the same connotations of privilege or need as the language of 'special rights'. As such, equivalent rights can be recognized horizontally between citizens and employed as a means to reconceptualize equality beyond the sameness model.[64]

IV. SIMILARITIES IN OBJECTIVES: DIFFERENCE, DISCOURSE, AND DIGNITY

As stated, I have chosen to introduce the philosophy of sexuate difference in order to supplement the intersubjective justification theory of human rights. I hold that Irigaray's insights on binary logic and strategies for reconceiving difference, teamed with Forst's insights and strategies for constructing rights, can go some way to producing the coexistence between subjects that both theorists desire. Indeed, both theorists' objectives—for the recognition of difference, a focus on discourse, and the recognition of dignity—are compatible.

Irigaray strongly advocates that difference must inform the rights owed to all people; that is, difference is not something to be abstracted away from. Irigaray claims that 'everyone has the right and duty to be what he or she is'.[65] Thus, the philosophy of sexuate difference can help decipher how to go about promoting the legitimacy and importance of difference itself. Through the philosophy of sexuate difference a new way to imagine humanity emerges, creating an alternative reference point which allows people to have their (potential for) difference(s) positively recognized. Each sex is perceived as autonomous and self-defined. The new reference point is humanity built from (at least) two, male and female, who are truly irreducible to each other. This is in lieu of understanding humanity as consisting of duplicate 'ones', that is, as greater or lesser copies of the subject.[66] Irigaray deems a retraining in civility necessary to achieve this goal, which means people must relearn how to be citizens as well as how to be civil *between* themselves. Specifically, 'civil society, in our time, requires public relationships to be places of reciprocity between individuals'.[67] This reeducation requires recognizing that others have needs which may not be applicable to one's own. It requires acknowledging the limit to one's own subjectivity. It requires engaging with the Other. Thus, this process is also a teaching exercise.[68]

In a similar vein, at the core of Forst's basic right to justification rests the grounding assumption that all people ought to be regarded as equals without rejection of their specific identity traits. Given that real issues of social justice emerge among particular, situated people with various identities, the basic right to justification is of vast importance among those who have heretofore not been seen to count. A person's individual and/or shared experiences will inform his or her claim to specific rights. Thus, a claim to equal recognition avoids reliance on a falsely neutral and singular subject position. This is a necessity, since the 'neutral' subject has been proved to be problematically biased time and again in much of feminist theory. Difference, then, is not something to be abstracted away from until mutual commonalities are found among all citizens; rather, differences should inform the needs of citizens and of various political communities, who then build the shared norms that all are to live by. All of this, as well as the historical context in which rights claims are raised, informs what rights will be owed to a state's citizens.

Furthermore, Irigaray and Forst share a focus on communication. This is most obvious for Forst in his insistence on discursive constructivism as the appropriate model for determining the laws and norms which all must agree upon and live by. Of course, each person is born into a situated context where norms governing behaviour and the primacy of certain social institutions already exist, but thanks to the process of discursive constructivism, those norms and institutions are always able to be questioned and revised. Thus, the standards that one's society lives by are not fixed or immutable; they ought to change when its citizens justifiably demand it. All humans live an intersubjective existence, so intersubjective justification is required for the norms governing this existence. This requirement places emphasis on the importance of communication, as well as the necessity of creating and living within *shared systems of meaning*.

Irigaray's focus is on the development of certain values, specifically 'values of communication, not only in the sense of transmission of information but as communication-between', where 'communication-between' means among subjects fundamentally diverse between themselves.[69] Here, perception and silence (so as to allow for listening and understanding) are as imperative in communication as the capacity to speak. To recognize this would contribute to a reeducation in civility. Thus, both Forst and Irigaray have a clear commitment to the idea that communication (and the necessary measures to ensure communication) between people is not only desirable, but is necessary in order to ensure the fairest social context for all. Therefore, respect for difference in the building of shared norms and a retraining in civility, via a focus on communication-between, which encourages respect for the Other, appear to go hand in hand.

Finally, Forst and Irigaray have compatible views on what it means to treat a person with dignity. Dignity, for Forst, is a status all human beings hold in their capacity as agents who give, ask for, and can receive justifications. All human beings, therefore, are equally owed the right to build the shared norms of their community.[70] On Irigaray's part, dignity means the recognition of the Other as irreducibly different to oneself and requires respect for the limitations of one's own subjectivity in the encounter with that Other. Thus, the protection of dignity requires laws which valorize difference.[71] The combination of these conceptions of dignity is compatible with the understanding of LGBT identities that I promote in this book: they are identities that are owed respect regardless of sameness or difference to the partial normative subject. It is respect in their own right. This gives LGBTs symbolic presence and visibility, the possibility of endignifying representations, and the ability to cultivate difference(s). From this we see that the project of re-cognizing and reimagining difference begins with the practice of *respect for the Other*.

V. A NOTE ON TOLERANCE

By reading Irigaray's and Forst's philosophies together, I do not seek to argue that all things which are tolerated ought instead to be respected. Rather, I seek to argue that the objection component to LGBT identity and to same-sex marriage is insupportable given an account of difference like Irigaray's. In other words, assessing the matter of LGBT nondiscrimination and access to marriage through the lens of Irigaray's *two* renders the objection component illegitimate and creates a duty to repudiate prejudice towards LGBTs, as towards nonwhites and various Others.

The objection component towards LGBTs and their practices thus ultimately stems from the failure to recognize and respect LGBTs with regard to the diversity-between-ourselves. To understand such a basic difference as sexuate difference in this way—as (at least) two—will pave the way for the possibility of recognizing other forms of difference as equally legitimate. This is not to say that people will then necessarily cease to think and act with prejudice towards LGBTs but that the *legitimacy* of the objection could not be maintained in any general sense. Tolerance is still the minimum pragmatic requirement, but Irigaray's conception of difference shows *why* LGBTs are owed positive equivalent appreciation: their identity is not reducible and should not be reduced to a comparison with the biased conception of a 'neutral' human subject. It is because LGBTs have a positive identity that they should not be begrudgingly tolerated.

Irigaray argues, 'Changing these habits is a long process, because it means changing attitudes, changing the cultural climate, stereotypes and customs, and so on. Yet it also requires an immediate response . . . we can all start respecting each other without forgetting who we are.'[72] To recognize that LGBTs and heterosexuals differ between themselves leads to the equal regard of both. In other words, this positive esteem of LGBT identity, regardless of how it similarly or dissimilarly relates to heterosexuality, amounts to the proper acknowledgement of LGBT dignity. The combination of Irigaray's insights on difference with Forst's approach to human rights thus demands not a form of 'tolerance' towards LGBTs at all, but *respect* in the sense required by equal regard. Where there is respect for LGBT dignity, there is the *positive acknowledgement of difference-among-ourselves.* Difference is not to be denied in the name of some false universal.

The result of this dual reading, then, is a combined feminist approach to human rights that can be articulated as follows: All people are to be acknowledged as potentially differing persons who exist intersubjectively. These people of potential differences, having basic equal status, are entitled to contribute to the establishment of certain norms that they will have to live by. However, to ensure the equal regard of human subjects who already exist in historically situated contexts, formally equal rights may not be sufficient. Laws which are formally *unequal* but *equivalent* can be enacted in order to ensure equal regard among all persons when required. These rights would allow disadvantaged persons an opportunity to become equivalent by means more appropriate to their contextualized situation. The basic commitment to equal regard, demanded in instances of identity discrimination, reveals that the denial of rights to marked persons is in fact prejudiced and insupportable. This is so because the basic demand is for a revised understanding of and encounter with *difference itself*. Thus, the combined approach I propose articulates the demand for recognition in difference while simultaneously making claims for equivalent political and legal recognition. In other words, the combined approach created by this dual reading offers the best chance at achieving equal regard between heterosexuals and LGBTs.

Ultimately, this combined feminist approach to human rights confirms that same-sex couples are owed the right to marriage if they request it. It does this by doubling the onus of proof and demonstrating that there are no reciprocal or general reasons for rejection based on a commitment to equivalence. It also sets a standard for determining the legitimacy of 'objection components' in matters requiring tolerance thanks to the rejection of phallocentric logic and a commitment to think (through) two. Thus, the combined approach attempts to dismantle the hierarchical normative privilege of certain identities and institutions thanks to the very perspective of difference at its core.

NOTES

1. As previously noted, a shift in terminology has occurred from *sexual difference* to *sexuate difference* in Irigaray's work. For the purposes of consistency, the term *sexuate difference* will be used throughout. See the introduction, note 20.
2. Luce Irigaray, *Thinking the Difference: For a Peaceful Revolution*, trans. K Montin (London: Athlone Press, 1994), intro.
3. Luce Irigaray, *Democracy Begins between Two*, trans. Kirsteen Anderson (New York: Routledge, 2000), 122.
4. Luce Irigaray, 'The Question of the Other', trans. Noah Guynn, *Yale French Studies* 87 (1995): 7–8; Irigaray, *Democracy Begins between Two*, 7–19.
5. Margaret Whitford, *Luce Irigaray: Philosophy in the Feminine* (London: Routledge, 1991), chap. 5.

6. Penelope Deutscher, *A Politics of Impossible Difference: The Later Work of Luce Irigaray* (Ithaca, NY: Cornell University Press, 2002), chap. 1 and conclusion.

7. Luce Irigaray, *Je, Tu, Nous*, trans. Alison Martin (New York: Routledge, 2007), 4.

8. Xu Ping, 'Irigaray's Mimicry and the Problem of Essentialism', *Hypatia* 10, no. 4 (1995): 76–89.

9. Luce Irigaray, *I Love to You*, trans. Alison Martin (New York: Routledge, 1996), 48; original emphasis.

10. Irigaray, *Thinking the Difference*, intro.; Irigaray, *I Love to You*, chap. 2; Deutscher, *A Politics of Impossible Difference*, chap. 1.

11. Kay Lalor, 'Constituting Sexuality: Rights, Politics and Power in the Gay Rights Movement', *International Journal of Human Rights* 15, no. 5 (2011): 690.

12. Irigaray, *Thinking the Difference*, 59.

13. Irigaray, *Democracy Begins between Two*, chap. 9.

14. Ibid., 127–28.

15. Alison Martin, 'Introduction: Luce Irigaray and the Culture of Difference', *Theory, Culture & Society* 20, no. 3 (2003): 4.

16. Irigaray, *Democracy Begins between Two*, 129.

17. Moira Gatens, *Imaginary Bodies: Ethics, Power and Corporeality*. London: Routledge, 1996), chap. 1.

18. Ibid., 15; original emphasis.

19. Ibid., 16.

20. Irigaray, *Je, Tu, Nous*, 8.

21. Martin, 'Introduction', 1.

22. Irigaray, *Democracy Begins between Two*, 12; emphasis added.

23. This is a primary concern of Irigaray's in *Between East and West: From Singularity to Community*, trans. S. Pluháček (New York: Columbia University Press, 2002).

24. Deutscher, *A Politics of Impossible Difference*, 171.

25. Irigaray, *Democracy Begins between Two*, 13.

26. Irigaray, *Between East and West*, 139.

27. Irigaray, *Democracy Begins between Two*, intro. See also Frederica Giardini, 'Speculum of Being Two: Politics and Theory after All These Years', *Theory, Culture & Society* 20, no. 3 (2003): 13–26.

28. Lalor, 'Constituting Sexuality', 690.

29. Irigaray, *Democracy Begins between Two*, 14.

30. Marguerite La Caze, 'The Encounter between Wonder and Generosity', *Hypatia* 17, no. 3 (2002): 1–19. La Caze understands generosity as the act of recognizing what is essentially similar between us. It seems to be in the spirit of La Caze's work to interpret 'essentially similar' as 'equivalent'. Equivalence is discussed in the next section.

31. Rebecca Hill, *The Interval* (New York: Fordham University Press, 2012), intro.

32. Many scholars have dedicated significant attention to the problem of heterosexism. Alison Stone claims that a self-critical sexuate culture can undermine rather than support the heteronormative family. See Stone, *Luce Irigaray and the Philosophy of Sexual Difference* (Cambridge: Cambridge University Press, 2006), 161–224. Rachel Jones argues that while *sexuate* difference has ontological priority in Irigaray's thought, she does not require or imply heterosexuality. See Jones, *Irigaray: Towards a Sexuate Philosophy* (Cambridge: Polity Press, 2011), chap. 6. La Caze argues that Irigaray's notion of wonder that is to be cultivated between the sexes can legitimately be extended to the encounter with difference in general, thereby circumventing the bias towards heterosexuality. See La Caze, 'The Encounter'. Finally, Hill also acknowledges the potential for heterosexism, yet she argues that Irigaray's space-between (or interval) contains the possibility of becomings other than those of sexuate difference. See Hill, *The Interval*, conclusion.

33. Luce Irigaray, *Speculum of the Other Woman*, trans. G. Gill (Ithaca, NY: Cornell University Press, 1985), 52.

34. Ibid., 31; original emphasis.

35. Luce Irigaray, *This Sex Which Is Not One*, trans. C. Porter (Ithaca, NY: Cornell University Press, 1985), 64.

36. Ibid., chap. 3; Moira Gatens, *Feminism and Philosophy: Perspectives on Difference and Equality* (Cambridge: Polity Press, 1991), chap. 6.
37. Irigaray, *This Sex Which Is Not One*, 43, 65.
38. Irigaray, *Speculum of the Other Woman*, 101; original emphasis.
39. Ibid., 32.
40. Georgia Warnke, *After Identity* (Cambridge: Cambridge University Press, 2007), 134.
41. Irigaray, *Speculum of the Other Woman*, 31.
42. Christine Holmlund, 'The Lesbian, the Mother, the Heterosexual Lover: Irigaray's Recodings of Difference', *Feminist Studies* 17, no. 2 (1991): 288.
43. Luce Irigaray, *An Ethics of Sexual Difference*, trans. Carolyn Burke and Gillian C. Gill (London: Continuum, 2004), chap. 1.
44. Irigaray, *This Sex Which Is Not One*, 24.
45. Ibid., 26. See also Gatens, *Feminism and Philosophy*, chap. 6. Another alternative morphology proposed by Judith Butler is the possibility of a lesbian phallus. She argues, 'What is needed is not a new body part, as it were, but displacement of the hegemonic symbolic of (heterosexist) sexual difference and the critical release of alternative imaginary schemas for constituting sites of erotogenic pleasure.' See Butler, *Bodies that Matter* (New York and London: Routledge, 1993), 91. While this is an interesting figuration, it is unclear whether such a notion can be adequately severed from its historical connotations (penis as phallus) in order to do the theoretical work it proposes.
46. Irigaray, *This Sex Which Is Not One*, chap. 11. See also Ofelia Schutte, 'A Critique of Normative Heterosexuality: Identity, Embodiment, and Sexual Difference in Beauvoir and Irigaray', *Hypatia* 12, no. 1 (1997): 40–62.
47. Margaret Whitford, *Luce Irigaray: Philosophy in the Feminine* (London: Routledge, 1991), chap. 1.
48. Nicola Lacey, 'Violence, Ethics and Law: Feminist Reflections on a Familiar Dilemma', in *Visible Women: Essays on Feminist Legal Theory and Political Philosophy*, ed. Susan James and Stephanie Palmer (Oxford: Hart Publishing, 2002), 117–35.
49. Ibid. Similar criticisms can also be found in an earlier piece by Lacey. See Lacey, *Unspeakable Subjects: Feminist Essays in Legal and Social Theory* (Oxford: Hart Publishing, 1998), chap. 7.
50. Lacey, 'Violence, Ethics and Law', 132; emphasis added.
51. Irigaray, *I Love to You*, 9.
52. Moira Gatens, 'Can Human Rights Accommodate Women's Rights? Towards an Embodied Account of Social Norms, Social Meaning, and Cultural Change', *Contemporary Political Theory* 3, no. 3 (2004): 281.
53. Whitford, *Philosophy in the Feminine*, chap. 1; Gatens, 'Can Human Rights Accommodate Women's Rights?'
54. These are reproduced in Irigaray, *Democracy Begins between Two*, chap. 6 and appendix.
55. Ibid., 125.
56. Drucilla Cornell, 'Gender, Sex, & Equivalent Rights', in *Feminists Theorize the Political*, ed. Judith Butler and Joan Wallach Scott (New York: Routledge, 1992), 290.
57. Ibid.
58. Ibid., 282.
59. Irigaray, *Je, Tu, Nous*, 14.
60. Cornell, 'Gender, Sex, & Equivalent Rights', 290.
61. Ibid., 282; emphasis added. A genre in this context invokes the idea of 'kind' or 'type'. The idea is that men and women are distinctive kinds of beings and should be recognized as such. They should not be recognized as being of one kind and its lack (see Jones, *Irigaray*, chap. 6). Jones argues, 'Irigaray's notion of '*genre*' is neither a simple expression of our biology, nor a wholly socio-cultural construction imposed on blankly malleable bodies' (191).
62. Cornell, 'Gender, Sex, & Equivalent Rights', 290; original emphasis.
63. Ibid.
64. Ibid.
65. Irigaray, *I Love to You*, 53.

66. Ibid., chap. 5.
67. Irigaray, *Thinking the Difference*, 86.
68. Irigaray, *Democracy Begins between Two*, chaps. 1 and 5.
69. Ibid., 9.
70. Rainer Forst, 'The Ground of Critique: On the Concept of Human Dignity in Social Orders of Justification', *Philosophy & Social Criticism* 37, no. 9 (2011): 965–76.
71. Irigaray, *Democracy Begins between Two*, chap. 1; Irigaray, *Between East and West*, chap. 8; Irigaray, *Je, Tu, Nous*, chap. 1.
72. Irigaray, *Thinking the Difference*, xvi.

Chapter Six

A Combined Approach

Aiming for LGBT Equal Regard

In the previous chapter, I argued that the philosophy of sexuate difference provides a valuable supplement to the intersubjective justification theory. Weaving together insights from both results in the production of a feminist human rights approach that aims to encourage sociopolitical and legal change in the present—a theory whose core is a utopian revolutionary rethinking of difference. While I considered that the politics of sexuate difference can be interpreted as promoting an implausible or unrealizable vision of a perfect future, I argued that utopian visions are necessary. The combined approach does not advocate one fixed ideal for the future. The point is to allow people in the present the possibility of imagining, constructing, and reconstructing some reality that all can acceptably live with. By employing a utopian rhetorical strategy, the imagining of a different future can 'change from impossible to possible, from "utopian" via feasible to matter of fact'.[1] That is to say, utopian visions are crucial for the process of transforming the present in the direction of a different, more just future. Indeed, even when utopian aspirations are (all too frequently) disappointed, it is still important to consider what one's political climate *should* be, not only what it is or can be.[2]

In this chapter, I will argue that it is essential to examine the role that the imaginary plays in issues of social justice. It is essential because prominent arguments which circulate as justifications for same-sex marriage will feed into the shared public perception of LGBT identities.[3] Therefore, circulating the *right* kind of argument for same-sex marriage is just as important, if not more so, as access to same-sex marriage itself. What constitutes the right kind of argument is its being likely to promote equal regard for LGBTs in accordance with the value of equality in dignity. Thus, I will defend the importance of the role of 'the imaginary' in political theory, considering how shifts in social imaginaries contribute to sociopolitical and legal changes. I will also address Cheshire Calhoun's supposition that sameness arguments are the better arguments to endorse by contrasting her claims with the combined approach. I will therefore demonstrate in detail how the combined approach would justify same-sex marriage and what meaning-generating narratives it would endorse, concluding that conceiving of same-sex marriage under the combined approach will best promote a just sociopolitical and legal context for LGBT people overall.

I. THE IMAGINARY

When I speak of 'the imaginary', I am talking about *how things are imagined.* It is foremost important to stress that imaginaries are plural. As indicated in the introduction, they can be philosophical, religious, political, economic, sexual, racial, ethnic, national, international, and so on. According to Marcel Stoetzler and Nira Yuval-Davis, imaginaries are simultaneously a necessary condition and the product of the dialogical process involved in the construction of knowledge. In other words, imaginaries simultaneously produce and are produced by the meaning-generating narratives that are employed in the production of knowledge. Imaginaries, which are made up of images, symbols, metaphors, myths, and narratives, help to structure forms of embodied identity and belonging and create social meaning and value. Imaginaries are also situated, which is to say that they are shaped and conditioned by the historical contexts in which they arise. These historical contexts include geographical borders, transnational ideological commitments, one's own historical position, one's corporeal subjectivity, and one's relations to others. As such, imaginaries correspond and are applied to particular bodies in particular ways, attracting strong affective investments. These multiple imaginaries, including the symbols, metaphors, and narratives which make them up, produce a more or less (but not always) consistent set of social norms taken up in a particular historical context.[4]

As defined in the introduction, a social norm is a shared expectation about the appropriate behaviour for a person or a group of people with a particular identity in a particular context. That is, social norms characterize some actions as appropriate and others as inappropriate and act as shared guiding rules for social conduct. To demonstrate with an example, consider the norms of heterosexuality. There are multiple and complex social norms which guide individuals' actions: seeking out *one* partner of the opposite sex (the norms of hetero-sex and monogamy); participation in certain social institutions (marriage); engagement in only particular kinds of sex acts (vanilla, in pairs, procreative); and so on. These norms are learned in conjunction with *meaning-generating narratives*, while they simultaneously (re)produce those same narratives. The idea here is that the dominant shared Western social imaginary makes our conception of the world, our sociopolitical relations, and so on, *whole* by inscribing them with meanings.[5] In this context, the dominant meaning-generating narrative is the narrative of romantic love. Thus, not only do norms guide our actions, but our narratives give us *reasons* for our actions. That is to say, the norms and narratives of romantic love give people reasons for structuring their intimate and familial lives in one particular way rather than another. They contribute to our sexual and social imaginaries. Importantly, a shared meaning-generating narrative which privileges heteronormative ideals necessarily dictates that certain behaviours are deviant, and those who deviate from normative heterosexuality are shamed in various ways.

There are two points to be explicitly reminded of at this time. The first is that nonnormative heterosexuals as well as LGBT people can suffer shame. Different transgressions have different levels of severity, and these levels are in constant flux. However, LGBT people have been *stigmatized* for their transgressions. They have been repositories for the undesirable traits that both homosexuals and heterosexuals exhibit. Importantly, to be stigmatized is to be identified permanently with one's disgrace.[6] Again, this is a difference in *kind* rather than in *degree* of deviation. While there is a continual shift between which acts normatively count as more or less deviant, when LGBT people transgress norms it is a reflection of *who they are*. In other words, the heteronormativity of the dominant shared Western social imaginary marks LGBT people as inherently deviant, perverse, immoral, and so on. Thus, while heterosexuals may act nonnormatively and may even actively reject heteronormative behaviours, they are unlikely to be stigmatized in the same way that LGBT people are stigmatized for doing so. Nonnormative heterosexuals still retain some, if not much, of their heterosexual privilege.[7]

Second, it is worthwhile to comment on the *shared* nature of these social norms. Many people actively attempt to dissociate themselves from the norms of heterosexuality and romantic love. In what sense can it be said that social norms are shared, then, given that people actively reject and dissociate themselves from such norms? Despite one's best intentions, norms act on and through bodies, even in rebellion. People are assumed to have certain attributes, demeanours, and so on, depending on the kinds of bodies they have and the way that they present themselves. Moreover, individuals appropriate their macro-level identifications by others and incorporate them into their self-identity.[8] In other words, macro-level identifications by others have direct consequences on one's own embodied self-perception, which in turn affects behaviour, and this is true whether or not a person explicitly endorses or rejects the dominant norms of his or her society. This effect is *prereflexive*, and it is these prereflexive modes of knowing that cause feelings of inferiority, guilt, and shame when an individual does not live up to the normative expectations of him or her, or even anger and resentment that one is expected to behave in a certain fashion. This is why I have explicitly pointed to the importance of second-order appreciation. To strive for the second-order appreciation of LGBTs is to strive for a shift in the normative perception of LGBTs.

As the example of normative heterosexual behaviour indicates, a social norm never stands alone. Normative heterosexual behaviour incorporates norms about heterosexual sex acts, relationship structures, gender identity, procreation, the family, religion, taboos, and so on, and each of these norms touches on the others. All norms form a part of larger clusters of norms which together constitute these broader social imaginaries.[9] The difficulty in achieving equality for oppressed groups such as LGBT people stems from the fact that the rights they seek do not simply challenge one norm or another but challenge whole clusters of norms simultaneously. Indeed, LGBT people are threatening precisely because they (seek to) challenge the norms which have heretofore served to regulate sexual and behavioural conduct in certain ways, ways that privilege a certain kind of identity (the phallocentric subject) and social relations (heteromasculine) above others.

Although LGBT people have been perceived as a threat to the dominant social order, it has been extremely difficult for these people to instigate changes in the dominant shared Western social imaginary and subsequently in the legal and political realms. Importantly, certain kinds of people have their imaginings act more forcefully in the establishment of social norms rather than others.[10] In the context of the West, those who most closely resemble the phallocentric subject or the 'benchmark man' have had this privilege. For example, to demonstrate the difficulty of women exerting influence in the dominant shared Western social imaginary, Moira Gatens points to the late eighteenth-century writings of Mary Wollstonecraft and Olympe de Gouges. Olympe de Gouges stressed that the terms *man*, *citizen*, and *all* in Thomas Paine's Declaration of the Rights of Man and Citizen could not be assumed to include women. She thus wrote, as an alternative, the *Declaration of the Rights of Woman and Citizen*. Mary Wollstonecraft similarly argued in *A Vindication of the Rights of Woman* that the 'rights of man' were incomplete since they did not reflect human rights, which would necessarily include women. Despite their attempts, neither Wollstonecraft nor de Gouges were able to significantly influence the Enlightenment interpretation of the social meaning(s) of 'personhood' and 'womanhood'. As such, the 'unfinished business' of the Enlightenment—women's equality—has remained problematic for political theory and practice into the present.[11]

This raises the question: Why and how have women's legal challenges managed to become more successful in recent years given women's former lack of power in influencing shared norms? For a start, contradictions between the 'citizenship narrative' and the normative place of women gained more focus, and there was a growing collective desire for change. The citizenship narrative of the dominant shared Western social imaginary—the story of what it takes to be a citizen of a Western society—cannot logically deny women (or marked persons) as equals; it ideologically holds all people to be free and equal in dignity with certain inalienable rights. However, this ideological commitment is at odds with the West's history of understanding women as the property of men and which required wives' obedience to husbands. Thus, Gatens claims it is here—in the 'human desires for an alternative future', teamed with 'emerging contradictions within and between social imaginaries'—that the motors of social change are to be found.[12] Alongside these two factors for change are three additional elements—*time*, *resonance*, and *critique*—which are crucial for emancipatory changes to the dominant shared Western social imaginary.

First, consider time. No change is immediate, it is always gradual. Meanings are constructed and reconstructed across time, thanks to the promotion of alternative narratives via collective social movements in the face of contradictions. This can account for the pattern of 'small change' leading towards LGBT legal reform. Small legal changes across a length of time appear to be caused by, coincide with, and encourage minor shifts in the dominant shared Western social imaginary, encouraging a piecemeal acceptance of LGBT people. In other words, the law and the imaginary mutually constitute each other. Whether it is producing a desirable image of homosexuality is an additional question to which I have answered in the negative. Presently, we are seeing a highly assimilative shift in the reception of the LGBT community.

The second important feature is resonance with aspects of dominantly held imaginaries. If a normative shift in relations between normative heterosexuals and the LGBT community is going to occur, then the claims of LGBTs will need to resonate with at least *some* aspects of the particular imaginaries from which the norms of heterosexuality derives its legitimation.[13] In other words, while LGBTs need to produce alternative meaning-generating stories in order to secure change, the alternative must be able to latch on to some parts of the dominant meaning-generating story that is already endorsed. This is also evident for LGBT rights claims in the example of small change. For example, the decriminalization of sodomy—the first step in LGBT law reform—was frequently justified based on arguments for *privacy*, a highly resonant, individualistic value. It was via the initial promotion of these highly resonant values that LGBT rights claims were able to gain uptake and gradually make the sexual identity of its members more central.

However, a new narrative can be too resonant with dominant norms, resulting in little significant changes for particular marked persons. The personhood account of human rights is of this variety, with its implicit endorsement of heteronorms in its justification of marriage. The personhood account's argument for same-sex marriage does not (seek to) pose a challenge to the primacy of marriage or its typical structure of intimacy and familial life. It simply seeks LGBT peoples' entry to the institution. Indeed, too much resonance is common in arguments which ground themselves in sameness. Consider as well the dominant activist narrative in support of marriage equality, also discussed in chapter 2. Arguments which claim 'all love is the same' have proven to be more resonant in the dominant shared Western social imaginary than arguments which stress the importance of treating citizens equally (or equivalently) despite their difference. Indeed, 'the advocacy of same-sex marriage rights has primarily invoked the importance of individuals being able to satisfy their romantic, companionate, and sexual needs',[14] and these needs have been framed according to heteronormative parameters. Some activists even argue that the traditional values of marriage will be strengthened once the inclusion of LGBT people occurs.

The argument from sameness is the argument that can most easily gain social uptake and provide meaning to a dominant mass of people who share the same social environment: it portrays the narrative of romantic love and 'happily ever after'. Consider again AME's advertisement supporting same-sex marriage, discussed in chapter 2. Recall that Ivan states, 'We're not activists; we're just people who want to get married, just like everyone else.' He goes on to say, 'People understand marriage, they know what it means, they know that it means two people want to be together for the rest of their lives.' The ad also features Ivan's sister, who asks, 'If two people love each other, regardless of who they are, who are we to judge or restrict their choices in what they do from day to day?' This ad frequently refers to love, life-long commitment, and happiness by Ivan and Chris as well as the members of their extended families. It is this type of argument that resonates most with presently shared norms; it stresses the 'relevant' similarities of same-sex couples to normative different-sex couples. GetUp! Australia's ad does this even more successfully since it taps into this narrative through images alone. That is to say, it *shows* the general public how normal same-sex relationships are; it doesn't *tell* them. In other words, this ad is successful although it does not present (and perhaps *because* it does not present) a sustained rational argument for same-sex marriage. However, images of sameness also (either implicitly or explicitly) endorse heteromasculinist values. They concede that heteronorms are a legitimate basis for comparison.

Because this tactic is likely to redraw the boundaries of inclusion/exclusion, meaning that only some LGBTs will be deemed 'acceptable', overly resonant arguments ought to be challenged. This is where the desire for change needs to manifest in collective resistance and critique. This involves pushing ambiguities 'to their limit through the reinvention or reinterpretation of aspects of those [dominant] imaginaries'.[15] Collective resistance can challenge mainstream norms by reading them against the grain and pushing back against the phallocentric logic that supports them. When this occurs, people are urged to think differently, and thinking differently creates the possibility for social change. Thus, while it is necessary to maintain some amount of resonance, it is important to explicitly critique *which* imaginations have typically been able to shift the way citizens conceive of their political communities and *who* has been able to influenced them. That is, heteromasculinist positioning must be challenged.[16]

Thus, while resonance is necessary, one ought to be wary of just how resonant the proposed alternative meaning-generating narrative is, especially since dominant masculinist interpretations have been the majority source of widely shared social imaginaries and norms contributing to the exclusion of marked persons. Therefore, critique is especially important when the task at hand is the attainment of equal regard for marked persons struggling to become recognized in their own right, that is, without comparison to the model of the phallocentric subject. It is important to note that the mere existence of contradictions in imaginaries does not guarantee that people will take up the task of critiquing these imaginaries. As previously mentioned, the capacity to maintain inconsistent belief sets is the hallmark of worldviews that attempt to justify oppressive social, economic, and political relations. Thus, it is clear that when one strives for sociopolitical and legal change, collectively exposing the contradictions between competing imaginaries is crucial. The combined approach attempts to achieve all this by constructing a perspective which promotes values such as basic human equality while it simultaneously advances its alternative vision for encountering difference.

These five factors for change—desire, contradiction, time, resonance, and critique—need to be balanced in order to bring about the best results for LGBT people. Contradictions and a widespread desire for change are both necessary, for without them there is no movement or reason for movement. Time is also crucial. A better argument will be expedient, but it will not be expedient at the expense of its goal. That is, if the most expedient argument fails to lead towards equal regard, we may not prefer it over a slower argument that does. In other words, we should not presume that the argument which brings about change the quickest is necessarily the best argument. In addition, there must be resonance in order to ensure that one's claims are heard at all. The oppressors need to be able to identify with the oppressed in some meaningful sense, which means that strict neutrality will not be a beneficial ground of appeal. Finally, there must be critique. What is wrong with marriage in its current form? Not only is it exclusionary, it also has normative dominance, pressing upon people one model of intimacy and care and positioning it as normal, ideal, and desirable. That is, it hides the fact that what it presents as normal is only one of many possible conceptions of normalcy.

II. CHESHIRE CALHOUN ON BECOMING AN ESSENTIAL CITIZEN[17]

According to Calhoun, the primary stake in LGBT equality politics is 'the liberty to represent oneself as gay or lesbian in the public sphere'.[18] In other words, what matters is to ensure that the rights gained allow LGBT people to take on positive public representations as nonheterosexual and to be respected and accepted as equal citizens. This requires dealing with the *imaginative* aspect of LGBT claims for equality and not only law reform. This is because norms have affective dimensions that can only be countered by bringing about a change in the way that LGBT people are imagined and *felt* about.

It is important to remember, as discussed in the introduction, that heterosexuality is allowed a place as a complex public phenomenon. It is an assumed way of being oriented in the social world: it is taken for granted in social interactions, advertising, film and television representations, modes of flirting, dating, and the like. Heterosexuality, but particularly *normative* heterosexuality, is publicly promoted and naturalized in a way that homosexuality is not. As previously mentioned, this means that heterosexuality *as marriage and the traditional, middle-class nuclear family* is privileged. Now, it is well observed that citizenship is constituted through heterosexual norms and practices, and Calhoun stresses that what it means to be a citizen is closely bound with the Western cultural conception of 'being fit for marriage' given the political myth that normatively imagined marriage and the nuclear family play 'a uniquely foundational role in sustaining civil society'.[19] The political myth of the foundational role of traditional marriage was highlighted in chapter 1. There we saw that the explicit place of marriage in the Universal Declaration of Human Rights 1948 (UDHR) and subsequent covenants rests on the supposition that 'the family is the natural and fundamental group unit of society and is entitled to protection by society and the State'. This political myth holds 'marriage' (including the family) to be a natural institution, existing prior to the creation of the modern state, and it has an important implication: 'It means that if a social group can lay claim to being inherently qualified or fit to enter marriage and found a family, it can also claim a distinctive political status', that is, the status as full or essential citizens.[20] In other words, when LGBTs come to be seen as legitimately entitled to marry, they will also be seen as essential citizens of a particular state. The crucial question that I shall seek to answer, then, is whether LGBT people can come to be perceived as essential citizens *without* endorsing this perspective of marriage.

Importantly, a connection can be made between the myth of marriage as a prepolitical institution, discussed in chapter 1, and the normative ideal of marriage, discussed in chapter 2. The normative ideal position also endorses the idea that marriage is not a creation of the state, but is something that the state is obliged to protect. Those who support the normative ideal position hold that 'the legal institution of marriage is founded on an antecedent moral conception of marriage'.[21] Thus, the state must protect and promote marriage because it has intrinsic moral worth. What marriage is 'about', according to this conception, is the unity of two persons, which requires monogamy, long-term commitment, sexual fidelity, companionship, economic support, and it also provides the ideal context for childrearing. There is normative tension regarding childrearing, though. On natural law accounts, 'marital unity is partly expressed through procreation and child rearing'.[22] This aligns with traditional heteronormative understandings of marriage and the nuclear family. Advocates of the natural law argument usually oppose same-sex marriage since they think heterosexual marriage ensures children's access to fathers, unites men's and women's complementary natures, and provides a psychologically healthy environment for children.[23] 'On more secular accounts', though, 'the stability of a relationship based on long-term commitment simply provides the ideal environment for child-rearing'.[24] The secular account, then, aligns more closely with dominant arguments which seek to demonstrate that same-sex couples are 'fit' for marriage.

As we saw in chapter 2, these kinds of arguments seek to show that when 'normal' LGBT people form relationships, they do so monogamously and with an eye to long-term commitment. They may also desire to have children and certainly seek to promote the core values of marriage, such as mutual caring and financial support. These LGBTs pose no threat to the institution of marriage. Rather, they would *strengthen* the values that marriage protects. Importantly, then, marriage continues to be understood as '*the* normative ideal for how sexuality, companionship, affection, personal economics, and child rearing should be organised',[25] and this is true even if activists would endorse the introduction of other forms of legal relationship recognition in addition to marriage. Such arguments ultimately aim to show that same-sex couples can fulfil/wish to fulfil the criteria necessary for the spiritual unity that marriage represents, just like different-sex couples. As such, they claim that they should be able to have their relationships equally recognized.

What the marriage-as-normative-ideal position and the political myth have in common is that both posit marriage as something antecedent to the modern state. The political myth holds that marriage ought to be state regulated and privileged since it provides the very foundation for the modern state. That is, the political myth holds that the state could not exist without the continuation of a particular type of familial union: traditional marriage and the nuclear family. The normative-ideal conception similarly finds that marriage ought to be legally protected since it has intrinsic moral worth, which is to say that the features of marriage, such as spiritual unity, long-term commitment, sexual fidelity, and so forth, are intrinsically morally valuable and so must be protected by the state. Thus, for both, 'marriage' exists prior to the state's regulation of it. In one case, marriage is worthy of protection since it is the bedrock of society; in the other, marriage is worthy of protection because it is the home of certain intrinsically valuable mores. It is easily possible, and even likely, then, for these two positions to become conflated and inform each other.

Importantly, on these accounts 'marriage' is something which states or citizens cannot define for themselves. In other words, there is a *correct* or *true* definition of marriage. If 'good' LGBT people can show that they are structuring their relationships and familial life according to the intrinsic requirements of marriage, whatever those requirements may be, no adequate reason remains for the continued exclusion of LGBT people from marriage. The debate thus concerns *which* aspects of the marital relationship have intrinsic worth and *who* can uphold these aspects, not *whether* marriage has intrinsic worth as such. This explains the divergence on childrearing and sex/gender roles between natural law accounts and secular accounts of the normative-ideal position. The political myth argues, likewise, that the nature of marriage was fixed before it was state regulated. Calhoun claims, 'The essential nature of marriage is fixed independently of liberal society—by God, or by human nature, or by the prerequisites for civilization.'[26] All who endorse this myth, whether implicitly or explicitly, therefore agree that the essential nature of marriage is independently fixed and intrinsically good, and it is the foundation for modern society. However, they may disagree on *what* independently fixes the nature of marriage. For example, if one maintains that the Judeo-Christian God determines what counts as marriage, then the answer to this definitional question will likely be found in scripture; if one maintains that 'human nature' or the 'prerequisites of civilization' fix the nature of marriage, the definition may be found in facts of human nature and political societies.[27]

Thus, 'marriage' and 'family' have been turned into matters of definition, and no challenge has been made to the normative position that these institutions hold. As such, it is possible to argue that 'marriage, even if not heterosexual marriage, is unlike other possible voluntary intimate arrangements', and is therefore worthy of hierarchically privileged state endorsement over other legally recognized unions.[28] A combination of the secular normative-ideal position and the political myth underscores this type of argument. Thus, this argument justifies the inclusion of LGBT people in the institution of marriage, positions them as essential citizens, and thereby provides a positive identity to LGBTs. LGBT people who argue in this vein aim to sustain the political myth by undermining the *necessary* heterosexuality of marriage and the family while simultaneously endorsing the other 'values' that marriage protects. This strategy is therefore highly resonant with dominantly held norms and is only marginally critical. It is resonant in its endorsement of meaning-generating narratives of romantic love, while it is critical of the exclusion of same-sex couples from marriage. Because of its high resonance, it is also an expedient argument.

Now, Calhoun acknowledges that if there is a public policy goal of promoting one particular kind of relationship, then 'to pursue marriage rights is to reject the value of pursuing possibly more liberating, if less conventional, sexual, affectional, care-taking, and economic intimate arrangements'.[29] Nonetheless, she endorses 'sameness' arguments which favour same-sex marriage. Her reasoning is as follows:

> Defending same-sex marriage on grounds of state neutrality with respect to individuals' voluntary associations requires only that same-sex marriages be legally permitted *regardless* of how they are morally viewed. Genuine equality for gays and lesbians, however, requires more than merely coming to be tolerated. It requires that we, as a culture, give up the belief that gays and lesbians are unfit to participate in normatively ideal forms of marriage, parenting, and family.[30]

In other words, a position from state neutrality cannot ensure full LGBT acceptance. On this view, same-sex marriage is simply a political and legal requirement. While a given society may tolerate LGBT people on political and legal grounds, Calhoun believes they will not come to be *respected* as legitimate and essential members of that society. Thus, if this argument is correct, we may conclude that only some form of the sameness argument stands a chance of affording (some) LGBT people respect.

It is my belief that traditional marriage and the nuclear family do not differ in any politically or morally significant way from other voluntary caring associations. This is why I reject the position that only one normative ideal of personal relationships and childrearing should be promoted. However, this action itself is not enough. This is because norms bite into the identities of individuals; they have imaginative and affective dimensions that can only be countered by bringing about a change in the way LGBT people are imagined and, consequently, *felt* about. Without a new meaning-generating story, neutrality arguments cannot challenge how LGBT people are morally viewed. A simple presentation of any claim as the 'truth', such as the claim that the normatively imagined family is *not* the bedrock of society, is unlikely to result in social uptake. That is to say, damaging representations of LGBT people cannot be modified with mere legal reform or by simply claiming that their representations are 'false'. Their falsity does not necessarily make them less meaningful.[31]

From Calhoun's perspective, gaining access to marriage while sustaining the political myth and perception of marriage-as-normative-ideal would be *better* for same-sex couples because there is still some kind of moral legitimacy attached to marriage, and only moral legitimacy can bring about a shift in the way LGBT people are perceived and treated. I agree with Calhoun that a simple denial of the political myth of marriage and an emphasis on the socially constructed nature of marriage is likely to be problematic in the aforementioned way, but I will argue that this does not present a problem for the combined approach. I will also argue that sameness arguments are *too resonant*. Retaining the hierarchically privileged status of marriage and opening it up to LGBT people seems unlikely to be the best way to have them recognized as essential citizens. The combined approach can do better. Thus, in order to reject the political myth of marriage and also attempt to achieve LGBT equal regard, I propose another meaning-generating narrative which can be socially shared. I propose the narrative of caring-love teemed with a neutrality justification. This narrative acknowledges that all persons at all stages of their life require, desire, and/or deliver care. We form relationships of caring-love between our (biological) families, our friends, and our intimate partners. We all require emotional and physical support, and we seek to provide this to the people we care about. Moreover, we are social creatures—we live intersubjective existences. Care is fundamental to our flourishing as intersubjective individuals. Care is universal, and care can (and does) come in many formulations. Importantly, it is not farfetched to assume that care is something all persons already value (or in the very least need) to some degree, so why not bring it into the spotlight?

III. JUSTIFYING SAME-SEX MARRIAGE IN THE COMBINED APPROACH

A theory like the combined approach would reject the political myth of marriage and deny that marriage has any intrinsic value. What the combined approach demands is the *equivalent* right to be recognized fully in those relationships which the state chooses to regulate. What unions should be recognized is an additional question; I propose that caring unions are suitable candidates, since care is a basic human need. Furthermore, those who do not choose to mimic the lifestyle patterns of traditional heterosexuals should not need to justify to anyone why this is the case. This allows for people to consider the ways that social norms and laws have pressed for one model of relationship recognition rather than others and creates an option for people to make other legitimate interpersonal choices based on what may suit their needs and desires.[32]

Given the constructivism at the core of the combined approach to human rights, there is no need to search for the 'true' or 'correct' definition of marriage. Rather, the institution of marriage is understood as a construction (or, rather, a reconstruction) according to norms which are justifiable on the grounds of reciprocity, generality, and historical context. The combined approach may recognize that several features of traditional marriage and nuclear family life are valuable to the state and its citizens, but it can also question whether this normatively privileged social institution is the *only* such valuable structure. This style of argument would still position LGBT people as essential citizens, but in a different way. They can be seen as essential citizens insofar as they are recognized as equal participants in the creation of norms that all must live by—participants who are partial and need not deny the differences that exist between themselves. LGBTs being deemed essential citizens stems from a rethinking of difference and a commitment to the basic right to justification.

Importantly, the combined approach *already* attempts to account for the imaginative aspects of LGBT people's claims for equality. That is to say, it is not a strict neutrality argument. The combined approach attempts to actively generate new stories about who 'counts' as an essential citizen and why. According to the combined approach, the essential citizen is any person capable of giving and receiving justifying reasons in respect of their (potential for) difference(s) *between* Others. This holds resonance with the strong ideal of the equal dignity of all persons. Calhoun worries that to deny the political myth amounts to asking for legal equality *in spite of* the fact that LGBT people are still largely viewed as immoral, perverse, enemies of the family, and the like. I agree that such an outcome would be problematic and undesirable. But this is not a consequence of the combined approach. The combined approach demands legal equality *in recognition of* the real and potential differences between subjects, given the criteria of reciprocity and generality.

Although dominant arguments in favour of same-sex marriage assert the normality of being same-sex attracted, the combined approach is specifically designed to ensure that LGBT people can gain rights without basing their appeal on sameness. First of all, Rainer Forst's basic right to justification shifts the onus of proof onto those who would deny same-sex marriage and maintain the status quo. Since there are no justifiable reasons to deny same-sex couples entry to this institution, legal reform is morally and legally required. The combined approach also proposes the notion of 'equivalent rights' to account for adequate recognition of (the potential for) difference(s). Determining when equivalent rights are appropriate would require an assessment of the sources of inequality; specifically, whether the inequalities were the result of a comparison to phallocentric systems of order. For example, LGBT people can demand equivalent rights because their identities have heretofore been wrongly compared to a biased model of human subjectivity. The combined approach holds that marked persons should not be made to feel shame for their inability to match this biased standard, especially since no legitimate justification can be offered for its continuation as an implicit marker of humanity.

In addition, the combined approach, with its emphasis on starting from the particular historical moment in which a rights claim emerges, illuminates contradictions between imaginaries. Real families are expanding and diversifying in form and have been doing so for decades. The acknowledgement of this fact rubs against our shared normative notions of what the (traditional) family looks like and forces us to think about care more actively. This is a productive contradiction because it can produce and support a perception of alternative and non-Eurocentric families as horizontally valuable based on the reconceptualization of difference in terms of an A/B figuration. It can therefore also produce a dominantly shared normative commitment to protecting such diversified families. This would be better not only for those who find themselves perceived as victims of 'broken' families (such as divorcees) but also those who may not desire to attempt a 'traditional' relationship at all.

The combined approach can therefore be seen to endorse a 'pluralization strategy', which promotes multiple kinds of familial and intimate relationships that could be deemed horizontally worthy of state protection. Such relationships could include monogamous but less binding intimacies, polyamorous sexual relationships, various relationships of care including two or more adults, and so forth. The combined approach therefore invites us to think about the ways norms and laws press one model of intimacy on people, and it challenges that model by denying the *prepolitical* value of marriage. The combined approach claims instead that many associations (including same-sex associations) are instrumentally valuable to society and as such they are worth regulating. The fundamental value at play here is care.

An interesting legal development which supports the aim of pluralization is the Relationships Act of 2003 (Tasmania). This relationship recognition scheme purposefully tries to distance itself from the marriage model. Relationships Tasmania state, 'The Tasmanian relationships registry moves us beyond this narrow view of relationships, placing the emphasis instead on love and commitment wherever it is found.'[33] It does this by allowing for the legal recognition of both 'significant relationships' and 'caring relationships'. Significant relationships are sexually intimate relationships akin to marriage but less legally binding—this is Tasmania's version of a civil union. The caring relationship is a relationship where two people, whether related or not by family, and of any sex, who are not in a relationship as a couple but do provide domestic support and personal care to each other, can be legally recognized.[34] This might be, for example, two single mothers who are not involved in a sexual relationship but have decided to throw in their lot together in order to alleviate financial burdens and burdens of child care. Or this may be two sisters who wish to have legal documentation proving that they are each other's next of kin so that other family members may not overrule their wishes in the case of a medical emergency. The recognition of these types of relationships, ones that are not romantic-love relationships, is an exciting development given the goals of the pluralization strategy. While this registry is still limited, it is clearly a step in the right direction and ought to be promoted, meaning it should be emphasized in the media, in advertising, in fiction, in personal anecdotes, in education, and so on. Indeed, caring relationships and the possibility of pluralization are important to consider, as it is unclear how many people, whether heterosexual or homosexual, would continue to desire and participate in traditional marriage if other kinds of relationships became horizontally valued in the dominant shared Western social imaginary.

Thus, what ultimately gets put into circulation via this type of argument is the conception that, although *traditional marriage* may be a significant institution which values nuclear familial relationships, affection, mutual support, and so on, marriage is not the *only* possible relationship type which may be worthy of equivalent sociopolitical and legal respect. In other words, the combined approach explicitly rejects the assumption that marriage should be regarded as hierarchically superior to other kinds of relationships. If one were to circulate the combined approach, one may claim that 'civil societies depend only in the most general way on its citizens having the capacities for and interest in casting their personal lot with others and sharing, in voluntary private arrangements, sex, affection, reproduction, economic support, and care for the young, the infirm and the elderly'.[35] It would hold this to be true while still advocating that, in a sociopolitical context, familial structures play an important role. Thus, the combined approach *does not deny the value of familial relationships*; what is important is that this role may be fulfilled by a variety of interpersonal structures. It has *resonance* with the growing recognition of the value and worth of nontraditional families (already common among some nonwhite groups), as well as with the well-established ideology of equality in dignity, without denying that traditionally structured marriage and family are valuable.

Ultimately, my argument for same-sex marriage, based on the combined approach, takes the following shape: There is a basic commitment to all people as having equal status qua members of the human community. There is a general acknowledgement that a potential for difference exists *between* us and that such difference is radically Other and irreducible to a standard of the 'same'. There is also the history of LGBT discrimination in the West, stemming from a designation of LGBT people as Other. This Othering occurs by comparison to the implicitly biased human subject (now identified as a false universal) dictated by phallocentric logic. As a constructivist theory, this argument denies the *intrinsic* status of marriage as a prepolitical, hierarchically, and morally superior form of union. Yet, many traditional and nontraditional features of intimate relationships may be deemed useful or valuable to the state and its citizens, and the state ought to recognize several unions as horizontally valuable. Furthermore, if same-sex couples demand entry to the institution of marriage specifically, the onus is on those who would deny their claim to give justifying reasons for this denial. In other words, LGBT people need not prove that they are just like heteronormative couples in order to be worthy of legal protections and benefits. They may also choose not to enter this institution without having to justify this decision.

The reasons opposing same-sex marriage will be deemed unjustifiable because they are predicated upon prejudiced beliefs that effectively deny people's basic human status. Thus, entry to marriage is a right owed to LGBT people since there are no reciprocal or general reasons to justify their exclusion and since failure to extend this right would be an action of disrespect towards those LGBT people who are rightly owed second-order appreciation. The second-order appreciation which LGBT people are owed in recognition of difference reflects their status as essential citizens who have the right to participate in the construction of the norms that all are to live by. Furthermore, this position promotes an alternative meaning-generating narrative which seeks to value multiple forms of intimacies and families and which matches the growth of alternative families in the West throughout recent decades. Given these empirical changes to 'normal' families, the combined approach's meaning-generating narrative may be likely to gain much traction if it is widely promoted. There are many varieties of families and intimate relationships emerging, and the combined approach seeks a positive encounter with real and potential difference(s). This position, then, generates positive, meaning-generating beliefs which will encourage social change in the present, and it also holds resonance with the liberal value of equal respect for basic human status.

However, the combined approach is less resonant than sameness arguments for same-sex marriage. That means it is less likely to naturally gain dominant uptake. But because the combined approach cultivates a new narrative which can generate shared social meaning and is more likely to result in the equal regard of LGBT people, it *must* be actively promoted instead of arguments based on sameness. The combined approach needs to become a dominant perspective, which cannot occur without the circulation of its alternative meaning-generating story. Even if arguments like those proposed in chapter 2 would more expediently realize the goal of legal marriage equality, it would do so at the expense of circulating arguments and images of LGBT people which may ultimately perpetuate their stigmatized identity as marked persons and fuel negative stereotypes. Thus, marriage equality would come at the expense of the goal of equal regard. This is unacceptable. It is for this reason that the combined approach ought to be promoted. While Calhoun argues for the most resonant approach, a combined approach undertaken in the justification of same-sex marriage is more appropriate. The combined approach reconceives difference and relationships *between* subjects such that marriage and 'competing' intimacies are considered outside of the order of the same. This entails a different commitment to the recognition of (the potential for) difference(s). It can counter the way that LGBT people are imagined and *felt* about.

IV. A NOTE ON PLURALIZATION

Thus far I have argued in favour of a pluralization strategy, but what would such a strategy look like in practice? It is important to state explicitly that there is no 'one size fits all' specification of pluralization. Because the combined approach utilizes an intersubjective justification theory, this means that it is up to the individual members of individual states to specify how pluralization should look. I have already mentioned Tasmania's Relationships Act 2003 and claimed that this illustrates an exciting possibility for further recognition. However, there are multiple conceivable models which could be employed. Creating multiple institutions which recognize a variety of caring relationships is one such possibility. One may also propose a system of contracts or something akin to 'minimal marriage'.

Marriage is an interesting institution, being both a form of contract and the designator of status. Elizabeth Brake's proposal for minimal marriage retains both of these features, but it is marriage largely deregulated. Minimal marriage recognizes care as a political good and designates status based on this recognition. It is also an inclusive form of marriage since the state cannot justify restricting marriage only to those participating in heterosexual, monogamous unions (on the grounds of political liberalism). Thus, the proposal for minimal marriage holds that 'individuals can have legal marital relationships with more than one person, reciprocally or asymmetrically, themselves determining the sex and number of parties, the type of relationship involved, and which rights and responsibilities to exchange with each.'[36] Brake insists that this is not simple contractualization. Several feminists have argued that replacing marriage with a free contract would not be beneficial to women insofar as they consistently have less bargaining power than men. Moreover, contractualization can legitimize oppressive forms of marriage.[37] If minimal marriage were wholly contractualist, it would argue against a state definition of marriage in any form. The terms and conditions would be wholly up to the individuals who participated in it. Instead, only those relationships that perform a certain function (the function of care) can count as marriages.

There is no denying, though, that minimal marriage is much closer to a system of contracts than present marriage law. Prospective spouses would be given a list of entitlements which they can assign as desired. In other words, each adult individual has a number of benefits which can be consensually given to one or several people. Similarly, that same individual may be consensually obliged to perform certain duties which are bestowed upon them by one or several people. For example, Jason may be Tom's next of kin and obliged to care for Tom's biological child in the event of his death, while Tom may be the next of kin to and be obliged to care for the children of Jason, Abbey, and Bridget in the event of their deaths. Tom may also be married to Cameron, insofar as Cameron receives the partner benefits of Tom's health care plan. Tom may also be married to Dianna, with whom he owns a house and shares day-to-day living expenses. Now, Brake does stipulate that minimal marriage would have to face reasonable limits. There are only so many people a person can genuinely care for. But the level of care that is required is unclear. Is the level of care sufficient if Tom only cares about Dianna's home life (ensuring that she does not live on the street, for example) without caring about her professional life in any capacity? Similarly, if Tom only cares that Abbey's and Bridget's children have a safe environment to live in the event of their death, but not about Abbey's or Bridget's general happiness, is this level of care sufficient? If it is, then a person may be potentially married to a large quantity of people, and minimal marriage looks very much like the contractualization of marriage indeed, for it is unclear that any two people's marriages would look alike.

Contractualization aside, would it be better in principle to attempt to reform marriage to make the institution more just or to provide a selection of institutions which recognize caring relationships to make society more just? This depends on the history of exclusion from marriage and the historical importance and role of marriage. It is a question of what work the name 'marriage' does, and a question of what narratives are circulated about care. As Brake rightly points out, resistance to calling other caring unions 'marriages' has been one central way to deny the significance, legitimacy, and value of such relationships. As such, she argues, 'Extending the application of "marriage" is one way of rectifying part of the discrimination against homosexuals, bisexuals, polygamists, and care networks.'[38] Thus, it may seem that minimal marriage is the way to go. Let us reform marriage so that it is a just institution. However, I am not sure that minimizing marriage will encourage the normative shift that I seek, and if this is true, then extending the nomenclature is not as useful as one would hope it to be. Legally, those who do structure their relationships differently would be recognized according to minimal marriage law, but what impetus is there to circulate counternarratives about alternative care networks? It seems to me that the best way to encourage equal regard is to recognize that there are no grounds on which to deny same-sex marriage while simultaneously pushing for the existence of more unions, like civil unions and caring relationships, which are open to people of any sex and vary depending on the benefits and obligations they confer. We should also recognize that some people do genuinely want legal recognition without being saddled by the nomenclature and the stereotypes and assumptions this calls to mind.[39] Changing 'marriage' is not necessarily to move away from the primacy of normative marriage, but creating alternative legally recognized unions and endorsing them may well be more likely to reduce the primacy of 'traditional marriage'.

Whether we open up marriage or whether we have marriages, civil unions, caring relationships, contracts, and more, what matters at the end of the day is equal regard. Equal regard is linked to symbolic representation of LGBT persons and can only come about via effecting shifts in the social imaginary. To achieve equal regard, we need to move away from sameness arguments, and we need to stress the remaining resonant elements of the debate. This involves the mobilization of counternarratives that resonate with but also critique and challenge aspects of the mainstream imaginary. The counternarrative is that of caring-love. Care is a basic human need, and it is a need which remains with us, on and off, throughout the entirety of our lives. Moreover, people are practicing care in various ways—this shouldn't be seen as anything less valuable than marriage. On this, Brake and I agree.

Importantly, at the heart of the combined approach is a counternarrative that involves a radical philosophical reconceptualization of difference itself. This counternarrative pushes for the recognition of plural intimacies and relationships of care, while simultaneously justifying why same-sex couples ought to have access to marriage. It does this by advocating equivalent rights. Thus, it is not true of the combined approach to say that defending same-sex marriage 'requires only that same-sex marriages be legally permitted *regardless* of how they are morally viewed'.[40] This is because, although the combined approach does seek state neutrality for intimate relationships, it does so based on LGBT people coming to be positively morally viewed or held with equal regard.

What is to be acknowledged is the following: arguments with high resonance to dominant norms may encourage new systems of social inclusion and exclusion; however, arguments with less resonance—like the combined approach—could work towards the end of equal regard. This is what has been and will always remain at stake in the same-sex marriage debate. Thus, access to marriage is not desirable if it fails to question the place of 'traditional' marriage as hierarchically ideal or 'normal'. Conceiving of same-sex marriage under the combined approach, then, will best allow for the greater sociopolitical and legal situation of LGBT people overall. It is for this reason that the combined approach must be promoted—so that the contradictions it reveals may yield the possibility for change in the present in the direction of a more just future. Same-sex marriage is merely one aspect among many which may contribute to greater overall respect for LGBT people.

NOTES

1. Marcel Stoetzler and Nira Yuval-Davis, 'Standpoint Theory, Situated Knowledge and the Situated Imagination', *Feminist Theory* 3, no. 3 (2002): 327.
2. Moira Gatens, 'Can Human Rights Accommodate Women's Rights? Towards an Embodied Account of Social Norms, Social Meaning, and Cultural Change', *Contemporary Political Theory* 3, no. 3 (2004): 275–99.
3. Cheshire Calhoun, *Feminism, the Family, and the Politics of the Closet: Lesbian and Gay Displacement* (Oxford: Oxford University Press, 2000), chap. 5.
4. Stoetzler and Yuval-Davis, 'Standpoint Theory'; Gatens, 'Can Human Rights Accommodate Women's Rights?'.
5. Susan James, 'Freedom and the Imaginary', in *Visible Women: Essays on Feminist Legal Theory and Political Philosophy*, ed. Susan James and Stephanie Palmer (Oxford: Hart Publishing, 2002), 175–95.
6. Michael Warner, *The Trouble with Normal: Sex, Politics, and the Ethics of Queer Life* (Cambridge, MA: Harvard University Press, 1999), 27.
7. This is, of course, unless they are accused of homosexuality and face misdirected homophobia.
8. Georgia Warnke, *After Identity* (Cambridge: Cambridge University Press, 20070, chap. 2.
9. Gatens, 'Can Human Rights Accommodate Women's Rights?'.
10. Ibid.
11. Ibid. See also Joan Wallach Scott, *Only Paradoxes to Offer: French Feminists and the Rights of Man* (Cambridge, MA: Harvard University Press, 1996), chap. 2, and Carole Pateman, *The Sexual Contract* (Stanford, CA: Stanford University Press, 1988), chap. 8.
12. Gatens, 'Can Human Rights Accommodate Women's Rights?'.
13. Ibid.
14. Cheshire Calhoun, 'Who's Afraid of Polygamous Marriage? Lessons for Same-Sex Marriage Advocacy from the History of Polygamy', *San Diego Law Review* 42 (2005): 1033.
15. Gatens, 'Can Human Rights Accommodate Women's Rights?' 287.
16. Stoetzler and Yuval-Davis, 'Standpoint Theory'.
17. My choice to focus on *Feminism, the Family, and the Politics of the Closet* deserves qualification. In a later article, Calhoun discusses the reasons why advocates for same-sex marriage and polygamy would do well to support each other's movements. While there is only a minor thread within the Judeo-Christian marriage tradition that has recognized same-sex marriages (which can be dismissed as a 'negligible blip'), polygamist relationships are 'part of a millenias-long *pluralist* Judeo-Christian tradition of marriage' (Calhoun, 'Who's Afraid of Polygamous Marriage?' 1029–30; original emphasis). Because the Judaeo-Christian tradition does not have a monolithic history of heterosexual monogamous marriage, and because Western liberal societies aim to protect individuals' liberty to pursue a plurality of goods, it seems that the state should, in fact, support nonmonogamous and nonheterosexual marriages. At first glance, this argument appears to contradict Calhoun's position in *Feminism, the Family, and the Politics of the Closet*. But this discussion of same-sex marriage is primarily concerned with the movement's *ideal* form of articulation when debated within academic circles. Importantly, Calhoun does not find these ideal (or utopian) arguments appropriate for the political realm as they are not *politically expedient*. Political expediency favours emphasizing sameness to heteronormative married couples and maintaining LGBT distance from polygamist (and indeed, polyamorous) partnerships. Thus, there are three reasons why I focus on Calhoun's earlier work. First, her position actually remains consistent between both texts: Calhoun ulti-

mately endorses the politically expedient approach to same-sex marriage, reserving the utopian argument for academic debates. Second, Calhoun consistently understands plural possible relationships by comparison to traditional marriage across the two texts. Heterosexual, monogamous marriage is the marker of legitimacy, and competing relationships must prove why they, too, are legitimate. Third, the earlier text is more substantive.

18. Calhoun, *Feminism, the Family*, 95.

19. Ibid., 123. See also Diane Richardson, 'Locating Sexualities: From Here to Normality', *Sexualities* 7 (2004): 391–411.

20. Calhoun, *Feminism, the Family*, 124.

21. Ibid., 110.

22. Ibid.

23. Warnke, *After Identity*, chap. 6.

24. Calhoun, *Feminism, the Family*, 110.

25. Ibid., 110.

26. Ibid., 127.

27. Ibid.

28. Ibid., 129.

29. Ibid., 113. This is Calhoun's *academic* position on same-sex marriage and polygamy. See Calhoun, 'Who's Afraid of Polygamous Marriage?'

30. Calhoun, *Feminism, the Family*, 130; emphasis added.

31. Gatens, 'Can Human Rights Accommodate Women's Rights?'

32. Elizabeth Emens, 'Just Monogamy?' in *Just Marriage*, ed. Mary Lyndon Shanley (Oxford: Oxford University Press, 2004), 79.

33. Relationships Tasmania, 'Caring Couples', accessed 2 November 2014, http://www.relationshipstasmania.com/caringcouples.html.

34. Ibid.

35. Calhoun, *Feminism, the Family*, 129.

36. Elizabeth Brake, 'Minimal Marriage: What Political Liberalism Implies for Marriage Law', *Ethics* 120, no. 2 (2010): 303.

37. Ibid. See also Mary Lyndon Shanley, 'Just Marriage: On the Public Importance of Private Unions', in *Just Marriage*, ed. Mary Lyndon Shanley (Oxford: Oxford University Press, 2004), 3–30.

38. Brake, 'Minimal Marriage', 323.

39. Kees Waaldijk, 'Small Change: How the Road to Same-Sex Marriage Got Paved in the Netherlands', in *Legal Recognition of Same-Sex Partnership: A Study of National, European and International Law*, ed. R. Wintemute and M. Andenæs (Oxford: Hart Publishing, 2001), 437–64.

40. Calhoun, *Feminism, the Family*, 130.

Conclusion

Reflections on Same-Sex Marriage

The key concern of this book has been whether or not same-sex marriage, articulated as a right, would be able to assist in ending social discrimination towards LGBTs. I have endeavoured to show that a feminist human rights framework can justify same-sex marriage without requiring assimilation and can also challenge the characterization of homosexuality as immoral. Indeed, I argued that a combined approach, which utilizes aspects of the politics of sexuate difference and the intersubjective justification theory, can provide a stronger and more transformative vision for the ultimate goal of equal regard than standard rights-based justifications of same-sex marriage. I asserted that what LGBTs require and what they are rightly owed is the end of stigmatization, the fostering of their identities, and the cultivation of difference. What matters, in other words, is LGBT people coming to be respected as sexual citizens.

In chapter 1, I analyzed whether it would be possible for activists to make a human rights claim for same-sex marriage based on the grounds set out in the Universal Declaration of Human Rights 1948 (UDHR) and the implications of doing so. I noted that two implications were particularly relevant: First, appealing to human rights need not challenge the characterization of homosexuality as immoral in order to be successful; second, appealing to human rights may be assimilative in character. I also considered the pattern of small change and the emerging transnational soft law norm of same-sex relationship recognition. We saw that law reform will only be perceived as acceptable if the legal change is small, and so not a threat to the dominant heteronormative way of life, or if it is accompanied by some other legal change which reinforces the superiority of the heteronormative way of life.

Eventually, however, these legal changes accumulate. This can result not only in a significant shift in the legal status of LGBTs over time but also in a shift in the normative status of LGBTs in society.

Just how significant this shift is depends on the arguments we circulate and the conceptions of homosexuality they assume. This indicates that serious assessment should be given to the symbolic weight of the push for marriage and the meanings attached to it as a normative institution which shapes and regulates behaviour. Importantly, empirical evidence elucidating instances of homophobic discrimination would attest that marriage itself is not a reliable indicator of changing attitudes towards LGBTs. I concluded that the same-sex marriage movement, as it stands, presents a bleak outlook for LGBT activists who seek equal regard. If LGBT acceptance is predicated on likeness to the heteronormative mainstream, and if law reform is only awarded in small, homogenizing normative steps, then *at best* this approach will redraw the boundaries of acceptability to include only *some* LGBT people. I therefore proposed that legal changes should be made *with regard for* sexual orientation, not *in spite of* sexual orientation.

In chapter 2, I went on to explore dominant justifications of same-sex marriage. These arguments primarily stress a romantic-love narrative, focusing on the 'relevant' similarities between same-sex and different-sex couples. I also considered in depth the personhood account of human rights, which was introduced briefly in chapter 1 and appeared to have some intuitive appeal as a justification for same-sex marriage based on the ground of liberty. The personhood account takes it to be a natural fact that normative agents reflect, assess, and make decisions in such a way that it accords with their perception of the good life. On this account, human rights are grounded in the protection of people's normative agency, where agency is to be understood as a capacity to conceive of and pursue this good life. Now, for something to be successful as a liberty claim, it has to pass certain constraints. Particularly, it has to be shown that the claim must significantly affect whether or not one functions as a normative agent. However, this is not shown to be true of marriage; rather, it is assumed. Same-sex marriage is supposedly justified under a paucity of options, but it remains unclear why this option should be deemed necessary for the good life. To accept this argument, a lot of normative content has to be assumed of marriage and its relationship to the good life. Yet this argument can be criticized for lacking any justification for assuming that marriage (or marriage-like relationships) are so valuable. Thus, even though the personhood account claims to justify same-sex marriage on the ground of liberty, it too is implicitly assuming the romantic-love narrative, which plays into the interpretation of marriage as passing the material constraint.

The personhood account is just one of many justifications for same-sex marriage which presume that the standard of sameness between same-sex couples and different-sex couples is relevant. But when arguments are circulated which stress the 'sameness' of different-sex and same-sex couples, this can only achieve a sham of equality and the illusion of progress, while real instances of homophobia, discrimination, marginalization, and hostility towards LGBT people continue. This is because same-sex couples *are* different to different-sex couples. They are different in at least one way, that is, the types of participants in the couple are not the same in both instances. I suggested that *at best* the assimilative approach simply redraws the boundaries of acceptability to include some LGBT people, but this does not amount to equal regard. Considering that a key goal of LGBT activists has been to end discrimination against LGBTs as a collective, it should be noted that potential nondiscrimination of some at the expense of others is not an acceptable outcome. Assimilative arguments are generally troublesome since they prevent the cultivation of difference(s) and the fostering of LGBT identities. Nonetheless, this exploration of the personhood account has provided two valuable insights. The first is that we need better philosophical justifications for same-sex marriage. An account justifying same-sex marriage ought to (a) oblige those who are able to introduce same-sex marriage to do so, irrespective of their personal inclinations; (b) not assume that marriage is an intrinsically worthy institution worthy of reproduction; (c) have a socially comparative element balanced by a critical component; and (d) take into account the history of LGBT discrimination. The second is that such a justification needs to be widely circulated and easily accessible. Presently, it is assimilative arguments that have the widest platform.

However, it was also necessary to explore whether rights discourse has the capacity to shore up equal regard for LGBTs in the first instance. This was the focus of chapter 3. There, we saw that although the unstable concept of legal personhood allows all human beings to be persons for some purposes, some people are far more effective legal actors than others. In fact, the 'healthiest' legal person possesses the attributes of the 'normal' human subject—white, heterosexual, male, able-bodied, rational, autonomous, and so on—and he sets the status quo in the legal sphere. This observation is crucially important when considering the politico-legal claims of LGBT people, and of marked persons generally, since the power to determine what is (or can be) normative is overwhelmingly claimed by the 'benchmark man'. This produces 'paradoxes' for marked persons. The first paradox was that when marked persons claim they deserve rights *as marked persons* this can result in the construction of their rights as 'special rights', as well as lock them into their identity as subordinates. The second paradox pertains to difficulties with the formal equality approach, which can result in marked persons failing to achieve adequate recognition in an already unequal society. Both problems may have perverse social and political effects. A third paradox emerges between marked persons as groups. Because of the diversity that exists within groups, the presentation of a united front can mean many people go unrepresented. Alternatively, and this is the final paradox, making an identity so thin that it can account for all differences can result in the inability to articulate concrete unifying issues, dissolving group identity.

However, there is no reason to presume that these paradoxes are irresolvable. If rights for LGBT people result in paradoxical consequences, then we should believe that our reasoning is faulty or that such consequences have occurred based on the adoption of false assumptions. Having investigated the ways that marked persons are constructed, I concluded that rights are delegated on a faulty system of recognition using a single-axis framework and but-for reasoning. To combat this issue, difference must be reconceived. A challenge must be posed to the way LGBTs are conceived in the dominant shared Western social imaginary alongside the call for legal reform. I proposed that we revise our approach to (the possibility of) difference(s), blurring the limits of categorical identifications and remaining open to difference(s) not yet experienced. Instead of applying binary logic to the categories 'heterosexual' and 'homosexual', I suggested the law would do better to understand such a difference as an A/B distinction. It is thus to be understood as truly different, not as the other of the same.

In chapter 4, I considered whether discursive constructivism could be utilized to build a feminist theory of human rights that would meet the aforementioned criteria. I analyzed the intersubjective justification theory proposed by Rainer Forst, noting that it goes some way to achieving this goal. The intersubjective justification theory holds that one fundamental human right lies behind all other rights claims: the basic right to justification. The basic right to justification is the primary right of all people to give and receive justifications for the norms that they are each to live by. To be treated with dignity, on this account, means to be treated as a person equally owed and owing justificatory reasons when called on. When this process is respected, people are able to act with and be recognized as having moral autonomy. This process of giving and receiving justifying reasons is what legitimizes the social norms which all are to live by. The criteria that determine a moral norm's legitimacy, and therefore establish a human right, are 'reciprocity' and 'generality'. However, reciprocity and generality cannot be taken alone. One must also consider the historically situated context in which specific rights claims arise and give weight to empirical considerations. This will bring to light any history of privilege or exclusion, which will then inform the legitimacy of norms and their justifications. All norms are constructed this way: they are established in an intersubjective realm of ongoing dialogue and exchange.

The intersubjective justification theory justifies same-sex marriage by claiming that 'a society where the institution of marriage is reserved for some couples and denied to others without reciprocally justifiable reasons violates the demands of reciprocity'.[1] The criteria of reciprocity and generality, as well as the history of sociopolitical and legal exclusion that has disadvantaged LGBTs, establish the conclusion that there is no reason to maintain LGBT inequality via a bar to marriage. As such, LGBTs are owed access to marriage as a matter of right. This theory need not consider the *value* of marriage whatsoever. What is significant is that some citizens have demanded justifying reasons for why they are excluded from a certain institution, and sufficient reasons are unable to be given. This approach is appealing for an additional reason, too. The intersubjective justification theory shifts the onus of proof from those making the claim to those who would continue to deny the claim. This reduces the likelihood of relying on a notion of sameness to gain rights and respect, which is to say, it prevents the need for LGBT assimilation. It forces those who are privileged to be accountable for their situation. The privileged must answer to the disadvantaged by providing generally acceptable reasons. Thus, if LGBTs demand equal access to marriage, it is upon those who would continue to deny this claim to justify why this is the case and to remedy the situation if such a justification cannot be provided.

However, some issues remain with the intersubjective justification theory. Although it is socially comparative, Forst's version does not offer a strong enough critical component. This is evidenced by Forst's appeal to the relevant sameness of same-sex and different-sex couples when evaluating the reciprocal acceptability of the claim for same-sex marriage. Fortunately, though, this assumption is not inherent to the theory. Secondly, Forst refers to justified differences in legal recognition as 'special rights', recalling the first paradox discussed in chapter 3. These two difficulties are born of the fact that Forst's intersubjective justification theory does not explicitly involve a reconception of difference, which amounts to a third overarching difficulty. A final issue is Forst's recommendation that same-sex marriage be tolerated in accordance with the 'respect conception of tolerance'. 'Respect' in this context means recognizing the other person as being entitled to equal rights simply as an active member of the sociopolitical community and *qua* human; it does not mean respecting their personal identities or practices as such. To be a candidate for tolerance, the practice or conviction must be deemed objectionable according to *reasons which are sufficiently defensible*. Grossly irrational and immoral prejudices must be excluded. But to tolerate LGBTs and their practices is not acceptable since the reasons they are deemed objectionable are not sufficiently defensible—they are based on prejudice. The stigma attached to LGBT identities and the shame attached to their sex acts can only be justified by a comparison to 'normal' heterosexual identities and sex acts, which is problematic since these standards can only be considered normal by reference to a past history in which they have been construed as normal. This is tautological, and thus invalid. More importantly, not only is tolerance an inappropriate response, it is likely that practicing tolerance would condemn LGBTs to a condition of sociocultural, stigmatizing 'deviance'. This is because tolerance only requires that someone shows restraint in his or her actions, without changing his or her way of thinking.

Taking the intersubjective justification theory as a prototype for building a feminist human rights account, I went on to consider the politics of sexuate difference in chapter 5. I proposed that the politics of sexuate difference offers reflections on encountering difference which can be entwined with the intersubjective justification theory in order to re-cognize and reimagine how LGBT difference should be encountered. That is to say, the intersubjective justification theory is *compatible* with a reconception of difference. When undertaken, this enhances the scope of the necessary critical component. Luce Irigaray strives to imagine difference through an A/B figuration rather than A/not-A binary logic, maintaining a position of openness to difference. From this, we can encourage a shift from recognizing the Other as 'different-from' to recognizing Others as 'diverse-between'. Thus, the politics of sexuate difference illuminates in greater detail why opposition to same-sex marriage should be characterized as prejudicial: we cannot keep imagining difference through the A/not-A binary schema, assessing the worth of LGBT people only insofar as they match a partial conception of ideal humanity. It is necessary to abandon the neutral universal subject altogether if one is to attempt the transformation of the dominant symbolic order of an entire culture and thus to shore up equal regard. As such, Irigaray seeks to think (through) two; this model is a purposeful and strategic approach to relieving matters of unjustified social and political exclusion.

Chapter 5 also called for equivalent rights. Equivalence is defined as 'of equal value' but not necessarily because of likeness. Equivalent rights ensure equal opportunity for those who have been systematically discriminated against. They seek to target and alter unjustified biased perspectives regarding homosexuality. I proposed two such equivalent rights in the fight for same-sex marriage: first, LGBTs should be given the equivalent right to be recognized fully in those relationships which the state chooses to regulate, and second, those who do not choose to mimic the life patterns of traditional heterosexuals need not justify to anyone why this is the case. When employing equivalent rights, it must be to the end of combating the prevalence of detrimental stereotypes and the shame which can be associated with them. The language of 'equivalence' is thus employed to ensure that these rights are perceived as legitimately owed rights rather than as special privileges.

Having supplemented the intersubjective justification theory with insights from the politics of sexuate difference, the combined feminist approach to human rights begins to take shape. It holds that all people are to be acknowledged as potentially differing persons who exist intersubjectively. These people of potential differences, having basic equal status, are entitled to contribute to the establishment of certain norms that they will have to live by. However, to ensure the equal regard of human subjects who already exist in historically situated contexts, formally equal rights may not be sufficient. Laws which are formally *unequal* but *equivalent* can be enacted in order to ensure equal regard among all persons when required. These rights would allow disadvantaged persons an opportunity to become equivalent by means more appropriate to their contextualized situation. The basic commitment to equal regard, demanded in instances of identity discrimination, reveals that the denial of rights to marked persons is in fact prejudiced and insupportable. This is so because the basic demand is for a revised understanding of and encounter with *difference itself*. Thus, the combined approach I propose articulates the demand for recognition in difference while simultaneously making claims for equivalent political and legal recognition.

In chapter 6, I explored the five factors necessary for change: widespread desire, contradictions in shared imaginaries, time, resonance, and critique. With reference to these five factors, I elucidated the justification that the combined approach would provide for same-sex marriage. It is clear that widespread desire for change exists in the West. It is both a desire for marriage, where it is not yet legal, and a desire for nondiscrimination even in states where same-sex marriage is available. It is also clear that there are contradictions in our shared imaginaries. In particular, the citizenship narrative of the West understands all people to be free and equal in dignity and rights, while the natural law conception of marriage (for example) holds that marriage is intrinsically good and requires one man and one woman by definition. These worldviews are in tension, and LGBT activists have been pushing these tensions to their logical limits by employing a variety of arguments and circulating a number of alternative narratives. One such narrative is the narrative of sameness, as we saw previously. Assimilative arguments attempt to demonstrate the similarities between same-sex and different-sex relationships while dismissing the differences as irrelevant. This type of argument has high resonance because it is so similar to the dominantly endorsed narrative of romantic love. This also means that endorsing sameness arguments is likely to be politically expedient. However, arguments can be too resonant with dominant norms, resulting in little change in the direction of nondiscrimination, and as such, I held that the most expedient argument is not always the best argument to endorse. Critique is essential in order to ensure change in the direction of equal regard.

The combined approach instead argues that there is a basic commitment to all people having equal status qua members of the human community. It acknowledges that a potential for difference exists between us and that such difference is radically other and irreducible to a standard of the 'same'. It also takes into account the history of LGBT discrimination in the West, which stems from a designation of LGBT people as Other. This Othering occurs through a comparison to the implicitly biased human subject, as dictated by phallocentric logic. Because it is a constructivist theory, this argument denies the intrinsic status of marriage as a prepolitical, hierarchically and morally superior form of union, but it also regards many traditional and nontraditional features of intimate relationships as useful or valuable to the state and its citizens. Thus, the state ought to recognize multiple unions as horizontally valuable. Furthermore, if and when same-sex couples demand entry to the institution of marriage, the onus is on those who would deny this claim to give justifying reasons for maintaining the status quo. In other words, LGBT people need not prove that they are just like heteronormative couples in order to be worthy of legal protections and benefits. LGBTs (and non-normative heterosexuals) may also choose not to enter this institution without having to justify this decision.

In addition, this position promotes an alternative meaning-generating narrative which seeks to value multiple forms of intimacies and families. Importantly, this matches the growth of alternative families in the West throughout recent decades. This is the narrative of caring-love. The narrative of caring-love acknowledges that all persons at all stages of their life require, desire, and/or deliver care. We form relationships of caring-love between our (biological) families, our friends, and our intimate partners. We all require emotional and physical support, and we seek to provide this to the people we care about. Moreover, we are social creatures—we live intersubjective existences. Care is fundamental to our flourishing as intersubjective individuals. Care is universal, and care comes in many formulations. Given increasing empirical changes to 'normal' families, the combined approach's meaning-generating narrative may be likely to gain much traction if it is widely promoted. There are many varieties of families and intimate relationships emerging, and the combined approach seeks a positive encounter with real and potential difference(s). This position, then, generates positive, meaning-generating beliefs which will encourage social change in the present, and it also holds resonance with the liberal value of equal respect for basic human status.

Thus, the combined approach should be endorsed for two fundamental reasons: it does not rely on assimilative arguments nor affirm the hierarchical and normative worth of 'traditional' marriage, and it circulates a new meaning-generating narrative which focuses on care as a universal need. The combined approach also demonstrates that it would, in fact, be better if a plurality of possibilities were opened up for legal recognition. This would include but not be limited to marriage equality. This possibility is particularly interesting to entertain, since it is unclear how many people, whether heterosexual or homosexual, would continue to desire and participate in traditional marriage if other relationship recognition became horizontally valued in the dominant shared Western social imaginary and by law. Thus, I conclude that same-sex marriage can be good for LGBT equality, so long as it is not hierarchically held to be *the* good. Indeed, if something like the combined approach is widely endorsed, then same-sex marriage will act as but one factor among many which may contribute to greater overall respect for LGBTs.

NOTE

1. Rainer Forst, 'The Justification of Human Rights and the Basic Right to Justification: A Reflexive Approach', *Ethics* 120, no. 4 (2010): 725.

Bibliography

Arendt, Hannah. *The Human Condition*. 2nd ed. Chicago and London: University of Chicago Press, 1998.

———. 'Reflections on Little Rock'. *Dissent* 6, no. 1 (1959): 45–56.

Australian Human Rights Commission. 'A Guide to Australia's Anti-Discrimination Laws'. Accessed 2 November 2014. http://humanrights.gov.au/info_for_employers/law/index.html.

———. 'Same Sex: Same Entitlements'. Accessed 2 November 2014. http://www.humanrights.gov.au/human_rights/samesex/index.html.

Australian Marriage Equality. '"A Failed Experiment": Why Civil Unions Are No Substitute for Marriage Equality'. Accessed 2 November 2014. http://www.australianmarriageequality.org/wp-content/uploads/2010/12/A-failed-experiment.pdf.

———. 'The Hintons, a Family That Supports Marriage Equality'. YouTube, 20 August 2012. Accessed 3 November 2014. https://www.youtube.com/watch?v=M7hwFD4Ii3E.

———. 'Just Like You—Love Knows No Difference'. Accessed 3 November 2014. http://www.australianmarriageequality.org/just-like-you/.

———. '12 Reasons Why Marriage Equality Matters'. Accessed 2 November 2014. http://www.australianmarriageequality.org/12-reasons-why-marriage-equality-matters/.

Beauvoir, Simone de. *The Second Sex*. 1949. Translated by C. Borde and S. Malovany-Chevallier. London: Vintage Books, 2009.

Beyond Marriage Allied Activists. 'Beyond Same-Sex Marriage: A New Strategic Vision for All Our Families and Relationships'. Accessed 3 November 2014. http://www.beyondmarriage.org/BeyondMarriage.pdf.

Boswell, John. *The Marriage of Likeness: Same-Sex Unions in Pre-modern Europe*. London: Fontana Press, 1995.

Brake, Elizabeth. 'Minimal Marriage: What Political Liberalism Implies for Marriage Law'. *Ethics* 120, no. 2 (2010): 302–37.

———. *Minimizing Marriage: Marriage, Morality and the Law*. Oxford: Oxford University Press, 2012.

Brown, Wendy. 'Suffering Rights as Paradoxes'. *Constellations* 7, no. 2 (2000): 208–29.

Buchanan, Allen. 'The Egalitarianism of Human Rights'. *Ethics* 120, no. 4 (2010): 679–710.

Buikema, Rosemarie. 'Monumental Dresses: Coming to Terms with Racial Oppression'. In *Teaching Race with a Gendered Edge*, edited by B. Hipfl and K. Loftsdóttir, 43–61. Budapest and New York: Central European University Press, 2012.

Butler, Judith. *Bodies That Matter*. New York and London: Routledge, 1993.

Calhoun, Cheshire. *Feminism, the Family, and the Politics of the Closet: Lesbian and Gay Displacement*. Oxford: Oxford University Press, 2000.

———. 'Who's Afraid of Polygamous Marriage? Lessons for Same-Sex Marriage Advocacy from the History of Polygamy'. *San Diego Law Review* 42 (2005): 1023–42.
Card, Claudia. 'Against Marriage and Motherhood'. *Hypatia* 11, no. 3 (1996): 1–23.
Cole, Elizabeth, Lanice Avery, Catherine Dodson, and Kevin D. Goodman. 'Against Nature: How Arguments about the Naturalness of Marriage Privilege Heterosexuality'. *Journal of Social Issues* 68, no. 1 (2012): 46–62.
Cornell, Drucilla. 'Gender, Sex, & Equivalent Rights'. In *Feminists Theorize the Political*, edited by Judith Butler and Joan Wallach Scott, 280–96. New York: Routledge, 1992.
Crenshaw, Kimberlé. 'Demarginalizing the Intersection of Race and Sex: A Black Feminist Critique of Antidiscrimination Doctrine, Feminist Theory and Antiracist Politics'. *University of Chicago Legal Forum* (1989): 139–67.
Croome, Rodney. *Why vs Why: Gay Marriage. Yes*. New South Wales, Australia: Pantera Press, 2010.
Dettmer, Lisa. 'Beyond Gay Marriage'. *Race, Poverty & the Environment: Weaving the Threads* 17, no. 2 (2010). Accessed 3 November 2014. http://reimaginerpe.org/node/5822.
Deutscher, Penelope. *A Politics of Impossible Difference: The Later Work of Luce Irigaray*. Ithaca, NY: Cornell University Press, 2002.
Dworkin, Ronald. 'Lord Devlin and the Enforcement of Morals'. *Yale Law Journal* 75, no. 6 (1966): 986–1005.
Emens, Elizabeth. 'Just Monogamy?' In *Just Marriage*, edited by Mary Lyndon Shanley, 75–80. Oxford: Oxford University Press, 2004.
Eskridge, William N., Jr. *Gaylaw: Challenging the Apartheid of the Closet*. Cambridge, MA: Harvard University Press, 1999.
———. 'A History of Same-Sex Marriage'. *Virginia Law Review* 79, no. 7 (1993): 1419–13.
European Union Agency for Fundamental Rights (FRA). *EU LGBT Survey: European Union Lesbian, Gay, Bisexual and Transgender Survey—Results at a Glance*. Luxembourg: Publications Office of the European Union, 2013. Accessed on 2 November 2014. http://fra.europa.eu/sites/default/files/eu-lgbt-survey-results-at-a-glance_en.pdf.
Family Research Council. 'Questions and Answers: What's Wrong with Letting Same-Sex Couples "Marry"?' Accessed 2 November 2014. http://www.frc.org/whats-wrong-with-letting-same-sex-couples-marry.
Fineman, Martha Albertson. 'Why Marriage?' In *Just Marriage*, edited by Mary Lyndon Shanley, 46–51. Oxford: Oxford University Press, 2004.
Forst, Rainer. 'The Basic Right to Justification: Toward a Constructivist Conception of Human Rights'. *Constellations* 6, no. 1 (1999): 35–60.
———. *Contexts of Justice*. Translated by J. Farrell. Berkeley: University of California Press, 2002.
———. 'First Things First: Redistribution, Recognition and Justification'. *European Journal of Political Theory* 6, no. 3 (2007): 291–304.
———. 'The Ground of Critique: On the Concept of Human Dignity in Social Orders of Justification'. *Philosophy & Social Criticism* 37, no. 9 (2011): 965–76.
———. 'The Justification of Human Rights and the Basic Right to Justification: A Reflexive Approach'. *Ethics* 120, no. 4 (2010): 711–40.
———. 'The Limits of Toleration'. *Constellations* 11, no. 3 (2004): 312–25.
———. *Toleration in Conflict: Past and Present*. Translated by Ciaran Cronin. Cambridge: Cambridge University Press, 2013.
Freedom to Marry. 'Marriage 101'. Accessed 2 November 2014. http://www.freedomtomarry.org/pages/marriage-101#faq1.
———. 'Why Marriage Matters'. Accessed 2 November 2014. http://www.freedomtomarry.org/pages/why-marriage-matters.
Gartner, Nadine. 'Articulating Lesbian Human Rights: The Creation of a Convention on the Elimination of All Forms of Discrimination against Lesbians'. *UCLA Women's Law Journal* 14 (2005): 61–87.
Gatens, Moira. 'Can Human Rights Accommodate Women's Rights? Towards an Embodied Account of Social Norms, Social Meaning, and Cultural Change'. *Contemporary Political Theory* 3, no. 3 (2004): 275–99.

———. *Feminism and Philosophy: Perspectives on Difference and Equality*. Cambridge: Polity Press, 1991.
———. *Imaginary Bodies: Ethics, Power and Corporeality*. London: Routledge, 1996.
———. 'Paradoxes of Liberal Politics: Contracts, Rights, and Consent'. In *Illusion of Consent: Engaging with Carole Pateman*, edited by. D. O'Neill, M. Shanley, and I. Young, 31–48. University Park: Pennsylvania State University Press, 2008.
GetUp! Action for Australia. 'It's Time'. YouTube, 24 November 2012. Accessed 3 November 2014. https://www.youtube.com/watch?v=_TBd-UCwVAY.
Giardini, Frederica. 'Speculum of Being Two: Politics and Theory after All These Years'. *Theory, Culture & Society* 20, no. 3 (2003): 13–26.
Griffin, James. 'Human Rights: Questions of Aim and Approach'. *Ethics* 120, no. 4 (2010): 741–60.
———. *On Human Rights*. Oxford: Oxford University Press, 2008.
Grosz, Elizabeth. *Sexual Subversions: Three French Feminists*. New South Wales, Australia: Allen & Unwin, 1989.
Hill, Rebecca. *The Interval*. New York: Fordham University Press, 2012.
Holmlund, Christine. 'The Lesbian, the Mother, the Heterosexual Lover: Irigaray's Recodings of Difference'. *Feminist Studies* 17, no. 2 (1991): 283–308.
Hull, Kathleen. 'The Political Limits of the Rights Frame: The Case of Same-Sex Marriage in Hawaii'. *Sociological Perspectives* 44, no. 2 (2001): 207–32.
International Lesbian, Gay, Bisexual, Trans and Intersex Association. *ILGA Constitution*. Accessed 3 November 2014. http://old.ilga.org/documents/ENG-ILGA%20Constitution-Nov08.pdf.
Irigaray, Luce. *Between East and West: From Singularity to Community*. Translated by Stephen Pluháček. New York: Columbia University Press, 2002.
———. *Democracy Begins between Two*. Translated by Kirsteen Anderson. New York: Routledge, 2000.
———. *An Ethics of Sexual Difference*. Translated by Carolyn Burke and Gillian C. Gill. London: Continuum, 2004.
———. *I Love to You*. Translated by Alison Martin. New York: Routledge, 1996.
———. *Je, Tu, Nous*. Translated by Alison Martin. New York: Routledge, 2007.
———. 'The Question of the Other'. Translated by Noah Guynn. *Yale French Studies* 87 (1995): 7–19.
———. *Speculum of the Other Woman*. Translated by Gillian C. Gill. Ithaca, NY: Cornell University Press, 1985.
———. *Thinking the Difference: For a Peaceful Revolution*. Translated by Karin Montin. London: Athlone Press, 1994.
———. *This Sex Which Is Not One*. Translated by Catherine Porter. Ithaca, NY: Cornell University Press, 1985.
Ivison, Duncan. *Rights*. Stocksfield, UK: Acumen Publishing, 2008.
James, Susan. 'Freedom and the Imaginary'. In *Visible Women: Essays on Feminist Legal Theory and Political Philosophy*, edited by Susan James and Stephanie Palmer, 175–95. Oxford: Hart Publishing, 2002.
Jay, Nancy. 'Gender and Dichotomy'. *Feminist Studies* 7, no. 1 (1981): 38–56.
Jennings, Rebecca. 'Lesbian Mothers and Child Custody: Australian Debates in the 1970s'. *Gender and History* 24, no. 2 (2012): 502–17.
Jones, Rachel. *Irigaray: Towards a Sexuate Philosophy*. Cambridge: Polity Press, 2011.
Kirby, Michael. 'Same-Sex Relationships: An Australasian Perspective on a Global Issue'. In *Legal Recognition of Same-Sex Partnerships: A Study of National, European and International Law*, edited by R. Wintemute and M. Andenæs, 7–21. Oxford and Portland, OR: Hart Publishing, 2001.
Kollman, Kelly. 'European Institutions, Transnational Networks and National Same-Sex Unions Policy: When Soft Law Hits Harder'. *Contemporary Politics* 15, no. 1 (2009): 37–53.
———. 'Same-Sex Unions: The Globalisation of an Idea'. *International Studies Quarterly* 51 (2007): 329–27.

Kollman, Kelly, and Matthew Waites. 'The Global Politics of Lesbian, Gay, Bisexual and Transgender Human Rights: An Introduction'. *Contemporary Politics* 15, no. 1 (2009): 1–17.

La Caze, Marguerite. 'The Encounter between Wonder and Generosity'. *Hypatia* 17, no. 3 (2002): 1–19.

———. 'Seeing Oneself through the Eyes of the Other: Asymmetrical Reciprocity and Self-Respect'. *Hypatia* 23, no. 3 (2008): 118–35.

Lacey, Nicola. *Unspeakable Subjects: Feminist Essays in Legal and Social Theory*. Oxford: Hart Publishing, 1998.

———. 'Violence, Ethics and Law: Feminist Reflections on a Familiar Dilemma'. In *Visible Women: Essays on Feminist Legal Theory and Political Philosophy*, edited by Susan James and Stephanie Palmer, 117–35. Oxford: Hart Publishing, 2002.

Lalor, Kay. 'Constituting Sexuality: Rights, Politics and Power in the Gay Rights Movement'. *International Journal of Human Rights* 15, no. 5 (2011): 683–99.

Lever, Annabelle. 'The Politics of Paradox: A Response to Wendy Brown'. *Constellations* 7, no. 2 (2000): 242–54.

Li, Xigen, and Xudong Liu. 'Framing and Coverage of Same-Sex Marriage in U.S. Newspapers'. *Howard Journal of Communications* 21, no. 1 (2010): 72–91.

Lundy, Sandra. 'Abuse That Dare Not Speak Its Name: Assisting Victims of Lesbian and Gay Domestic Violence in Massachusetts'. *New England Law Review* 28 (1993–1994): 273–311.

Marriage Equality. 'Sinéad's Hand'. YouTube, 19 August 2009. Accessed 18 October 2014. https://www.youtube.com/watch?v=6ULdaSrYGLQ.

Martin, Alison. 'Introduction: Luce Irigaray and the Culture of Difference'. *Theory, Culture & Society* 20, no. 3 (2003): 1–12.

Meuhlenberg, Bill. *Why vs Why: Gay Marriage. No.* New South Wales, Australia: Pantera Press, 2010.

Miriam, Kathy. 'Toward a Phenomenology of Sex-Right: Reviving Radical Feminist Theory of Compulsory Heterosexuality'. *Hypatia* 22 No. 1 (2007): 210–28.

Naffine, Ngaire. 'Can Women Be Legal Persons?' In *Visible Women: Essays on Feminist Legal Theory and Political Philosophy*, edited by Susan James and Stephanie Palmer, 69–90. Oxford: Hart Publishing, 2002.

Neilsen, Mary Anne. 'Background Note: Same-Sex Marriage'. *Parliament of Australia: Department of Parliamentary Services*, 10 February 2012. Accessed 2 November 2014. http://parlinfo.aph.gov.au/parlInfo/download/library/prspub/1409734/upload_binary/1409734.pdf;fileType=applica%20tion/pdf.

———. 'Marriage Amendment Bill 2012 [and] Marriage Equality Amendment Bill 2012 [and] Marriage Equality Amendment Bill 2010'. *Parliament of Australia: Parliamentary Business*, 18 June 2012. Accessed 2 November 2014. http://www.aph.gov.au/Parliamentary_Business/Bills_Legislation/bd/bd1112a/12bd158.

Okin, Susan Moller. *Justice, Gender, and the Family*. New York: Basic Books, 1989.

———. 'Sexual Orientation, Gender, and Families: Dichotomizing Differences'. *Hypatia* 11, no. 1 (1996): 30–48.

Paetzold, Heinz. 'Respect and Toleration Reconsidered (Under Consideration: Rainer Forst's *Toleranz im Konflikt: Geschichte, Gehalt, und Gegenwart eines umstrittenen Begriffs*)'. *Philosophy & Social Criticism* 34, no. 8 (2008): 941–54.

Pateman, Carole. *The Sexual Contract*. Stanford, CA: Stanford University Press, 1988.

Ping, Xu. 'Irigaray's Mimicry and the Problem of Essentialism'. *Hypatia* 10, no. 4 (1995): 76–89.

Polikoff, Nancy. *Beyond (Straight and Gay) Marriage: Valuing All Families under the Law*. Boston: Beacon Press, 2011.

———. 'We Will Get What We Ask For: Why Legalizing Gay and Lesbian Marriage Will Not "Dismantle the Legal Structure of Gender in Every Marriage"'. *Virginia Law Review* 79, no. 7 (1993): 1535–50.

Rawls, John. *A Theory of Justice*. Cambridge, MA: Belknap Press of Harvard University Press, 1971.

Raz, Joseph. *The Morality of Freedom*. New York: Oxford University Press, 1988.

Relationships Tasmania. 'Caring Couples'. Accessed 2 November 2014. http://www.relationshipstasmania.com/caringcouples.html.

Rich, Adrienne. 'Compulsory Heterosexuality and Lesbian Existence (1980)'. *Journal of Women's History* 15, no. 3 (2003): 11–48.

———. 'Reflections on "Compulsory Heterosexuality"'. *Journal of Women's History* 16, no. 1 (2004): 9–11.

Richardson, Diane. 'Locating Sexualities: From Here to Normality'. *Sexualities* 7 (2004): 391–411.

———. 'Sexuality and Citizenship'. *Sociology* 32 (1998): 83–100.

Rosenblum, Darren. 'Queer Intersectionality and the Failure of Recent Lesbian and Gay "Victories"'. *Law & Sexuality* 4 (1994): 83–122.

Rossi, Leena-Maija. '"Happy" and "Unhappy" Performatives: Images and Norms of Heterosexuality'. *Australian Feminist Studies* 26, no. 67 (2011): 9–23.

Russo, Vito. *The Celluloid Closet*. New York: Harper & Row, 1987.

Schutte, Ofelia. 'A Critique of Normative Heterosexuality: Identity, Embodiment, and Sexual Difference in Beauvoir and Irigaray'. *Hypatia* 12, no. 1 (1997): 40–62.

Scott, Joan Wallach. 'Deconstructing Equality-versus-Difference: Or, the Uses of Poststructuralist Theory for Feminism'. *Feminist Studies* 14, no. 1 (1988): 32–50.

———. *Only Paradoxes to Offer: French Feminists and the Rights of Man*. Cambridge, MA, and London: Harvard University Press, 1996.

Shanley, Mary Lyndon. 'Just Marriage: On the Public Importance of Private Unions'. In *Just Marriage*, edited by Mary Lyndon Shanley, 3–30. Oxford: Oxford University Press, 2004.

Sheill, Kate. 'Losing Out in the Intersections: Lesbians, Human Rights, Law and Activism'. *Contemporary Politics* 15, no. 1 (2009): 55–71.

Stoetzler, Marcel, and Nira Yuval-Davis. 'Standpoint Theory, Situated Knowledge and the Situated Imagination'. *Feminist Theory* 3, no. 3 (2002): 326–27.

Stone, Alison. *Luce Irigaray and the Philosophy of Sexual Difference*. Cambridge: Cambridge University Press, 2006.

Tasioulas, James. 'Taking Rights out of Human Rights'. *Ethics* 120, no. 4 (2010): 647–78.

Thornton, Margaret. *Dissonance and Distrust: Women in the Legal Profession*. Oxford: Oxford University Press, 1996.

United Nations Human Rights Committee (UNHRC). *Toonen v. Australia*, Communication No. 488/1992, U.N. Doc CCPR/C/50/D/488/1992 (1994). Accessed 2 November 2014. http://www1.umn.edu/humanrts/undocs/html/vws488.htm.

Waaldijk, Kees. 'Civil Developments: Patterns of Reform in the Legal Position of Same-Sex Partners in Europe'. *Canadian Journal of Family Law* 17 (2000): 62–88.

———. *More or Less Together: Levels of Legal Consequences of Marriage, Cohabitation and Registered Partnership for Different-Sex and Same-Sex Partners: A Comparative Study of Nine European Countries*. Paris: Institut National d'Etudes Démographiques, 2005.

———. 'Others May Follow: The Introduction of Marriage, Quasi-Marriage and Semi-Marriage for Same-Sex Couples in European Countries'. *Judicial Studies Institute Journal* 5 (2005): 104–24.

———. 'Small Change: How the Road to Same-Sex Marriage Got Paved in the Netherlands'. In *Legal Recognition of Same-Sex Partnership: A Study of National, European and International Law*, edited by R. Wintemute and M. Andenæs, 437–64. Oxford: Hart Publishing, 2001.

———. 'Standard Sequences in the Legal Recognition of Homosexuality—Europe's Past, Present and Future'. *Australian Gay and Lesbian Law Journal* 4 (1994): 50–74.

Warner, Michael. *The Trouble with Normal: Sex, Politics, and the Ethics of Queer Life*. Cambridge, MA: Harvard University Press, 1999.

Warnke, Georgia. *After Identity*. Cambridge: Cambridge University Press, 2007.

West, Angela. 'Prosecutorial Activism: Confronting Heterosexism in a Lesbian Battering Case'. *Harvard Women's Law Journal* 15 (1992): 249–71.

Whitford, Margaret. *Luce Irigaray: Philosophy in the Feminine*. London: Routledge, 1991.

Williams, Amanda. '"This Is the True Face of Homophobia": Gay Man Viciously Beaten in Paris Posts Picture of His Injuries to Facebook in Protest Move That Has Now Gone Viral'.

Daily Mail, 27 May 2013. Accessed 28 May 2013. http://www.dailymail.co.uk/news/article-2307288/Paris-gay-attack-victim-Wilfred-Bruijns-Facebook-injuries-picture-goes-viral.html#ixzz2UZH3Bjz1.

Wolfson, Evan. 'Marriage Makes a Word of Difference: Why We Can't Call It Something Else'. *Portland Mercury*, 14 June 2007. Accessed 3 November 2014. http://www.portlandmercury.com/portland/marriage-makes-a-word-of-difference/Content?oid=344646.

Yep, Gust A., Karen E. Lovaas, and John P. Elia. 'A Critical Appraisal of Assimilationist and Radical Ideologies Underlying Same-Sex Marriage in LGBT Communities in the United States'. *Journal of Homosexuality* 45, no. 1 (2003): 45–64.

Index

AHRC. *See* Australian Human Rights Commission
AME. *See* Australian Marriage Equality
appreciation, 102n14, 103n50, 122; first order, 85, 107; second order, 85, 100, 102n14, 107, 129, 142
Arendt, Hannah, 16, 17, 20, 30n13
assimilat/ed/ive/ion, 2, 6, 7, 9, 14, 17, 21, 29, 35, 39, 52, 63, 67, 81, 91, 93, 131, 149, 150, 152, 155, 156
Australia, 1, 13, 17, 24–26, 26, 31n23, 32n48, 63
Australian Human Rights Commission, 25
Australian Human Rights Commission Act 1986, 18
Australian Marriage Equality, 17, 21, 36, 38, 39, 132
Austria, 23, 27–28, 92
autonomy, 2, 42, 43, 44, 55n48, 60, 109, 120, 151; moral autonomy/morally autonomous, 84, 85, 97, 107, 152

Baehr v. Lewin, 32n54
basic right to justification, 8, 82, 84, 95, 97, 120, 139, 152
Beauvoir, Simone de, 2, 58
Belgium, 1, 14, 22, 26, 30n9
benchmark man, 57, 60, 63, 72, 75, 76, 130, 151
Beyond Marriage, 54n21, 62, 67
binary, 52, 57, 59, 67, 100, 106, 108, 109, 110, 116, 118, 120, 152, 154. *See also* dichotomy/ous
bisexual, 2, 73, 144
Brake, Elizabeth, 54n21, 67, 78n29, 143–145
Brown, Wendy, 19, 57, 63, 64, 66, 68, 69, 72, 74
Buchanan, Allen, 49, 54n31
burden of proof, 92. *See also* onus of proof
Butler, Judith, 125n45

Calhoun, Cheshire, 8, 20, 49, 78n30, 127, 134, 136, 137, 138, 139, 142, 146n17
Canada, 1, 14, 28
Card, Claudia, 19, 54n21, 67
care, 6, 17, 21, 24, 49, 50, 62, 67, 81, 87, 89–90, 94, 105, 133, 138, 140–141, 143–145, 156; caring couple, 24; caring-love, 6, 8, 138, 145, 156; caring relationships, 6, 21, 24, 78n29, 89, 90, 140, 143, 144, 145
children, 4, 25, 38, 39, 40, 45, 46, 49, 50, 65, 68, 70, 87, 89, 135, 144
citizen/ship, 4, 6, 14, 17, 20, 21, 24, 28, 29, 54n21, 61, 62, 67, 82, 85, 89, 91, 92, 93, 97, 100, 116, 119, 120–121, 130, 131, 132, 134, 136, 139, 141, 149, 152, 155. *See also* essential citizens
civil union, 13–14, 24, 25, 30n2, 39, 47, 98, 140, 144, 145

combined approach, 6, 8, 10, 123, 127, 133, 138, 138–140, 141–142, 143, 145, 149, 154–156
communication, 82, 121
Constitution of the Kingdom of the Netherlands, 23
constructivism, 6, 8, 76, 82, 84, 96, 121, 139, 141, 152, 155. *See also* discursive constructivism
contract, 143–145
Convention on the Elimination of all forms of Discrimination against Women, 53n1
Convention on the Rights of the Child, 53n1
Convention on the Rights of Persons with Disabilities,2n1
Cornell, Drucilla, 70, 106, 117, 119
Crenshaw, Kimberlé, 70, 73, 76
Croome, Rodney, 17

de facto, 13, 14, 25, 26, 27, 39, 47
Defense of Marriage Act (DOMA), 1, 26, 28, 32n54
Denmark, 1, 23, 26, 30n9
dichotomy/ous, 58, 59, 75. *See also* binary
difference(s), 2, 5, 18, 29, 40, 61, 73, 101, 109, 112, 119, 120, 121, 139, 142, 150, 152, 156; cultivating difference, 5, 18, 119
dignity, 2, 14, 16, 29, 38, 40, 51–53, 61, 84, 91, 106, 111, 117, 118, 119, 120, 121, 122, 127, 130, 139, 141, 152, 155; endignify/ing, 15, 63, 121
discourse, 13, 22, 57, 58, 59, 60, 64, 68, 73, 74, 107, 110, 114, 118, 120; rights discourse, 13, 22, 35, 57, 60, 63, 73, 74, 75, 81, 115, 116, 151
discursive constructivism, 8, 76, 82, 96, 121, 152
DOMA. *See* Defense of Marriage Act
duty, 2, 16, 17, 43, 51, 99, 112, 120, 122

ECHR. *See* human rights, European Court of
England, 1, 27
equality, 2, 14, 16, 19, 21, 22, 40, 44, 45, 51–53, 60–61, 62, 63, 88, 91, 92, 97, 109, 119, 127, 130, 133, 134, 137, 139, 141, 150, 156; equal regard, 2, 3, 6, 8, 10, 14–15, 17, 29, 40, 44, 49, 52, 57, 61, 62–63, 67, 74, 83, 85, 89, 91, 93, 95, 100, 101, 105, 117, 119, 122, 123, 127, 133, 138, 142, 144–145, 149, 150, 151, 154, 155; equality feminism, 109; formal equality, 14, 61, 63, 66, 67, 93, 94, 95, 102n42, 151; principle of equal respect, 44, 53; substantive equality, 61, 62, 63, 64, 66, 67
equivalent/ce, 2, 40, 61, 90, 97, 99, 111, 112, 117, 118, 122, 123, 124n30, 131, 141, 154. *See* rights, equivalent rights
Eskridge Jr., William N., 39
essential citizens, 134, 136, 138, 139, 142
European Agency for Fundamental Rights (FRA), 30n9
European Union (EU), 14, 28, 116

family: traditional family, 2, 3, 71, 117, 118, 140; nuclear family, 3, 4, 10, 93, 134, 135, 137, 139
Family Research Council, the (FRC), 20, 64
feminism/t, 2, 6, 15, 19, 59, 67, 68, 70, 81, 82, 83, 90, 105, 120, 123, 127, 143, 149, 152, 154; sexual difference feminism, 8, 106, 107
Finland, 1, 26
Forst, Rainer, 6, 8, 82–101, 102n14, 103n48, 105, 106, 107, 117, 119, 120, 120–121, 122, 139, 152, 153
FRA. *See* European Agency for Fundamental Rights
France, 1, 9, 22, 26, 30n9
Freedom to Marry, 38

Gartner, Nadine, 68
Gatens, Moira, 71, 74, 95, 115, 130
gay, 13, 19, 31n29, 36–37, 38, 39, 51, 57, 67, 69, 70, 71, 73, 76, 93, 134, 137
gender, 19, 59, 62, 66, 68, 69–70, 73, 76, 93, 100, 105, 110, 113, 114, 118, 130, 136
generality, 8, 84, 86, 88, 89, 91, 95, 96, 139, 152
Germany, 1, 22, 26, 98
Griffin, James, 17, 35, 41–51, 54n31, 55n37, 55n41, 55n59, 86, 87

heteronormative/ity, 2, 3, 5, 6, 7, 9, 10, 14, 15, 21, 26, 29, 35, 47, 61, 62, 63, 65, 67, 76, 88, 93, 100, 101, 118, 124n32, 128, 129, 132, 135, 141, 146n17, 149, 150
heterosexism, 69, 93, 113, 124n32
heterosexual/ity: compulsory heterosexuality, 3–4, 68; heterosexual privilege, 40, 52, 62, 67, 71, 91, 129; heterosexual relationships, 3, 37, 38; heterosexuals, 5, 7, 17, 21, 37, 51, 60, 62, 64–65, 67, 90, 93, 99, 119, 122, 123, 129, 138, 154; nonnormative heterosexuals, 60, 76, 129; normative heterosexual/ity, 38, 58, 67, 78n29, 81, 100, 108, 112, 114, 128, 130, 131, 134
Hill, Rebecca, 124n32
homo-sex, 19, 22, 31n19, 100, 101; decriminalisation of, 17, 18, 22, 24, 26, 31n23, 92
Hull, Kathleen, 32n54
human rights, 7, 14–21, 22, 23, 28, 29, 30n12, 57–76, 106, 119, 122–123, 130, 149; European Court of (ECHR), 15, 27, 28, 92; intersubjective justification theory of. *See* intersubjective justification theory; Human Rights (Sexual Conduct) Act 1994, 92; personhood account of; personhood account; Universal Declaration of (UDHR); Universal Declaration of Human Rights; United Nations Human Rights Committee (UNHRC), 17, 31n23

ICCPR. *See* International Covenant on Civil and Political Rights
Iceland, 1, 23, 26
ICESC. *See* International Covenant on Economic, Social, and Cultural Rights
identity/ies, 4–5, 7, 16, 19, 28, 44, 52, 58, 63, 68, 70, 71, 72, 73, 75, 82, 85, 94, 98, 99, 108, 109, 111, 112, 114, 118, 119, 120, 123, 128, 129, 130, 137, 149, 151, 153; cisgendered identity/ies, 70; civil identity/ies, 112; collective/group identity/ies, 72, 76, 102n42, 151; cultural identity/ies, 97; embodied identity/ies, 4, 128; female/feminine identity/ies, 3, 109, 113; gender identity/ies, 62, 69, 113, 130; heterosexual identity/ies, 100; identity as Other, 58, 60; identity-based discrimination, 15, 17, 118, 123, 154; identity-based rights claims, 57; lesbian identity/ies, 68, 70, 113; LGBT identity/ies, 2, 5, 18, 29, 60, 61, 71, 81, 99, 100, 108, 111, 115, 128, 129, 130–131, 131, 140, 145, 152, 156; marginal identity/ies, 68; marked identity/ies, 58; masculine identity/ies, 3; political identity/ies, 29, 58; principle of identity, 58; racial identity/ies, 73; sexual identity/ies, 3, 5, 19, 61, 68, 131
ILGA. *See* International Lesbian, Gay, Bisexual, Trans and Intersex Association
imaginary, 10, 27, 28, 110, 116, 125n45, 127–133, 145; dominant shared Western social, 4, 5, 6, 8, 10, 13, 19, 27, 29, 67, 71, 100, 108, 111, 115, 128, 129, 130–131, 131, 140, 145, 152, 156
immoral/ity, 6, 14, 18, 81, 83, 97, 119, 129, 139, 149, 153
indignity, 59, 82, 83, 91, 105
International Convention on the Elimination of all forms of Racial Discrimination, 53n1
International Covenant on Civil and Political Rights (ICCPR), 15–16, 18, 53n1
International Covenant on Economic, Social, and Cultural Rights (ICESC), 16, 53n1
International Lesbian, Gay, Bisexual, Trans and Intersex Association (ILGA), 15, 35
intersectionality, 68–72, 72, 73, 76
intersex, 35, 73
intersubjective justification theory, 6, 8, 81–101, 102n42, 105–106, 106, 116, 120, 121, 127, 143, 149, 152–154, 154
Ireland, 1, 37
Irigaray, Luce, 6, 8, 10, 11n20, 101, 106, 107–114, 115, 116, 117, 118, 120–121, 122, 123n1, 124n23, 124n32, 154

Jennings, Rebecca, 68, 78n38

Jones, Rachel, 124n32, 125n61
'Just Like You: Love Knows No Difference', 39

Karner v. Austria, 27, 92
Kollman, Kelly, 22, 27, 28, 29, 32n55
Kortmann Commission, 24

La Caze, Marguerite, 124n30, 124n32
Lacey, Nicola, 115, 125n49
Lalor, Kay, 31n23
Lawrence v. Texas, 28
lesbian, 3, 19, 31n29, 36, 38, 64, 68–69, 70–71, 73, 78n38, 93, 113–114, 125n45, 134, 137
Li, Xigen and Xudong Liu, 35
liberty, 7, 16, 17, 18, 29, 30n13, 31n18, 40, 42, 43, 44, 45, 46, 48, 49–50, 52, 134, 146n17, 150
love, 2, 5, 21, 38–39, 61, 62, 113, 128, 129, 131, 132, 136, 140, 150, 155. *See also* care, caring-love
Lundy, Sandra, 69
Luxembourg, 1, 22

marked persons, 52, 57, 58–59, 63, 66, 68, 72, 73, 74, 75, 76, 101, 108, 111, 118, 123, 130, 131, 133, 139, 142, 151, 152, 154
marriage: Marriage Act 1961, 24, 25; minimal, 143, 144; normative ideal of, 49, 61, 135, 136, 138; prepolitical myth of, 20, 21, 48, 134, 135–136, 138, 139; symbolism, 9, 14, 17, 29, 40, 150; traditional, 4, 9, 10, 36, 87, 93, 98, 134, 135, 137, 139, 140, 141, 144, 145, 146n17, 156; true definition, 21, 136. *See also* Defense of Marriage Act
Marriage Equality (organization), 36
Martin, Alison, 110
Miriam, Kathy, 3
miscegenation, 16, 17
Modern Family, 37
moral/ity, 2, 6, 8, 18, 31n23, 44, 49, 51, 55n59, 82, 84, 85, 86–91, 91, 92, 96, 106, 114, 119, 135, 137, 138, 139, 141, 145, 152, 155. *See also* autonomy, moral autonomy
Muehlenberg, Bill, 64

Naffine, Ngaire, 60, 72
narrative, 4, 6, 35, 65, 128, 130, 131, 132, 138, 142, 144–145, 150, 155, 156; meaning generating, 4, 5, 6, 8, 127, 128, 131, 133, 137, 138, 142, 156
Netherlands, 1, 9, 14, 23–24, 24, 26, 30n2
Netherlands Advisory Commission for Legislation, 23
New Normal, the, 37
New Zealand, 1, 14
non-discrimination, 2, 7, 52, 76, 81, 92, 108, 122, 150, 155; principle of, 16, 52
normative agency, 42, 43, 44, 46, 47–48, 49, 50, 51, 52, 53, 86, 150
norms, 4, 5, 6, 8, 26, 28, 60, 66, 67, 70, 84, 87, 88, 95, 97, 118, 121, 123, 128–130, 131, 132, 133, 134, 136, 137, 139, 140, 142, 145, 152, 154, 155; European norms, 27, 28; heteronormative/ity. *See* heteronormative/ity; international norms, 27, 32n55; moral norms, 82, 84, 86, 88; political norms, 57, 82, 84, 86; sex/gender norms, 70, 100, 105; sexual norms, 113; shared norms, 84, 97, 120, 121, 130, 132; social norms, 4, 59, 60, 111, 118, 128, 129, 130, 138, 152; soft law norms; soft law; transnational norms, 27, 28; universal norms, 86, 89, 96
Norway, 1, 14, 23, 26

objection component, 83, 97–98, 99, 107, 122, 123
onus of proof, 6, 91, 93, 105, 119, 123, 139, 152. *See also* burden of proof

Paetzold, Heinz, 9, 103n50
paradox: of rights, 7, 57, 63–76, 83, 94, 102n42, 106, 151, 152, 153; of the tolerant racist, 99–101
parenting, 13, 49, 61, 65, 137
partiality, permitted domain of, 43, 51
patriarchy/al, 2, 4, 107; heteropatriarchal, 49
personhood account, 7, 35, 41–43, 44, 47–48, 50, 51–52, 55n37, 83, 86–87, 131, 150
perverse/ion, 19, 60, 67, 70, 113, 118, 129, 139, 151

phallocentric/sm, 4, 5, 75, 100, 101, 107, 108, 109, 110, 110–111, 113, 114, 118, 123, 130, 132, 133, 139, 141, 155
phallus, 125n45
pluralization, 140, 143–145
Polikoff, Nancy, 67
polyamorous, 90, 140, 146n17
Portugal, 1, 30n9
prejudice/d, 9, 19, 39, 83, 97, 99–101, 106, 122, 123, 142, 153, 154
principle of non-discrimination. *See* nondiscrimination, principle of
privacy, 17–19, 119, 131
procreation/ive, 59, 113, 128, 130, 135

race/ial, 16, 20, 23, 52, 58, 62, 69, 70, 73, 99, 100, 108, 112, 128
racism/t, 99–101
Rawls, John, 82
Raz, Joseph, 55n48
reciprocity, 8, 84, 86, 88, 89, 91, 94, 95, 96, 98, 120, 139, 152
registered partnership. *See* civil union
Relationships Act 2003, 24, 140, 143
Relationships Tasmania, 140
reproduction (sexual), 65, 66, 68, 113, 114, 141
respect, 2, 8, 40, 42, 44, 45, 49, 50, 51, 53, 61, 67, 68, 78n38, 84, 88, 98, 101, 107, 121, 122, 137, 142, 152, 156; for difference, 2, 6, 40, 109, 111, 112, 118, 121; for LGBTs, 15, 63, 81, 119, 122, 134, 137, 145, 149, 156; for the Other, 106, 111, 112, 118, 121; legal respect, 141; principle of equal respect, 44; respect conception of tolerance. *See* tolerance; self-respect, 84, 85; sexual citizens, 14
Rich, Adrienne, 3, 68, 69
Richardson, Dianne, 10n5, 54n21, 67
rights: basic right to justification, 8, 82, 84, 95, 97, 120, 139, 152; equivalent rights, 106, 116, 118–119, 138, 139, 145, 154; natural right, 41, 83; rights rhetoric, 22, 29, 57; special rights, 64, 65, 78n29, 83, 95, 101, 105, 106, 117, 119, 151, 153

sameness, 2, 5, 7, 29, 35, 40, 61, 66–67, 76, 83, 89, 90, 93, 105, 109, 117, 119, 121, 127, 131, 132, 137, 138, 139, 142, 145, 146n17, 150, 152, 153, 155
Scotland, 1
sex: (act), 3, 17, 22, 24, 26, 31n19, 31n29, 39, 49, 53n7, 57, 58, 61, 62, 65, 67, 68, 93, 100, 105, 113–114, 118, 128, 130, 131, 137, 140–141, 153; (biological), 3, 16, 17, 19, 23, 39, 52, 58, 59, 60, 62, 65, 69, 73, 75, 100, 105, 108, 109, 110, 111, 112, 113, 114, 118, 120, 124n32, 125n45, 128, 136, 140, 143, 144; sexism, 69; sexual difference, 8, 11n20, 59, 106, 107, 110, 123n1, 125n45; sexual freedom, 19; sexual identity, 5, 19, 131; sexual imaginaries, 128; sexual morality, 92; sexual orientation, 5, 13, 14, 15, 16, 17, 19, 23, 24, 31n23, 39, 58, 61, 62, 71, 93, 100, 110, 113, 150; sexual stereotype. *See* stereotype/ing; sexuality, 21, 49, 57, 68, 70, 86, 111, 113, 114, 118, 135. *See also* heterosexism, homo-sex
sexuate difference, 6, 8, 11n20, 105–106, 106, 107–114, 115, 116, 117, 118, 120, 122, 123n1, 124n32, 127, 149, 154
shame, 59, 59–60, 62, 85, 100–101, 128–129, 139, 153, 154
Sheill, Kate, 19, 64, 68
small change, 14, 21, 22, 24, 26, 29, 131, 149
soft law, 22, 26, 92; soft law norm, 7, 13, 21–22, 27, 29, 149
social comparison/socially comparative, 7, 8, 35, 52, 53, 61, 65, 66, 67, 81, 83, 88, 90, 91, 94, 101, 105, 150, 153
space between, the, 112, 116, 124n32
Spain, 1, 23, 30n9
stereotype/ing, 15, 64, 69, 70, 71–72, 73, 113, 114, 115, 117–118, 122, 142, 144, 154; sexual stereotypes, 115
stigma/tize, 2, 7, 57, 59, 60, 69, 98, 99, 100, 105, 129, 142, 149, 153
Stoetzler, Marcel, and Nira Yuval-Davis, 10, 128
Stone, Alison, 124n32
Sweden, 1, 14, 23, 26, 30n9
Switzerland, 1, 22, 31n29

Tasioulas, James, 54n31, 55n59

thinking (through) two, 8, 110–111, 115, 116
Thornton, Margaret, 57
tolerance, 8, 83, 87, 96–101, 103n48, 105, 106, 107, 122–123, 153; coexistence, 96; esteem, 96, 97, 98, 99, 103n50; permission, 96, 98, 99; respect, 96, 97, 99, 107, 153
Toonen v. Australia, 18, 31n23, 93
transgender, 2, 65, 69, 73, 79n45
Treaty of Amsterdam, 15, 16, 17

UDHR. *See* Universal Declaration of Human Rights
United Kingdom (UK), 69
United Nations (UN), 15, 22, 64
United Nations Declaration on the Rights of Indigenous Peoples, 53n1
United States (US), 1, 13, 16, 26, 27, 28, 30n13, 37, 62
United States v. Windsor, 27
Universal Declaration of Human Rights (UDHR), 15, 16, 17, 20, 20–21, 30n13, 48, 51, 52, 134, 149
utopia/n, 8, 10, 115, 127, 146n17; utopian rhetorical strategy, 115–116, 116, 127

Waaldijk, Kees, 13, 14, 22, 26, 30n2, 31n29, 39
Wales, 1, 26
Warner, Michael, 54n21, 59, 60, 67
Warnke, Georgia, 4, 72
West, Angela, 69
Whitford, Margaret, 115
Wolfenden Report, the, 18, 31n23
Wolfson, Evan, 38